Healthy Faith

Healthy Faith

A STRATEGIC LIFESTYLE PLAN TO TRANSFORM YOUR HEAD, HEART AND HANDS

Bill Nichols, PhD

*This book is dedicated to
my best friend and the love of my life, Phyllis.*

*"Many women do noble things,
but you surpass them all."
Proverbs 31:29 NIV*

Acknowledgements

❦

MANY OF THE TRUTHS AND stories in *Healthy Faith* came from far more people than I can possibly acknowledge here. I'm indebted and grateful to all of them but especially to the following people.

First and above all, I thank my beloved wife, Phyllis Clark Nichols, who is a novelist, seminary graduate, and my patient writing coach. Without her persistent pushes, tender encouragements, and thoughtful ideas, I would not have started or finished this book.

Secondly, I thank my fellow faith-writers, colleagues, and teachers whose thorough research and thoughtful insights are the book's backbone. My understanding of what a healthy faith is and what it takes to have one were most profoundly influenced by those men and women. I'm particularly thankful to John Newport, my friend and supervising professor for my PhD. His remarkable work, *Life's Ultimate Questions,* was life-changing for me. I'm also greatly indebted to a few of my fellow teachers: Russell Dilday, Bill Hendricks, Jim Denison, Joel Gregory, Milton Ferguson and Dean Dickens. I thank Abraham Verghese M.D., Ruth Berggren M.D., Marvin Forland M.D., Don Anderson and C.W. Brister, my friends and renowned advocates in medicine, comprehensive patient care and pastoral ministry. They significantly influenced my thinking about the holy significance of caring for people who are sick, treating them as more than physical creatures.

Thirdly, I am respectfully indebted to these particular authors who wrote what I consider faith-classics: C. S. Lewis' remarkable, ground-breaking *Mere Christianity*, Paul Tillich's brilliant study of faith in *Dynamics of Faith*, Francis

Collins' unprecedented work *The Language of God,* John Edward Carnell's comprehensive *An Introduction to Christian Apologetics,* Ronald Nash's scholarly and sensible *Faith and Reason: Searching for a Rational Faith,* Bernard Ramm's level-headed *The Right, the Good and the Happy,* Harry Emerson Fosdick's thought-provoking and pastoral *The Meaning of Faith,* Philip Yancey's popular and imaginative *Reaching for the Invisible God,* James Denison's practical and biblically instructive *Wrestling With God,* Timothy Keller's intellectually supportive *The Reason For God,* and Charles Colson's inspiring and back-to-the-basics *The Faith Given Once, For All.*

Fourthly, I'm beholden to those mentioned in the book whose names are not real but whose lives and painful stories were very real.

Finally, I bow my knee and my heart in humble gratitude to my Heavenly Father who has been, and is, and will always be faithful to me because that is His nature. I thank you for trusting me with such a personal and critical part of your private life. Since you're reaching out for help for yourself or someone you love, I take your trust seriously. I count it a privilege and holy responsibility to do all I can to help you find a healthy faith and to experience God's faithfulness to you.

Table of Contents

Introduction

❦

WHEN MY '68 VOLKSWAGEN BUG and the eighteen-wheeler crashed, my car went airborne, spinning round and round like a child's toy. My world spun out of control and went dark and silent. The car landed right-side up with a spine-rattling thud and jerk. I was alive, in pain, and blood was everywhere.

Fearing a fiery explosion, a truck driver who saw the accident stopped and pulled me from the wreckage. I lay shivering in seventeen-degree temperatures on the frozen grass in the median, keeping my eyes closed to block the intense sunlight in my face. The voice from the silhouette that stepped near me and shaded me from the light asked what I did for a living. His question at such a time shocked me, but I answered, "I'm a minister."

Looming above me, he then asked, "So, what do you think of your faith now?" He didn't wait for an answer but quietly walked away.

Very few people escape experiencing a traumatic crash along the way. Most of our crashes are not with eighteen-wheelers. They're with family members, friends, co-workers, health issues, or other unexpected, uninvited dilemmas. Nonetheless, they leave us with wounds, scars and the wreckage.

Since my accident, I've thought many times about that stranger's penetrating question, "So what do you think of your faith now?" Before then, that kind of question was merely hypothetical and interesting. But afterwards, it felt intensely personal and practical.

Since you're reading this book, my guess is that it's personal for you, too. You or someone you love has experienced some painful crash, leaving you with doubts and some of your own tough questions about faith, questions like—Why did this terrible thing happen? Am I being punished for something I've done in the past? How can I know if God is real? Why doesn't my faith work? Was my faith not strong enough?

During my years as a teacher in a graduate school preparing ministerial students, as a hospital chaplain, as a pastor and counselor, I heard many heartbreaking stories from people experiencing a faith crisis. Those hundreds of stories and questions led me to three distinct conclusions about people and faith. First, every one of us has some kind of faith. Second, most of us have the kind of faith that's practically useless, especially when difficulties come. Third, a few of us have found a unique kind of faith that's what I call *healthy*—healthy because it's a faith that works the way it's supposed to in the best and worst of times. It's the kind the Bible talks about.

If your faith doesn't equip you to handle difficult situations with confidence and give you a sense of inner peace in the midst of your troubles, then your faith is not healthy, and you need a new kind of faith. Maybe you've observed another person's faith and simply want more of what they have. Or, you may be weary and wary of a faith that was ineffective when you needed it most. Regardless of your reason for reading this book, if you're looking for a vibrant, healthy kind of faith that gives you helpful answers to your hard questions, makes a positive difference in your daily life, and gets you in touch with God, this book is designed to help you.

When I taught at seminary, I had access to an extensive library of books on faith. Before long I had read practically every academic and popular book on the subject, and I continue to research this topic. But when asked by a faith-crushed counselee to recommend a book that would help her develop a faith that would make a difference in her daily life, I couldn't do it. Not because there are no good books on faith. To the contrary, there are many.

Some of the books I considered recommending to her were written by my friends, fellow teachers, and other outstanding people of faith. I knew that many of those books would provide valuable information, inspiration and encouragement, but that's not what she wanted. What she needed was a book that would provide her a comprehensive, uncomplicated, practical, step-by-step plan that would produce a healthy faith.

Since her plea for help, far too many other people have asked me the same question. When I told my wife the kind of book those seekers needed just was not out there, she asked me a convicting question, "Well then, why don't *you* write it?"

So I did. I recalled what I learned from highly respected men and women who lived a healthy faith for years, and I put together what I learned from the academic, counseling and pastoral roles of my life to come up with an approach to help people develop the healthy faith they really wanted and needed.

When we talk about faith, we wrestle with some of life's most difficult issues that the world's sharpest minds have debated, discussed and written about for centuries. I could use imposing religious words, fashionable spiritual lingo, trendy psychological jargon, and traditional philosophical terminology. To some, that would be intellectually stimulating, but it wouldn't change much, if anything. So I completely avoided such verbiage and tried to make every sentence relevant, easy to understand, practical and down-to-earth honest.

If you want a graduate course or an encyclopedia on faith, you've come to the wrong place. This book is nothing like that. It's a compact, practical, workable plan. I wish the plan were effortless and filled with shortcuts, but it's not. I will try to be as sympathetic as I can; but, at the same time I will be as straight-forward and down-to-earth as I am when I counsel with people face to face.

For years, I have served on the Advisory Board of the Center for Medical Humanities and Ethics at the University of Texas Health Science Center in San Antonio. This institution is one of our country's premiere medical schools and research centers. Serving in this capacity has kept me close to the medical field, to many of the ethical issues involved in medicine and healing, and to the professionals who are influencing thought and practices in those fields.

We live in a time when health and health-related issues are on the front pages of newspapers, on television news segments, and even in the apps on our phones. We visit our doctors when our bodies are not well, and we expect a prescription or treatment that will address the symptoms as well as the cause of the illness. We visit our doctors for check-ups, and they order tests to see how truly healthy we are. The doctor often comes up with a plan for us to improve our health. So we follow through with the plan and follow-up with the doctor. We do all these things because we desire to be healthy—we desire our bodies to work the way God designed them.

The same is true about our faith. We want the kind of faith that is healthy and that will work the way God designed. So on occasion, we all need a faith-examination to see if our faith is working or why it isn't working, and that's part of what I'll help you do in this faith-development plan.

I do not offer you sugar-coated success-stories, self-help clichés, keys to self-actualization, pious religious mumbo-jumbo, or the promise of a quick-fix. This faith-development plan is an uncomplicated and workable strategy intended for someone who is serious about making healthy changes. It's not a casual read. It's a call to action.

Not wanting to minimize or dismiss your pain and struggle, I offer this plan with sincere compassion and understanding. I'm committed to helping you make some tough choices that can change your faith and life. What you'll be challenged to do may be different from what you expected to find in a book on faith. But, this is a different kind of book. How's it so different?

First, it's *highly compact*. Without having to read the many books listed in the bibliography, you'll benefit from the key insights about faith from some of the most respected minds of all times. One of the book's most noticeable limitations is its intentional brevity in dealing with such major issues.

Second, it's *result-oriented*. I suspect you're not interested in becoming a scholar or an expert on faith. You just want a no-gimmick, effective plan that will work for you. But, don't get confused by the words, *work for you*. Yes, it *will* produce radical changes in your faith and life, but it's not magic. It's no one-time pill that will cure all your ailments, solve all your problems, and protect you from all evils. It won't. The plan will work for you when you work the step-by-step plan.

Third, it's *evidence-based*. It's not a theory. I do not offer you an innovative list of impressive ideas or intellectual speculations. I'm talking about timeless biblical principles and practices you can count on. This book is about the kind of faith based on hard facts, honest data, and tested evidence. It's about real people and real results.

With this basis of evidence come assumptions—solid building blocks that come from historical data and centuries of life experiences. I've questioned and tested these assumptions myself. They've become the foundation of my faith, and they drive my understanding of what a healthy faith is and what steps it takes to get there.

Building-block Assumptions

1. *You were created.* You are not an accident of nature. You're part of God's creation. Your creator is real and personal and has a purpose for you. You are born with some of his unique characteristics such as your conscience, your free-will, your desire to have loving relationships, your ability to reason, and your sense of being more than physical.

2. *You will experience evil.* You live in a world where bad things happen to good and bad people. You will wrestle with questions as to why there is so much evil and why good people suffer. Without a healthy faith when confronted with evil, your response will be confusion, anger, bitterness, self-centeredness and self-destruction.

3. *You have a free will.* You're born with a conscience, through which God guides you. Your conscience gives you the ability to make free, unselfish and responsible decisions or to make selfish and irresponsible decisions. You can't always control what happens to you, but you can choose how you will respond. Without your conscience, your physical instincts or animal urges, such as your desire for food, safety, pleasure, and power, would take over. Your free-will gives you the ability to respond in a meaningful way.

4. *You have a personal God.* God not only created you, he cares about you and desires a personal relationship with you. So that you and he could communicate and relate to one another, he created you to be like him

in many ways. But in some ways, he's not like you at all. He is holy. In part, holy means, he's very different from you and me. This holy-difference means you and I can't begin to completely figure out what he's like or what he will do; but you can know that he's more powerful and loving than your mind can imagine.

Even in his holiness, God is personal. The very word *personal* is made up of two words, *per* and *sonal*. They literally mean: (per) through and (sonal) sound, or *to speak through*. Part of what that means is that God wants to communicate with you. The best way to know about God and his ways is to look at the life and words of Jesus, whose name means one who liberates or sets free. It is in the Bible, God's personal record of some of his activities in history, where you can learn some of the characteristics of your personal God and the principles that he built into his creation—principles that can give you a healthy faith.

One of the best examples of someone who was able to use his personal relationship to God and his free-will to find peace and meaning in the face of a horrible situation was Viktor Frankl. Before he was sent to Auschwitz and other Nazi concentration camps during World War II, Frankl was a successful neurologist, psychiatrist, a loving father, devoted husband and a faithful man of God. While a prisoner of war, he lost every possession and every member of his family. His mother, father, brother and wife all died in the camps or in the Nazi gas ovens.

After the war, Frankl was released and wrote *Man's Search for Meaning*, his internationally-famous testimonial volume which exposed his horrific Holocaust experiences. Daily he endured excruciating torture, starvation, bestial labor in freezing conditions and the constant expectation of extermination. While thousands around him became depressed and eventually committed suicide, Frankl's faith gave him the ability to live above his afflictions. He called his way of triumphing over his dilemma a *will to meaning*. He was able to find a greater meaning or higher value in everything good or bad that happened to him. He decided that the one thing his torturers could not take from him was his right to choose, his free-will, his ability to make a godly difference in the face of any impossibility or pain. Frankl had a healthy faith that worked.

More than likely you'll never have to face what Frankl did. But, probably you and your loved ones will face some highly personal and painful crises. Now is the time for you to get prepared. Get ready for some self-examination, some diagnoses, and some action. The plan before you involves five steps that can lead you to the healthy faith you want.

1. Resolve the Confusion—Five Misunderstandings about a Healthy Faith
2. Refocus Your Mind—Five Prescriptions of a Faith-healthy Mind
3. Reclaim Your Heart—Five Heart-healthy Requirements
4. Restructure Your Behavior—Five Action-changing Principles
5. Revitalize Your Lifestyle—Three Ultimate Decisions

Read carefully, and if you follow these steps and work this plan, you'll learn more about yourself than you've ever known, and you'll come away with an understanding of what healthy faith is. You'll get answers to some of your toughest questions about God and suffering. You'll discover how your mind and emotions and your view of yourself influence your faith. At the end of each chapter are five exercises that will help you to grow and maintain your faith. One of those exercises includes conversation with a trusted friend, family member or mentor. Be thinking of someone who could fill that role for you. And when you've finished, you'll be proud of yourself for having done this work. You'll feel and act healthier than you can even imagine right now.

Back to where we started, you may be wondering what my answer would be to the stranger whose shadow loomed over me as I lay in the median on that icy December day when he asked, "So, what do you think of your faith now?"

I would tell him, "I'm more grateful for my faith than I've ever been. Thank God, it works!"

Resolve The Confusion

Five misunderstandings about a healthy faith

"Perfection of means and confusion of ends seem to characterize our age.

ALBERT EINSTEIN, THEORETICAL PHYSICIST

"I had to give up my childhood faith because my studies convinced me that all this talk about faith is no more than emotional, wishful thinking."

SONYA, COLLEGE SOPHOMORE

"Your job is to guide them . . . into healthy faith.".

TITUS 2:1

FROM ANCIENT TIMES, BLOOD-LETTING WAS an accepted medical practice. One of medicine's oldest practices probably originating in ancient Egypt, it was used widely in Greece, where doctors such as Erasistratus (3rd century B.C.) wrongly believed that all sicknesses came from an overabundance of blood. Physicians believed extracting their bad blood would cure the sick.

You wouldn't be surprised that blood-letting is still used by witch-doctors in primitive remote tribes, but you might be surprised that until the nineteenth century blood-letting was an accepted medical procedure by American physicians. In 1799 our first president, George Washington, developed a throat infection and underwent blood-letting by a team of our nation's finest physicians. After ten hours of withdrawing 3.75 liters of his blood, President Washington died.

When a physician's treatment is based on false medical concepts, the outcome can be dangerous. When our faith is based on misconceptions, we turn our backs on God, and our faith does not work when we need it most.

The first step in your path to a healthy faith is to get rid of five common misconceptions that prevent people from developing a healthy faith. Do you hold any of these false ideas? Let's get started.

CHAPTER 1

What are the Characteristics of a HEALTHY Faith?

*"Take time to define what health means to you and what you are willing
to do or willing to give up doing to bring better health into your life."*

Dr. Melanie Greenberg, Clinical Psychologist

*"Those now who live by faith are blessed (healthy) along
with Abraham, who lived by faith—this is no new doctrine!
And that means that anyone who tries to live by his own
effort, independent of God, is doomed to failure."*

Galatians 3:8-10

What do people want most? Money, love, power, fame? You might be surprised. Health is at the top of many lists of the basic human desires. Who doesn't want a healthy body and mind? The problem is there's so much confusion about what it means to be healthy that we can be perilously sick and still think we're healthy.

In my experience, most unhealthy people had no idea as to just how sick their bodies or minds were until a crisis hit. Often, they had destructive warning-signs for a long time but got so used to them they assumed they were normal.

The same is true for faith. If you don't have an accurate understanding of what a healthy faith is, over time, you get so used to your unhealthy symptoms, that you don't think of your faith as sick until it fails you miserably.

How can you know if your body is healthy or not? If you had a list of recognized characteristics of a healthy body, you could compare your body to that list and have a more realistic perspective. Fortunately, just as there are some commonly-accepted characteristics of a healthy body, there are seven distinct characteristics of a healthy faith.

Let's see just how healthy or unhealthy your faith is. Study each of the descriptions below and ask yourself, "Is this a good description of me and my faith? Which parts of my faith are in good shape and which need help?"

CHARACTERISTICS OF A HEALTHY FAITH

1. YOU HAVE A HEALTHY FAITH IF IT'S
EVIDENCE-BASED

A healthy faith is based on reliable evidence, not wishful thinking, superstitions, myths or fairytales. It's founded on time-tested, trustworthy findings including a real, personal God who acted in real historical events and in real people's lives. Your faith is not healthy because of bright ideas, the latest fad, or popular theory, but because of solid research and dependable evidence.

Your faith is able to handle challenges. It's secure because it's well-informed and well-equipped, not naïve or easily manipulated. It's not closed-minded, stagnant or disrespectful of different views. You don't get angry or upset when people disagree with your beliefs. You're willing to listen and learn from others. Your faith is so secure it welcomes new ideas and doubts. It's ready for hard questions and difficult situations. Is this a description of your faith?

2. YOU HAVE A HEALTHY FAITH IF IT'S
HONEST AND ETHICAL

A healthy faith is an honest faith. It gives you the ability to be truthful, open and unafraid to admit your weaknesses and stand up for your beliefs. You're not secretive, two-faced or boastful. You don't harbor guilt or anger or answer hardships or unkind acts by being bitter, resentful or revengeful. Because of your faith, you respond to such adversities with sympathy, sorrow, forgiveness and compassion. You are truthful when it would be easier and less painful to tell a lie.

A healthy faith is ethical. It gives you a stand-up-to-culture moral character. You're not selfish, deceitful or lazy. You practice a pure, godly life-style. You don't take advantage of others or use others. Because of your faith, you have the ability to do what is good and right when you're tempted to do what is bad and wrong. Your faith has not made you perfect, but when you do something wrong or hurtful, your faith enables you to quickly confess your sin, do what you can to correct the wrong, and get back on track quickly. Your faith gives you a clear and grateful conscience.

Your faith makes you the same person in public as you are in those areas of your life that only God and you can see—your private-life, your secret thoughts, and your prayer-life. You don't try to impress people by play-acting, bragging, name-dropping, or doing all the talking. Your faith sets you free to be unselfish, passionate, warmhearted, caring and outwardly expressive about your beliefs and your God. Is this a description of your faith?

3. YOU HAVE A HEALTHY FAITH IF IT'S
PRODUCTIVE DESPITE PROBLEMS

A healthy faith is productive, not passive or self-indulgent. It doesn't allow life's problems to stop you from being fruitful. You expect crises, disappointments, heartaches, injuries and roadblocks. They may slow you down, but they don't keep you from keeping on. You see them not as interruptions but as normal elements of living.

Your faith is relationship-driven, not reward-driven. You have a personal, loving relationship with God and others which causes you to see yourself as a person on a mission. You don't just live for your own good. You have values that are bigger and more important than you. You don't see yourself as being here by accident. You believe that God loves you and has work for you to do. When hard times come, your faith supplies you with the courage and tenacity to carry out your purpose. At times you get down and are disappointed, but nothing can stop you from demonstrating your love. Your faith keeps your head and heart and hands on your long-range goals and not your short-term challenges. Is this a description of your faith?

4. YOU HAVE A HEALTHY FAITH IF YOU ARE
AWARE OF GOD'S PRESENCE

A healthy faith is God-conscious. You don't just know about God, seek to follow godly values, or just believe in the idea of God. You know God personally, intimately, in a way you can't adequately express in words. You *hear* his inaudible voice. You're aware of his presence in your daily life. Although he's invisible physically, you have a personal relationship with God.

You're not worried, fearful, embarrassed or anxious about invisible things. Your faith makes you comfortable thinking and talking about things that are real although you cannot see or touch them.

Your faith is not narcissistic. It is humble, unselfish and compassionate. You're more interested in what God wants than anything else. His will is your greatest desire. When you pray to God, it's like a conversation between two people who love and respect one another. You don't try to talk God into your way of thinking or into doing what you want. In your decision-making process, you listen and watch for God to communicate with you through the Bible, your conscience, other people and the rest of his creation.

Like the invisible wind, you sense God's Spirit (his presence) in your life because you sense the difference he makes. Is this a description of your faith?

5. You have a Healthy Faith if it's
VULNERABLE AND PERSONAL

A healthy faith takes personal risks. It gives you the ability and willingness to have close personal relationships with others and God. You don't withhold feelings, thoughts, actions and love from people who care about you. You openly give yourself in loving relationships.

Although you know there will be times when people will lie to you, take advantage of you and even abuse your trust, you still get close to people. Even when people let you down, you don't give up on them. You look for ways to forgive, support, encourage and win their trust and love. Your faith makes you gentle and merciful. Is this a description of your faith?

6. You have a Healthy Faith if it's
RESPONSIBILE AND SYMPATHETIC

A healthy faith is responsible. Your faith causes you to be fully answerable for your own behavior, emotions and attitude. You're not a blamer or whiner. You don't justify bad decisions, thoughts and behavior by comparing yourself to others. You own up to your errors. You don't criticize or point out others' faults to make yourself look better. You are not judgmental, condemning, constantly looking for something wrong in others. When something goes wrong, you don't try to make others feel guilty.

No matter how hard or unfair your past was, you hold yourself accountable for your decisions, spirit, and behavior today. You don't depend on others to make you feel good.

Your faith causes you to feel sympathy, to encourage others, to look for compassionate reasons why people fall short. You're not angry or hateful toward those who do wrong. You're understanding. You remember your past failures and how God forgave you. Your focus is on future opportunities for you and others, not past failures. Is this a good description of your faith?

7. YOU HAVE A HEALTHY FAITH IF IT'S
COMFORTABLE WITH LIMITATIONS

A healthy faith is calm and level-headed under pressure. It keeps you from being hot-headed, melodramatic, or sensational. You do all you can to help in difficult situations, then you accept your limitations and place those problems you can't change in God's hands. You're able to face threats, hatred, unanswered questions, or changes calmly. You're quick to admit that you don't have all of the answers to all the questions about faith. Your faith gives you permission to not be right all the time. It allows you to candidly admit your incomplete understanding without feeling embarrassed.

Your faith is not uptight when it's surrounded with lots of imperfections, disappointments, and failures. It's not rigid. You don't get upset with challenges to what you think, how you feel, and what you do. You're hurt and sometimes angry when unfair and painful things happen to you and those you love; but, you don't let your anger make you bitter, mean-spirited or critical.

Although your faith is in a God who is perfect, you know you're imperfect, yet he loves you and accepts you with all of your limitations. You are grateful that he doesn't try to control you or force you to love him. So, you follow his example by encouraging others rather than trying to control or coerce them. Your awareness of your weaknesses makes you more humble, compassionate and forgiving.

A CHECKLIST FOR A HEALTHY FAITH.

Now that you have this list, you'll want to put it to use. I've personally found the list helpful in several ways. Whether I'm taking my regular, personal faith-examination, which I find is essential for me to do, or listening to someone with faith-concerns, this inventory is a good check-list. As you move through the plan, I trust it will do the same for you.

EXERCISES TO BUILD AND MAINTAIN YOUR HEALTHY FAITH

To develop a healthy, vibrant faith that works in good times and hard times, you need to know what one looks like. In Chapter One, you have gained an understanding of the characteristics of a healthy faith, so now it's time to make certain that yours is not just a passive understanding. So sit quietly with your Bible, and pen and paper, and let's get started.

RECORD: Either on an index/flash card you can stick in your pocket, or a notepad that is easily accessible during the day, or on your phone, record the Seven Characteristics of a Healthy Faith.

REMEMBER: Keep the list you have recorded handy, and read it three times a day for seven days, always trying to memorize the list.

REFLECT: In your quiet time, read again the characteristics of a healthy faith, and then open your Bible to Romans 5: 1-5. These verses explain to you what your life will be like because you have a healthy faith. Meditate on some of the rewards of demonstrating your faith. Talk to your Father about how you feel about your faith and thank Him for the rewards that come with faith.

RE-EXAMINE: Begin to pay close attention to how you respond to conflicts or other uncomfortable situations in your daily activities. Notice if your thoughts, feelings, and actions are similar or contrary to the characteristics of a healthy faith.

RELATE: Spend some time discussing these characteristics and your desires for your own faith with someone you trust.

Now that you have a clearer understanding of the word *healthy* as it relates to faith, you know where you're headed. You have a clear goal. For you to develop a healthy faith, there's another key word that needs clarification. It's one of the most misunderstood words in English. It's that powerful little word *faith*. Everybody uses it. But, it's not what most people think.

Because the word faith is so misconstrued, it usually causes more trouble than help. So many twist it to mean whatever they want that it's often equated with sick religion, foolish thinking, quacks, magic, and superstition. More than likely, you'll never find a healthy faith until you get a more accurate understanding of the word faith. Let's take a closer look at that in Chapter Two.

Pray this prayer to your Heavenly Father.

Dear Father, I need the courage and willingness to read this book and to work the plan. I humbly ask you to provide encouragement, understanding and the patience I need to begin my faith-building journey. Amen.

CHAPTER 2

What are the four essential parts of FAITH?

❧

"Today the term 'faith' is more productive of disease than of health."

PAUL TILLICH, CHRISTIAN PHILOSOPHER AND THEOLOGIAN

"Faith is the firm foundation under everything that makes life worth living."

HEBREWS 11:1

SHE COULD HARDLY EXPLAIN HER problem through her weeping. I felt so sorry for her. At thirty-three, she had desperately looked for love for years but had not found it. She'd met many men but had her heart broken every time. When I finally pieced together her story, it was clear why she couldn't find love. She didn't know what real love looked like. It's the same with faith. You'll never find it if you're looking for the wrong thing.

You know my name is Bill. You've got the right name. But, if you were trying to find me in a crowded, public place for the first time, just having my name wouldn't be enough. After all, I'm a rather ordinary looking fellow; and, there are lots of Bills out there. With no more than the name, no matter how persistent your search, you'd probably find the wrong Bill and never find me. What you would really need is to start out with a good, first-hand, here's-what-he-looks-like description. But, you'd need to be careful where you get your description. Some might innocently give you a misleading, second-hand description that someone passed on to them, by someone who passed it down to them, by . . . Well, you can just imagine how distorted the description could get over a just a few years.

What comes to your mind when you hear …?

- I have faith in God. I am a person of faith.
- My faith is Presbyterian. He's of the Catholic faith.
- I have faith in the Bible. I don't have faith in the stock market.
- My faith is weak. My faith is strong. I wish I had more faith.
- If you have enough faith, you can move mountains and cure diseases.
- He had faith and prayed for healing. He died anyway.
- Without faith, you can't please God or make it to heaven.

Ask ten people, "What exactly is faith?" You'll probably get ten different answers. No wonder people have such a hard time developing faith.

Another reason the word faith is so confusing is that it's not something just pious people have. Everyone has faith. Faith is not a religious thing. Faith is a human thing. Having faith is like breathing, thinking, and feeling. It's part of your birth-package. You didn't have to learn to think or feel. You do them naturally, automatically.

That's the way faith is. From your childhood until now, you've performed thousands of tiny and large acts of faith. You're a person of faith. You make faith-decisions all the time. The question is not, do you have faith, but what kind of faith do you have? Is it useful or useless, effective or ineffective, child-ish or mature, healthy or sick?

Most of us start out with a simple, child-like, fairytale understanding of the word faith. It's cute to hear the way some kids talk about their faith. I re-member when Tommy came to my office because his mom felt he was ready to join the church. When she left us alone to talk, I asked the bright little five-year-old, "Tommy, your mom said you have faith in God. What does that mean to you?" With a surprised look on his face, he sat up straight and answered, "If you don't have faith in God, your parents will get mad at you, and you won't get anything for Christmas." His answer probably made you chuckle. It did me.

We all laugh when we hear the funny things kids say about God and faith. After all, they're just kids. But a childish view of faith is neither cute nor adorable when it's held by an adult. It's a serious subject because we adults have to deal with grown-up faith-issues and tough faith-decisions having critical consequences for our lives and others.

In a way, our childish faith is like my first dog. When I asked my folks for a dog, they gave me a stuffed dog, Butch. Both of my parents worked long hours and didn't have time to take care of a real dog, so they figured that a furry, cuddly, marble-eyed imitation would be a lot less trouble. Don't get me wrong, as a little boy, I loved Butch. He was comforting to hold, and I liked playing make-believe with him. But, as I matured, I realized that Butch didn't do anything except sit there. I became discontented with having a stuffed animal for a friend. I wanted a real dog. Fake dogs were for babies. I wanted a living, breathing, barking, full-of-life dog.

A childish faith never satisfies the adult mind. To get to a healthy faith, you must put aside any childish notion you have about what faith is, what you think it is, what you've been told it is. It's time to start fresh and get back to the original, clear meaning of faith.

Getting a handle on the word *faith* is not easy because there are so many ever-changing definitions and ways people use and misuse the word. Originally, *faith* was a common, everyday word, not a religious word. Faith was a commitment to an uncertain future. It was a risky action. It was depending on something or someone other than yourself. Faith was stepping out on to something that appeared to be safe but was not safe for sure.

I grew up in south Florida and never saw snow or ice until I went to college. The first time I saw a frozen lake, I was nervous about following my ice-skating friends on to that once lake of water. Eventually I weighed the risk, made a decision and with all my weight, stepped onto that ice. At the moment I left the dry ground and put my full weight on that ice, faith happened.

Faith is not wishing, hoping, wanting or believing strongly. To equate faith with mere wishful thinking is to distort the word. That kind of faith never works and generally produces unhealthy results.

The Bible says, "Now faith is the *substance* of things hoped for, the *evidence* of things not seen." Hebrews 11:1. Notice, faith is not just hoping for something. Real faith is built on something real, something with substance. Faith has a foundation, a solid rock underneath our hopes, beliefs and wishes. *The Message* translation of that same scripture is, "Faith is the *firm foundation* under everything that makes life worth living. It's our handle on what we can't see. The *act of faith* is what distinguished our ancestors, set them above the crowd."

I've found that some feel embarrassed, others elated, when they learn the original meaning of the word faith and how it's used in the Bible. I remember one woman's emotional appreciation, "I can hardly believe how confused I was about what faith is. It's no wonder I've had so many problems with my faith. I feel like I've been blind and now I can see."

If you think about the many ways the word *faith* is used today, it's no wonder people have so much trouble understanding what faith is.

- Mother Teresa's sacrificial work helping impoverished people in India is said to be a result of her faith.
- David Koresh, the Waco, Texas-based Branch Davidian cult-leader, led his followers in an intense gun battle where four federal agents, seventy-six Branch Dravidians, twenty children, and two pregnant women died. News reporters said Koresh and his followers were motivated by their faith.
- Frank Short was one of the finest Christian men I've ever known. When he died of cancer, his doctors and nurses told me Frank had an unusual faith that enabled him to face death with extraordinary courage and joy.

It's amazing how the word faith is used to explain or describe a wide range of touching, strange, good and bad activities we do. When you think about your faith, as it relates to everyday activities, important relationships and God, it's no wonder the word faith often confuses, misleads, and creates anger, skepticism, fanaticism, intellectual rejection and overly-emotional commitments that are far from what real faith is.

As you work on developing your healthy faith, decide now to use the word faith the way it was used originally and how it is used in the Bible. To help you clarify and permanently embed that meaning in your mind, remember faith always has these four elements—a risk, decision, action and object.

1. The Risk

The essence of faith always involves *risk*. It's never completely safe. It's never a sure thing. Faith is about the future, which you cannot see or know. It includes questions, uncertainties and some level of fear. Faith is an adventure. If you say, "I'm absolutely certain about this," it's not faith. You may be acting in a courageous, unselfish, obedient or even noble way, but that's not faith. Faith always includes uncertainty or risk.

The Bible has many true stories about personal faith. One of my favorites is about Noah, who was called to build a large boat, the ark, in the middle of a desert even though he couldn't see the future. The Bible writer says, "He was warned about something he couldn't see, and acted on what he was told." Hebrews 11:7. Noah's future was unclear, but he acted on the little that he did know. He risked his life. If you haven't recently read the story, I invite you to read it in its entirety in Genesis 6-9.

As you work through this plan, you'll learn how to take risks, but not foolish, stupid risks. Faith always involves risking something to get something better. No matter how healthy your faith becomes, it will always include questions, uncertainties and some fear. Real faith is never an easy or safe way, but it's always the best way.

2. The Decision

Second, real faith always includes a personal *decision*. Faith is your response to a challenge. It's a choice. It's an act of your free-will, not just a thought or desire. Faith is not, "I hope so." Where there's no choice or decision, there's no faith.

Noah was warned there was going to be a flood and that he and his family would drown if he didn't build the ark. Part of Noah's faith was his personal response to the challenge, the threat of danger and possible death. His choice was not to follow popular opinion, but to personally decide to step out from the crowd. It was his choice. Because of his response, he and his family didn't die. He tried to convince others, but they would not believe him. They, too, had faith. Like Noah, they weighed the risks and made their decisions. It was a decision, but it was the wrong decision.

3. The Action

Third, faith always involves *action*. Faith is not just what you think, believe, feel or decide. For faith to happen, it must also include what you do. Throughout the Bible, faith without action is considered useless, dead, or not faith at all.

Noah *faithed*. That is, he weighed the risks, made a decision after considering the evidence, and then built the boat. Faith didn't happen until he acted, until he stepped out and went to work. He couldn't see the future, but he depended on God. He put his future in God's hands.

For Jesus, the words *faith* and *follow* were synonymous. If you had faith, you followed him. You took action. If you were a person of faith, you were called a follower or a person of the *way*. You walked in the *way* of Jesus. There's no faith without action. The Bible says, "Faith by itself, if it is not accompanied by action, is dead." James 2:17

4. The Object

Fourth, faith always includes an *object*. That is, there is always something or someone you're committing to, making the risk for, depending on, or following. This final element of faith makes a big difference. What is the *object* on which you're about to place your full weight? If it's a plane, you'd better check out the quality of the aircraft. Your faith is not much good if the plane is not safe. Is it dependable? How dependable? Every faith-decision you make will include some object on which you depend. It may be a plane, a chair, a belief, a person or God on which you put your full weight.

Americans who are deaf usually use American Sign Language to communicate. ASL has a graphic sign for the word faith. It clearly pictures the full meaning of the word. To communicate the word or idea of faith in ASL, you position your hands like you're holding on to a rope for dear life. You are completely dependent on that rope. If you let go, you will fall to your death. Obviously, the key element in the sign is the rope.

But, faith includes all four parts - the *risk* of depending on something other than yourself, the *decision* to grab hold, the *act* of putting all of your weight on that rope and the *object* of your faith, the quality of the rope itself. What a memorable picture of the real meaning of faith. God is our rope. He is that trustworthy, dependable object of our faith that we cling to. Put simply, for me, faith is depending on something or someone completely. For Christians, faith is depending on God completely.

Exercises to Build and Maintain your Healthy Faith

You've just finished reading about the essentials of faith, but reading isn't enough, so let's get busy.

RECORD: Remember how you recorded the Seven Characteristics of a Healthy Faith in Chapter One? In the same manner, record the Four Essential Parts of Faith. Think about your personal definition of faith and record it.

REMEMBER: Read the Four Essential Parts of Faith several times daily until you have committed them to memory. Keep reviewing the Seven Characteristics of Faith from Chapter One.

REFLECT: Read the story of the woman who desired healing in Mark 4: 24 – 34 and made a faith decision. With the four essential parts of faith in mind, meditate on these verses. Put yourself in the place of the woman. What did she do? What did Jesus do?

RE-EXAMINE: Recall a faith decision you have made recently and how it included the four essential parts of faith. Recall how Jesus' faith decision to give himself on the cross demonstrated all the parts of his faith.

RELATE: Discuss with someone your definition of faith and which one of the four faith essentials is most difficult for you.

Since you now have a better understanding of what a healthy faith looks like and what the word faith actually means, it's time to take a closer look at the person who is actually going to do the work in this plan. I'm talking about YOU.

Another reason many people get confused about their faith is they live with some serious misconceptions about what makes them who they are. For you to develop a healthy faith, you're going to have to engage your entire SELF—all three parts of you. But, what is this SELF I'm talking about? What makes up your SELF? Let's find out in Chapter Three.

Pray this prayer to your Heavenly Father.

Dear Father, I know you love and believe in me. Your Bible says you know my heart and my mind. Your son said we should ask if we want to receive anything. Please give me the wisdom and sensitivity to examine myself, to ask myself the hard questions, and the sensitivity to your Spirit to help me. Amen.

CHAPTER 3

How well do you know your *SELF?*

☙

*"The question is not whether or not we shall live by faith.
The question is—by what faith shall we live? What
range and depth and quality shall they have?"*

Harry Emerson Fosdick, Pastor, Author, Theologian

*"Love the Lord your God with all your heart and with all your
soul and with all your strength and with all your mind."*

Luke 10:27

"The only thing worse than being blind is having sight but no vision."

Helen Keller, Christian Political Activist, Author

Although Helen Keller was completely deaf, blind, and mute from the age of two, she became one of our nation's most inspiring and famous leaders. In 1964, Helen received the Presidential Medal of Honor, the highest civilian award in America. One of the main reasons Helen overcame such difficult challenges and had such a productive life was her self-image. She saw more in her *self* than a person who was deaf and blind. She used that decisive insight to become an author, political activist, fund-raiser, Christian, and internationally-recognized advocate for people with disabilities.

Like Helen Keller, how you look at your *self* will greatly determine the kind of faith you will have. Understanding who you are, what it is about you that determines your way of thinking, how you feel and what you do, will help you understand what you need to do to get a healthy faith.

Stop and look inside your SELF. If you're like most people I've talked to about their self-images, you haven't thought much about what makes you who you are. If you haven't, your self-image is probably a product of your past experiences—the good and bad comments made about you, the true and false beliefs you accepted, and the encouraging and painful circumstances you experienced. Before you go any further, you need to stop and look inside your *self* and get rid of any misconception you may have picked up along the way. This is not an easy job, but you can do it with a little help.

To help you examine your self-image more thoroughly, ask yourself some revealing questions like these:

- What makes me think what I think, feel what I feel, and do what I do?
- How do I decide what's right and wrong or good and bad?
- Is there a god who cares about me? If not, how did I get here?
- What's going to happen to me after my body dies?
- Is death the end of me, or is there more?

For thousands of years people have viewed the *self* in two main ways—*a spirit trapped in a body* or *a child of the living God*. I invite you to review the key characteristics of these classic two views and decide which is closest to the way you see your *self*?

A Spirit Trapped in a Body

Almost no one believes we are just physical bodies that live for a few years and cease to exist when we die. Most people around the world believe they are made of two main parts—physical and spiritual, body and spirit. But the way we view these two parts is crucial to our self-image and faith.

Your body is your biggest problem. The body-spirit view looks at your physical and spiritual parts as arch-enemies living in an on-going battle between your evil and good parts. From this point-of-view, your body and other material things cause all of your problems. You suffer because you are partly physical. All physical things eventually fight each other, break, decay, die and cause suffering. But, you can avoid suffering. How? If you don't allow yourself to be attached or attracted to any *thing,* you can become spiritual. Being spiritual is simply being spirit-oriented, not thinking about, caring for or relating to the physical world.

You're a free spirit. If you hold this view, you believe your spirit is the important, real, lasting, valuable part of you. It's the real-you. It's like a tiny bundle of energy or spark that broke-off the energy-source of the universe. It's not in any way a part of what makes up your body—your physical form, brain, thoughts, feelings, and actions. Your spirit is separate from all that. It's that impersonal part of you that's trapped in the prison-house of your body.

When your body dies, all that made up your body dies with it and ceases to exist. The only part of your *self* that survives death is your immortal spirit. At death your spirit is freed to be absorbed back into the energy-source from which it came. Your spirit is like a drop of water that splashes up into the air for a short time and then falls back into the ocean and is no longer your spirit. You personally no longer exist.

Your conscience is your god. According to this view, you should see your *self* as a immortal spirit that is independent, self-sufficient, responsible-to-no-one. You have no set of rules but your own. You have no god but your own conscience. You are spirit. If you stop thinking about physical things, stop getting emotionally involved with things, you would be free from everything that can cause you to suffer.

Any physical pain or any other feeling or desire you have is a result of your attraction to the physical world. If you have this body-spirit view, you would probably misquote and misinterpret the scriptures that instruct believers in this way, "Do not love the world or anything in the world." I John 2:15. The kind of faith that's built on this view of the *self* is radically different from one built on the view I call a *Child of the Living God.*

A Child of the Living God

Since everyone is someone's child, I wasn't surprised to learn that most people around the world believe in a god that is, in some way, their super-natural parent. How they picture that child and god may differ significantly. The largest group of God-believers is the Hebrew-Christian community. Those of us in this group don't agree on every detail, but our commonly-held Bible provides some commonly-held characteristics of the *self.* Those characteristics will help you decide if this is your view. I hope it is.

Take a look at some of the ways that the child-of-God view is appreciably different from the body-spirit view.

The Body-Spirit View

*   Your personal mind is your best source for an accurate self-image.
*   Your body is your spirit's evil enemy. It's your spirit's prison-house.
*   Physical death is the end of your body, thoughts, feelings and past.
*   Your spirit is an impersonal, immortal, body-less piece of energy.
*   Your spirit and body become non-existent when your body dies.
*   You're free if you are godless and dependent on no one and no thing.
*   Being spiritual is being free from desires, other-worldly, anti-physical.

The Child-of-God View

*   God and the Bible are your best sources for an accurate self-image.
*   Your body is a good partner of your mind and heart.
*   When your physical body dies, you get a transformed body like Jesus.

- Physical death is not the end of your thoughts, feelings and past. Each part of you lives for eternity as part of your new body.
- Your spirit is not separate from you. Your spirit is the combination of your three parts.
- Your spirit (you) will live forever with your new heavenly body.
- You're free if you're dependent on God, who is able to free you. You see your *self* as child who needs help, not independence.
- Being spiritual is thinking, feeling, and acting like God, who is Spirit.

Be careful where you go for help. I remember when I was struggling with my own self-image. To try to get a clearer picture, I asked myself some of the same big-picture questions I mentioned before such as, what's most important to me? What makes me think the way I think, feel the way I feel, do what I do? What's going to happen to me when I die? What elements make up who I am? After asking myself those kinds of questions, I realized it was critical to know where my answers came from and if they came from a reliable source. Plenty of people are willing to give their answers.

We all look to someone for help. Some choose to look into their own minds, as if their minds were pure from others' beliefs. Some turn to others' beliefs and theories. Those of us who hold the child-of-God view are not willing to put our faith in ourselves because we know our limitations. Neither will we depend on others for something so important because we know others have similar limitations. We begin with the most reliable source possible—God himself. And, how can you get answers from him? Fortunately, you have several ways to find the mind and heart of God on a subject like this. You can -

- Go to directly to him through prayer
- Study Bible stories and learn how God related to his children
- Look to Bible stories to see how God's children related to their Father
- Read the words of Jesus and those written about his personality
- Examine other Bible-believers' insights into the biblical view of the *self*
- Listen to your heavenly Father's still, small voice as you read his living word in search of his view.

Better than the best explanation. You'll never find an explanation in the Bible about the human *self*. As usual, God's word gives us helpful descriptions and declarations not speculations and explanations. If you want to know the biblical view of *self*, don't look for a long intellectual exhortation, a series of complex propositions, or a collection of other-worldly sounding phrases like *universal energy-force*.

God's way of describing what makes up your *self* is to give you some pictures you can remember, rather than explanations you'll forget. The first picture he gave us was the Bible-writers' picture of his creation of the first human. The Bible says we were made in *God's image or likeness*. Genesis 1:27. I call it a picture because, like a painting of person, it's not the actual person. But it's a close-enough resemblance or likeness to the real thing that you see the essence, but it leaves room for other qualities you may not see.

The biblical word-picture, *made in the image of God*, is an amazingly-simple yet profound description. According to the Bible, you should say to yourself something like this, "I was put together in such a way that I have some of the same characteristics of my heavenly Father. I'm no little god, but when you see me, you might say to yourself, 'the way he talks and acts reminds me of the God of the Bible.'"

Have you ever heard someone say, "That boy is the spitting-image of his father?" That doesn't just mean the son has some noticeable physical characteristics of his father. It also means he thinks the same way, likes the same things, and is excited about the same values.

The second picture God gave us to help us better see ourselves was the life and words of Jesus. No one knows all God meant in that famous descriptive phrase, *made in God's image*. But it seems clear to me and to many others that, in part, what God meant was he gave us the ability to think, feel, behave and make choices like he does. Even though we have a free-will like God has, we don't always choose correctly. In some miraculous, God-only way, Jesus was God in flesh. He was both God and human. From his human side, Jesus was the only person that not only had the ability to think, feel and behave like God, he actually always did behave like his heavenly Father.

The Bible says that Jesus was tempted in every way we are but was without sin. Hebrew 4:15. His life and words and relationship to his Heavenly Father give us a good picture of what made Jesus who he was and what makes us who we are. He saw himself as a child who thought humbly, felt grateful, acted like a servant, was tempted, and yet chose to be his Father's servant.

Therefore, as you work on developing your healthy faith, you're going to learn how to use each of your three God-created parts: your mind, feelings and behavior. Collectively, those God-like parts make up what we call *you,* your *soul, spirit or self.* Think of it this way, God doesn't have a spirit. He is spirit. When you see how he thinks, feels, and what his body does, you see his Spirit in action. We're made the same way.

So, you can see why any act of real faith must include all three of your parts. If any part of you is left out, your act of faith will not be you. It will be only a part of you. It will be incomplete, not a real commitment of your total self.

When I was in high school, I ran track and I wanted to join the cross-country team. But, I'd never run a long-distance race, and my body wasn't ready. The coach said he thought I could probably make the team if I would commit to work hard on a few important items. He gave me a written routine to follow. It included a list of some changes I needed to make and some disciplines I needed to follow related to my heart, respiration, leg muscles, eating and sleep habits. His plan worked. I made the team. After running a few long-distance races, no one had to tell me the importance of following the regimen to stay fit and conditioned.

The same is true for gaining and maintaining a healthy faith. It takes the same kind of comprehensive commitment and discipline. You'll also have to make some changes to one or more of your three parts.

If you're like most people, your faith depends more on one part of you than the other two. For example, if it's your habit to put your faith in someone mainly or solely because it feels right, then you probably say things like, "I put my faith in that person because my heart told me that it was the right thing to do. I try to follow my heart not my head." For you, it's important to feel good about a person before you make a significant commitment. But why just trust your heart? Why not also engage all of your parts, all of the resources you have? Wouldn't it be better to give your mind, heart, and experience equal attention in making a faith-decision? Of course it would.

That principle came home to me a few years ago when I read about an extreme case of an imbalanced personality. Sometimes we can learn more about our own less serious problems by examining someone's more acute situation.

In his Kansas courthouse testimony, the psychopathic serial killer, Dennis Rader shocked the world. With cool and dispassionate details, he described how he brutally murdered ten people. As he named himself, BTK (Bind, Torture and Kill), he revealed no conscience or sense of remorse. Those who knew him before he was discovered portrayed him as a nice fellow. He was highly intelligent, well educated, fun to be around, and a hard worker.

But if you took a closer look, you'd see that he was an exceptionally sick person. One of his three parts was absent—his heart. He had no feelings for people. He had no conscience. You might think he was doing pretty well operating on sixty-six percent of himself. You might even conclude he should be able to live a happy and normal life using two out of his three parts. But, obviously, his life was far less than normal. It was horrible. Of course, this is an extreme case. But, it's a classic reminder of the serious potential of ignoring any one part of our personality.

Over the years, you may have developed excellent skills in using your mind and experiences in making decisions. You may be so successful in using only those parts that you don't pay much attention to how you feel about your decision or what your heart says to you. To some degree that happens to all of us.

Dr. Abraham Verghese, Vice Chair for the Theory and Practice of Medicine at the Stanford School of Medicine and author of the award-winning novel, *Cutting for Stone*, is a friend of mine and an internationally-recognized advocate for comprehensive, person-centered, patient care. When I heard him speak at the University of Texas Health Science Center in San Antonio, he addressed his fellow physicians and other healthcare workers about the importance of treating patients as multi-dimensional people. He cautioned them about the growing tendency for healthcare workers to look at their patients as iPatients or machines that need to be fixed, not people who need care.

Certainly not all doctors see their patients as iPatients, and most of us don't look at ourselves as physical creatures only; however, most of us tend to depend more on one part of our total self than we do the other two. But, when it comes to your faith, it is wise to take a good look at your three parts and ask yourself these questions, "Which part of me do I depend on most when I'm making a decision or acting on faith? Do I rely mainly on my HEAD, HEART, or HANDS?" Below are brief descriptions of your three parts.

HEAD – THE MENTAL PART OF YOU

The mental part of you has a rational and moral side. It's that part that thinks through things before you make a decision and instinctively knows right from wrong because of your conscience. This part of you is made up of your thoughts, beliefs, mind, values, morals, conscience, judgments, understandings, reasoning, logic and analysis. You are, to some degree, what you believe. In the same way, your faith is, to some degree, what you believe.

HEART – THE EMOTIONAL PART OF YOU

Your heart is that inner, private part of you that houses your emotions, desires and will. It's the part of you that refers to your how you feel, what you want, what brings you comfort, pleasure, hope and satisfaction. When you put your faith in someone, part of what you do is put your feelings, desires, and trust in that person. An important element of faith is emotional.

HANDS – THE PHYSICAL PART OF YOU

Because our hands are so active doing things, the hand often symbolizes our physical behavior. You're not only what you think and feel, you're also what you do. The physical part of you refers to your behavior, experiences, deeds, conduct, actions, evidence, work, discipline, self-control, obedience. When you have faith in someone, you're mainly referring to how you behave or act towards that person. Faith is more about action than believing and feeling.

No doubt, you recognize which of your three parts plays the most dominant role in your decisions and which plays the least. In the remaining steps of the plan, you're going to learn how to effectively use all three parts. And, especially you're going to learn how to effectively use those parts you now use the least. Whether you're trying to decide on what to do about a crisis in your life or an opportunity before you, you need to make a balanced faith-decision if you want to make a healthy-decision.

EXERCISES TO BUILD AND MAINTAIN YOUR HEALTHY FAITH

Hopefully in this chapter you've learned something about the self and even yourself. So, let's see how well you know yourself.

RECORD: Trying to limit yourself to two or three sentences, record your answers to the following questions:

* What makes me think what I think, feel what I feel, and do what I do?
* How do I decide what is right and wrong or good and bad?
* Is there a god who cares about me? If not, how did I get here?
* What's going to happen to me after my body dies?
* Is death the end of me or is there more?

REMEMBER: Memorize the two main views of the self and the three parts of yourself.

REFLECT: Read the story of Jesus' washing his disciples' feet in John 13: 1-17. Picture yourself as one of those disciples, and make a list of five words that would describe Jesus' self-image.

RE-EXAMINE: Look at the list of words that described Jesus' self-image. Compare those descriptive words to your own self-image. Think about which part of the self you depend upon to make decisions.

RELATE: With your trusted person, discuss your recorded answers to the five questions listed above. Listen for their answers. Discuss how your past experiences have influenced your self-image and how you want to change the way you view yourself. And lastly, if you're making a major decision, discuss how you might use the three parts of the self to make that decision.

On your journey to a healthy faith, there's another common misconception we need to clear up. It's a problem that causes many a great deal of confusion—the lack of personal faith-diagnosis. Too frequently people try to fix their ineffective faith by simply attempting to get more of the same kind of ineffective faith they already have. They have no idea as to what specific areas of their faith are unhealthy; so, they're confused about how to make changes.

When William first came to see me, he didn't hold back. "I don't want to be disrespectful. You're a minister and all that. But, I want you to know from the getgo that I'm through with this whole faith thing. Every time I turned things over to God, they just got worse. It's not that I don't want to believe in God. I do. It's just that, and I'm ashamed to say it, but I can't see that it's ever helped me. It just doesn't work." When I asked William why his faith wasn't working for him, his answer was what I usually hear, "I don't have a clue."

Doesn't it make sense? If you're trying to fix a problem, you'd better start with a good diagnosis of the problem. You better know what the real problem is. Don't spend your time treating your kidney if it's really your heart that's causing the problem. In the same way, before you can properly treat your sick faith, it's best if you make a good faith-diagnosis and pinpoint what's causing the sickness. How can you do that? Keep reading. But before you do …

Pray this prayer to your Heavenly Father.

Dear Father, I love you and need you. I don't feel that I deserve your help, but I come to you as your child. Forgive me for disappointing you. I'm sorry. I want to become more like you. Help me see myself as your child. Help me think like you do, have a heart like yours, and behave like your son, Jesus. Thank you for your grace and patience. Amen.

CHAPTER 4

How do you take a
faith DIAGNOSIS?

ൿ

*"Let's give ourselves a chance at precise diagnosis before we treat…
'Find the enemy and win the firefight' is a good philosophy for
infectious diseases as it is for war. Diagnosis matters."*

DR. ABRAHAM VERGHESE, PHYSICIAN AND AUTHOR

"Diagnosis is not the end, but the beginning of practice."

DR. MARTIN H. FISCHER, PHYSICIAN AND AUTHOR

*"Search me, God, and know my heart; test me
and know my anxious thoughts."*

PSALM 139:23

IN DR. SANJAY GUPTA'S NOVEL *Monday Mornings*, the surgeons at Chelsea
General answer for their bad outcomes from the previous week at their
Monday Mornings' Morbidity and Mortality conference, known as M & M.
During those interrogative and introspective sessions, the surgeons face their
diagnostic and surgical errors, mistakes, and failures with their peers.

One M & M session focused on a surgeon's diagnosis of a jogger, who complained of a sore hip. After his examination of the runner, the surgeon simply gave the jogger some Tylenol for the tenderness and sent him home. In a short while the man returned for emergency surgery because the surgeon discovered that the runner's sore hip was actually pain from a deadly form of bone cancer which was overlooked in the initial diagnosis. The misdiagnosis resulted in a bad outcome, a really bad outcome. The jogger died. Misdiagnoses or no diagnosis can have serious consequences not only in health-care but in faith-care.

People often avoid examining their faith-problems because they know diagnosis can be embarrassing and demanding. Nobody likes to change. Even if we know we have a problem, we habitually find ways to explain it away or minimize it. But, now is the time to stop that hurtful habit. Now that we've cleared up these misconceptions about what healthy faith is and you've learned some things about your *self*, you're about to begin some exercises designed to help you make significant and helpful changes to your faith.

But, you can't effectively treat the specific troubles with your personal faith until you first clearly identify them. If you don't, you'll continue to ignore and hide your weaknesses, and change won't happen. That's what happened to Tiffany.

Tiffany was fifty-three-years-old when her mother was in a car accident and ended up in the emergency room. Tiffany prayed that God would save her. Sadly, shortly after her prayer, her mother died. Tiffany stopped going to church. She blamed God for her mother's death. She became so angry and hateful no one could stand being around her. She couldn't sleep so she asked her doctor for medication. He agreed with one condition. She had to see a counselor first. It didn't take long to figure out that her anger towards her *heavenly* Father was rooted in her anger towards her alcoholic, abusive *earthly* father.

From Tiffany's earliest memories, she heard her mother say over and over again, "All men are the same. They look good at first, but underneath they're mean and you can't trust them." One night, after Tiffany's drunken father beat her mother more brutally than ever, her father left and never returned.

For years Tiffany's anger towards her father grew. She kept playing her mother's tape over and over again in her mind. Tiffany came to picture God as nothing more than a big, old, cruel "man" in the sky. She blamed her father for hurting and abandoning her and her mother. With help, Tiffany recognized and confronted her personal problems. Over time she regained her faith.

Like Tiffany, all of us do a good job of hiding our problems underneath years of smiles, tears and busy activities. You may never experience what Tiffany did, but most of us can remember experiences with people and bad events that left us with the serious toxins of emotional scars, distorted thinking, self-destructive feelings, painful memories and hurtful habits. We can keep a lid on them for a while, but generally, in time, something happens that blows the lid off our cover, and our buried feelings and thoughts gush out like a break in a sewage pipe. Our hidden poisons leak out into our activities and relationships.

You know as well as I do that you could spend hundreds of hours and even years going through therapy or trying to figure out for yourself exactly what things in your childhood may have caused you to act the way you do. Unfortunately, you may never know all the details around what caused your childhood problems; and, even if you do, like Tiffany, there comes a time when we all have to stop blaming our past and take charge of our own lives.

We have to stop making excuses and start making changes. Since you're beginning this plan, now is a good time to stop letting your past control you. It's time to make a list of your toxins that keep you from having a healthy faith and say to them, "I'm not going to allow you to control me any longer. Today, I will begin to change all that."

As you look for the particular problem areas of your faith, remember, no one has a background or faith-history just like yours. So your diagnosis of your faith-condition will be uniquely yours. You may say, "But, I don't know how to make a good diagnosis of my faith. I know my faith is far from what it should be and what I want it to be, but I don't have a clue as to exactly what areas of my faith have problems, and I certainly don't know how to fix them."

Don't worry. That's normal. It's not easy for anyone to diagnose his or her own problems. But, with a little help you can do it. Whether you're trying to diagnose the problem with your faith or trying to find the cause of a physical sickness, two words stand out – honesty and self-awareness.

First, honesty is crucial. If you try to hide or minimize your symptoms or play like everything is fine, you'll only hurt yourself. So, say to yourself, "This is my chance to make a big change in my faith. I really want this to work, so I'm going to be seriously honest with myself about myself. And, why not? No one will see my answers but me."

Second, self-awareness is a sign of healthiness. Not being aware of one's *self*, our thoughts, feelings or behavior, is considered a common symptom of some level of mental illness. We refer to people who don't have self-awareness as "being out of touch" with reality. So, what you're doing in this diagnosis is a significant task. You're bringing back into your awareness those parts of your faith that may be hidden or buried.

From the beginning, I said this plan would work only if you work the plan. So, begin your self-diagnosis by using the seven characteristics of a healthy faith as a check list in Chapter One. Go back to the list and re-read each of the seven characteristics slowly and carefully. But this time, do more than just say to yourself, "I'm pretty good at that characteristic, but I could use a little improvement on that other one." Don't do that. It's time to go way beyond that. Work at being as thorough and specific as you can with your self-evaluation. As you read each of the three statements below, ask yourself this one question. Put your answers in the margin of the book or on a note pad.

The Question: Is this a good description of me and my faith, or is this where I'm weak and need help?

You can do this quickly and with just a few words. Here's an example of how one person answered the above question after reading the three different statements.

Statement 1. A healthy faith is well-informed and well-equipped. It's ready for hard questions and difficult situations.

Sample answer: I'm not at all prepared to answer any of the hard questions I have about faith or the questions I've heard others ask. I want help on this, but I feel very ill-equipped and don't really know where to start.

Statement 2. A person with a healthy faith doesn't harbor guilt or anger or answer hardships or unkind acts by being bitter, resentful or revengeful.

Sample answer: I feel a great deal of guilt about some things in my past. I'm angry inside about some things that someone did to me, and I can't seem to get over it. I would love to be able to respond in a healthier way.

Statement 3. A person with a healthy faith is aware of God's presence. You don't just know about God or just believe in the idea of God. Your kind of faith makes you cognizant of his presence in and around you.

Sample answer: I want to be like that. A few of my friends at work talk to God like they're best friends. They even tell me how he has answered their prayers. I would love to know God that way, but I don't know how.

As you work, sentence by sentence, through each of the seven characteristics, make a written list of the areas where your faith needs the most growth. Throughout the rest of the plan, you'll use this list to assist you in focusing your efforts and prioritizing your faith-building-exercises.

EXERCISES TO BUILD AND MAINTAIN YOUR HEALTHY FAITH

Hopefully by now, you have a better understanding of what a healthy faith is, and perhaps you have learned some things about yourself that will help you diagnose where you are in faith matters because faith matters.

RECORD: Retrieve your written list of the Seven Characteristics of a Health Faith. Using a scale of one to five, diagnose your faith. Use a one if this characteristic of your faith is weak or non-existent. Giving yourself a five means that you are completely satisfied with your faith in this area. Now look at your scores, and see your strengths and weaknesses.

REMEMBER: Review again the lists you have made from Section 1: the Seven Characteristics of a Healthy Faith, the Four Essential Parts of Faith, the Two Views of the Self, and the Three Parts of the Self. Do you have those memorized? Could you explain them to someone who might not know?

REFLECT: Open your Bible to the story of Zacchaeus in Luke 19: 1-9. Think of yourself as Zacchaeus. Climb the tree. Look hard for Jesus, and listen for his invitation. Think of how Zacchaeus saw himself and how he demonstrated the Four Essential Parts of Faith.

RE-EXAMINE: Think of one person you know who has a healthy faith and a healthy view of himself or herself. What does that person do that causes him/ her to come to your mind? Would you come to someone else's mind answering this same question? Think about why you would or wouldn't.

RELATE: Share not just your thoughts, but also your feelings about your faith diagnosis with someone you trust.

Since the beginning of this book, I've tried to be honest with you about the necessity of working the plan and not just reading about it. It's commonly known that permanent change in any area of our lives almost never happens suddenly and even less frequently just because we greatly desire it or even pray for it. That's especially true when it comes to something as important as your faith.

Before you move to Step 2 in the plan, you need to get rid of one other major misconception that keeps many from having a healthy faith. Remember, your faith is not a one-time thing, it is dynamic and living and changing. When most people I know first put their faith in God or in someone, they were excited and grateful for the positive feelings and changes they experienced. But after a short time, problems surfaced again they didn't expect. They felt disappointed, confused and even angry about the ineffectiveness of their new faith. They thought their faith would keep working like it had when it started or maybe even become more effectual. Some gave up on faith all together. Others put it on the back-burner. What does it take to keep your faith consistent, growing and permanent? You'll find answers in the next chapter.

Pray this prayer to your Heavenly Father.

Dear Father, I am grateful that you already know the secrets of my heart, yet you still love me. Please open my inner eyes so I can see what you want me to see. Show me the areas of my faith where I need to make changes and give me hope of having a healthy faith. I want to make you proud of me. I am your child. Amen.

CHAPTER 5

How do you produce permanent CHANGE to your faith?

"The only way you can sustain a permanent change is to create a new way of thinking, acting, and being."

Jennifer Hudson, Singer, American Idol winner

"Unless you change and become like little children, you will never enter the kingdom of heaven."

Matthew 18:3

"You cannot change what you refuse to confront."

Marc Chernoff, Personal development author

Sincerity does not produce lasting, noticeable changes in our faith. Most fail because they don't regularly perform the exercises needed to produce and maintain permanent change. Since you will certainly face unexpected challenges to your beliefs, feelings, body and relationships, you must never, for any significant length of time, put your faith-workout on hold. If you keep your faith consistently and permanently fit, you can handle anything life hurls at you. If you don't, it's not your faith that will let your down. It's you that will let it down. Decide now to do every one of these items.

1. *Wanting always precedes doing.* We don't intentionally do anything very long unless we are first motivated to do it. What's motivating you? List a few things that are high on your want-list that will motivate you to do the items needed to produce permanent change. They could be things you want for yourself, others or from God.

2. *Set a specific time and place* – Your second essential exercise is to take a small amount of time out of your current busy schedule, find a specific quiet space and set that time-period every day to do some prescribed faith-building exercise. Your Quiet-exercise-time does not need to be long; but, it does needs to be a dedicated-time, a holy-time that you protect. This may be the hardest part of your growth-plan. So, do what you must to make it happen.

3. *Make a daily check-list* – Permanent changes to your mind, emotions, and behavior will begin to happen when you make your faith-building exercises such a priority in your schedule that you make a daily check-list. That's what you do for other things you feel are too important to miss. You have a list of other responsibilities that are vital to your life and work. But, you must put your daily faith-building exercises on that same list, not on a separate list of things you'll do if you have time left over.

3. *Write achievable goals* – By setting your own exercise time, place, goals, specific exercises and daily steps, you will make this faith-plan a partnership. You won't see it as my plan for you to perform, but our plan to work together. I'll offer some practical suggestions, and give you a number of exercises at the end of each chapter. You can't do them all in one week or one month. So, you'll have to make your own schedule and set your own goals.

As you make a daily check-list of small steps that are achievable activities designed to help you reach your weekly goals, make your goals big enough to stretch you, yet small enough to be practically attainable. You may be tempted to try to take on too much at one time. Don't do it. Just as you don't build muscle in one or two trips to the gym, you don't build your faith-muscle in a couple of days or even a week. Trying to achieve too much too fast will set you up for disappointment, frustration and failure. Take your time. Patient progress produces permanent habits.

4. *Get Support* – Pride and unrealistic expectations can derail your growth. Every respected approach attempting to bring permanent personal change includes the need for support from someone according to my studies. Usually, those who try to stop some bad habit or addiction or try to make some personal change without help, fail.

   You need to talk to someone regularly about your exercise, for some people it will be daily. Your coach or support-person may be a spouse, close friend, caring family member, colleague, a member of your faith-community, a teacher you trust or maybe someone who wants to work the exercises with you.

   Your time together will only take a few minutes. Talk about your plan. Ask your friend to help you be accountable by listening and giving you feedback. Set a time to report your progress. Your reporting could be in person or by phone or some other form of communication. Let me assure you, the probability of permanent change in you will increase to the degree you share your progress, report your activities, and celebrate your achievements with someone.

5. *Talk to your biggest advocate.* Before you begin to set up the items in the workout described above, talk to your biggest advocate—your Heavenly Father. No one wants you to succeed more than he does. Share with him your thoughts, feelings, past failures and hopes. Tell him why you're doing this workout. Promise him that you will do the work. Ask for him to work in your

6. *Get up when you fall down.* It's easy to get discouraged if you stumble or fall. Change is often one step forward and two steps backward. You will see permanent change if you continue to practice these essential elements and do your exercises. Learn from your falls and stumbles.

Talk about them with your support-friend and together discover what cause them and how you can avoid them. Never give up.

MOVING ON TO STEP 2

Now that we've cleared up a few of misconceptions about a healthy faith, you're ready to move on to developing your three main parts: your mind, your heart, and your behavior. As you work on making each of these parts healthy, you'll get practical exercises that will strengthen and prepare you to produce the permanent kind of faith you've been seeking.

Pray this prayer to your Heavenly Father.

Dear Father, I come to your with a grateful heart. I love you and need you. As you know, I am weak, but you are strong. I ask you to teach me what I need know and do what you want me to do. I give you my mind, heart and body to accomplish the task ahead. Amen.

Refocus YOUR MIND

℄

Prescriptions for a faith-healthy mind

"Every function of the human mind participates in the act of faith."

PAUL TILLICH, THEOLOGIAN AND AUTHOR

"The heart cannot worship what the mind rejects."

JOHN SHELBY SPONG, EPISCOPAL BISHOP AND AUTHOR

*"Set your minds on things above, not on earthly things. For you
died, and your life is now hidden with Christ in God."*

COLOSSIANS 3:2

WHEN AN X-RAY IS NOT focused properly, it doesn't accomplish the job for which it was designed. The radiologist cannot properly diagnosis the problem. The physician cannot make a good decision about what to do. The patient stays sick. The clear solution to this problem is simple, refocus the X-ray machine.

Life is so full of painful, disappointing, and confusing confrontations that it is not unusual for our minds and faith to get out of focus. And, when that happens, we don't function the way we were designed to function. We don't know what to do, how to think, why we feel the way we do, what is right or wrong, or why we cannot get in touch with God.

Since your mind plays a critical role in developing your healthy faith and relationship to God, what you may need to do is *Refocus your Mind*. That's what Step Two is intended to do. Without a healthy mind, you'll never get a healthy faith. Each of the chapters in this Step is designed to help you take a new look at the way you think, reevaluate your beliefs, and make adjustments when needed.

CHAPTER 6

How do you UNDERSTAND your mind?

༉

"Religion needs intelligence to save it from becoming a ruinous curse."

HARRY EMERSON FOSDICK, PASTOR AND AUTHOR

"Put your mind on your life with God. The way to life—to God!—is vigorous and requires your total attention."

LUKE 13:23

DO YOU UNDERSTAND THE DIFFERENCE *between your mind and your brain?* Your brain and mind are not the same. Your brain is that three-pound mass of gray and white matter that collects, organizes, and manages the physical activities of your thoughts, feelings, body and actions. As your body's control-center, it has around fifteen billion neurons connecting to thousands of other neurons that communicate with each other through long protoplasmic fibers called axons. Your axons carry messages to the cells throughout your body. When stimuli outside and inside your brain arouse different parts of you, these signals release neuron-chemicals and electrical signals that regulate your body, control movement, and influence every part of you.

If you want to learn about the brain and how it works, I suggest you read Ray Kurzwell's *How to Create a Mind: The Secret of Human Thought Revealed*. Kurzwell is one of the world's leading authorities on how the brain works and how to create artificial intelligence. He and his colleagues believe we can create an artificial brain that will be more intelligent and useful than the human brain. He uses the terms brain and mind synonymously.

Like many other students of both our human and spiritual lives, I use the word mind for something different from the brain. You are more than a physical brain. You have a brain, but there is much more to you than your brain. That does not diminish the value of studying the brain and finding new ways of using intelligence to help improve life. But as amazing as your brain is, your mind is even more amazing.

Your mind is different from your brain. Unlike your brain, your mind is not physical. It has no neurons or axons. You cannot see it or touch it. You *have* a brain like you *have* a foot. But, you don't *have* mind. Your mind is part of who you are. We don't know exactly how our minds work, but we know it's one of the three vital parts of us.

Mysteriously, your mind knows everything that happens inside you. Think of your mind, not as a thing, but as an invisible part of you that uses all of your thoughts, feelings and memories to influence every part of you. It is that mental part of you that lives beyond physical death.

When your brain analyzes situations, your mind is aware. When your heart feels and desires, your mind knows. The Bible talks a great deal about God's mind—how he thinks, what he chooses, and what's most important to him. When he created humans, he made them in his image. Part of what that means is that we were made with a free-will to choose and with the capacity to think in a similar way to how God thinks. That's the only way you will have a healthy mind—choosing to think like he thinks. So, how can you begin to think in a God-like or spiritual way and not just in a creature-like or physical way?

The word spiritual does not mean strange or other-worldly. When we say a rock is material, the *-al* ending means *like*, or *has some of the characteristics of* matter, thus, materi-al. When we say God is spiritual, the *-al* again signals that God is *like, or has some of the characteristics of* spirit (the word for wind, air or breath). To say, God is spiritual, means he is in some ways like the wind or the air we breathe. We can't see him, but he is real and necessary for life.

For you to have a healthy mind means you think in a spiritual way. That does not mean you think in an anti-physical or weird way. It means you are seeking to think, make decisions and value things and people the way God does. What he thinks and how he evaluates things are your standard.

What does your mind have to do with your conscience and faith? The word *conscience* is another term for mind. We say, "My mind is telling me something's not right." At other times, we might say, "My conscience is telling me something's not right." We use the words interchangeably because they refer to the same activity or inner-sense.

The word *conscience* (con-science) literally means "with knowledge" or "to know within." Your conscience or mind is that invisible part of you that instinctively knows what's right and wrong. It's that God-given, built-in part of you that receives and processes inaudible messages or silent voices that say things to you like, "Nobody has to tell me this. I know it's wrong to hurt innocent people, and it's good to help those who are hurting." Those kinds of inaudible voices come from your conscience.

Your mind is primarily relational. Although your mind analyzes situations and performs many different rational activities, its main function is to build meaningful relationships with others and God. It is designed more for loving others than figuring them out. Your mind is working at its best when it relates in a loving way to others and God than when it simply makes sense out problems and provides answers. To have the mind of God is to have more than good sense.

How does your mind work? We know very little about the inner-workings of our minds, but the Bible and experience tell us that our minds are influenced by several inaudible voices that come to it. When I refer to inaudible voices, I am speaking about rational, functioning individuals. I am not referring to people who have hallucinations and suffer from some form of mental illness.

When your mind receives these different inaudible voices or messages, it processes them and makes decisions. For example, if God speaks to your mind in a still small voice, your conscience gets the message, processes it, then makes a faith-decision as to what to do with the message.

Since your mind is spiritual and there's nothing physical just like it, let's use something physical and familiar to you that will give you a little insight into how your conscience works. Think about your television. It's basically a receiver and processor for many invisible signals that are sent to it. It receives invisible signals and converts them into visible pictures and sounds. If it's working right, we get a clear image. Although your conscience is not lifeless and mechanical like a television, in some ways, it reminds me a little bit of the way our conscience works.

Your conscience is like a receiver and processor. When you have a crisis, a loss, an opportunity, or any change, your mind, heart, and body all get the message something has happened. Depending on what happened, each part of you begins to send messages to your conscience. Your conscience's job is to receive the messages, interpret and evaluate them and make a response.

You have several different inner voices or signals that send messages to your conscience. Each voice tells your conscience how you should respond to what's happening. If you are aware of the various voices and know how to properly process and prioritize them, you'll make healthy faith-decisions. If you don't, you'll make unhealthy faith-decisions and suffer the consequences. Take a look at seven voices that influence your mind and affect your faith.

1. The voice of REASON
2. The voice of GOD
3. The voice of your MORALS
4. The voice of your DESIRES
5. The voice of your EMOTIONS
6. The voice of your WILL
7. The voice of your PAST

1. *The voice of REASON.* If someone told you he was able to jump off a tall building and gently float safely to the ground, an inaudible voice

would say to your mind something like, "That statement is absolutely unreasonable, illogical, or just plain ridiculous." You have a built-in ability to know when something does or does not make sense. God gave you the innate capacity to reason, evaluate, or judge.

2. *The voice of GOD.* I've never heard the audible voice of God like those recorded in the Bible and some today, but I regularly hear his still, inaudible, gentle voice in my mind and heart. The Bible teaches that our Heavenly Father created us the way he did because he wanted to be able to relate to us like loving parents relate to their children. One way he relates to us is by speaking to our conscience.

    Our Heavenly Father sends messages that most of us never hear because we don't understand how our conscience works, and we assume the voice or thought we received is from some other source. But it is possible for you to learn how to hear his still small voice. When you do, you will have a stronger faith, be more at peace, make better decisions, and be closer to your Father because you'll know he is present and is guiding you. In the next chapter you will learn how to discern the voice of God.

3. *The voice of your MORALS.* Another voice that speaks to your conscience is the inner voice of your three primary morals. By morals, I am not referring to something you've learned from religion or culture, but to the part of your conscience that is beyond your five senses, animal instincts and ability to make rational or logical choices. A moral is a God-given attitude or DNA-like code that's written into your conscience.

    Morals are those *more-than* factors that give your conscience its ability to love, to be unselfish, responsible, honest and sacrificial and, yes, to know the difference between good and evil, right and wrong. Unless your built-in morals get perverted or confused by outside information and images, they continually speak to you about what's best for you. As we move forward, you'll learn about your three primary morals and how you can use them to help build your faith.

4. *The voice of your DESIRES.* Another voice you often hear speak to your conscience is the voice of your desires. "I want to feel safe. I would like to be loved. I want to know why these things happened." All of us have built-in human needs or wants such as the desires for safety, love, fulfillment, and purpose. They must be satisfied or our minds respond negatively.

For example, everyone is born with a basic desire or need to be loved. If you reach out to someone in love and they attack you hatefully, your conscience immediately receives a voice from your pool of desires that may say something like, "Conscience, what I just experienced was painful. I'm hurt. I feel sad and angry. I need to be loved. What are you going to do to satisfy my need?"

As you move forward in the plan, you'll learn more about each of your desires, the powerful influence they have on your mind and your faith and how you can better control them.

5. *The voices of your FEELINGS.* Some say the most powerful voice that speaks to your conscience is the voice of your feelings, your emotions. God gave us several emotions like love, anger and fear that we'll examine later. But for now, just remember, if any of your basic desires or needs is not met, your conscience automatically gets a message from one of your primary feelings.

For instance, if unexpectedly you don't feel safe or secure, your conscience immediately receives a message from your reservoir of emotions that may say something like, "Conscience, I feel insecure. I'm afraid. Do something about it." When you're frightened, your mind may allow your emotions to take over your will. Suddenly your emotions take charge and express themselves as anger. As we move through the plan, you'll learn more about each of your emotions, the influence they have on your mind and your faith and how you can better control them.

6. *The voices of your PAST.* Occasionally, when I see an eighteen-wheeler coming towards me on the highway, I hear a voice from my past

accident with that eighteen-wheeler saying "Be careful. This could be deadly. Remember what happened the last time." Voices from your past can be so painful and unwanted that your mind may put them in one of its closets so you don't have to see, hear, or remember them. Although you may be completely unaware of them, they're still in your mind. Other voices from your past may be so pleasant and encouraging that you repeat them over and over.

It's important to be aware of all of these different kinds of voices so that they don't control or distort your faith-decisions without your knowing it. Whether the idea you hear comes from one of your past experiences, people you have long forgotten, or some image you stored away in your mind, how your conscience deals with your past voices is important to your faith.

7. *The voice of your WILL.* No one can control your will but you. You'll experience many influences, but ultimately you will make your own faith-choices. Your free-will makes the decision about what you do with the voices, information, and images you receive. Your *will* is another God-given gift built into your DNA. You don't have to learn to make a choice, but you do have to learn how to make good choices

You will make your faith-choices one of three ways. You can let others make your choices for you. You can partner with God in making your choices. You can choose to go-it-alone as to what to think, whom you will love most, what matters most and much more. Choosing is easy. Making healthy faith-choices is the challenge. Later we'll talk more about your will and how it sometimes works independently and at other times in cooperation with God or others.

The voices, ideas, or impulses we've just reviewed can assist you or make it more difficult for you to build a healthy mind and faith. When you interpret them properly and put them to work for you, you'll be better equipped to (1) avoid hasty, superstitious, and contradictory beliefs, (2) test your own beliefs and practices to make sure they are truthful and honorable and not just commonly-held false prejudices, (3) better formulate and communicate your faith, (4) remove or lessen intellectual barriers to your faith, (5) stimulate discussions with people with competing beliefs, and (6) have more peace of mind about your personal, emotional and spiritual commitments.

EXERCISES TO BUILD AND MAINTAIN YOUR HEALTHY FAITH

Hopefully by now, you have a better understanding of the difference between your brain and your mind, and how your mind and the voices that control you will influence your faith.

RECORD: Record the list of the conscience's seven basic voices.

REMEMBER: You are constantly and continually listening to these voices. Rank these voices in the order you think you listen to them, with one being the strongest and seven the weakest.

REFLECT: Open your Bible to Psalm 26:2-3 and to Philippians 4:8-10. After reading these scriptures, close your eyes and ask God, "What do you want to say to me? What can I learn about your mind and my mind from these scriptures?"

RE-EXAMINE: As you make decisions, big or small, throughout the day, try to discern which voice is speaking to you. Ask yourself if that is the voice you should be listening to when making these decisions.

RELATE: With your trusted friend, discuss the role of these seven voices in your life and in your decision-making. Evaluate the voices you listen to most, and discuss with your friend what changes you feel you should make.

Now that you have a better understanding of what your mind is and how it works, the next chapter explains how you can DISCERN the voice of God.

Pray this prayer to your Heavenly Father.

Dear Father, Thank you for your patience in my search to learn about my mind and your mind. I sincerely want to have a healthy mind and to discover what you want me to do. I give you my mind to be attentive to your voice. I give you every part of me to be used any way you wish. I am your humble servant. Amen.

CHAPTER 7

How do you DISCERN
the voice of God?

*"The intellectual side has to give its free assent before
the spiritual can exercise its full capacities."*

HORACE G. HUTCHINSON, AUTHOR, *CREATURES OF CIRCUMSTANCES*

"Listen and hear my voice; pay attention and hear what I say."

ISAIAH 28:23

SHE PULLED A HANDGUN OUT of her purse. She explained that God told her last night to kill her husband because he had been unfaithful. Before she killed him, she came to ask me, her pastor, if she would go to hell for taking his life. She didn't kill her husband, but she still believed God spoke to her. Did he?

A physician in our congregation, who had a stable, successful practice, told his wife God had been telling him to leave his practice and go to India as a medical missionary. His wife had not heard anything from God. Was he hearing God's voice or not? Eventually, she believed God also spoke to her. They sold their home and practice and moved to India. Did they hear the voice of God?

When you go through crises, experience confusion, or face a major decision, wouldn't you like to hear God's voice for comfort and direction? Of course you would. But how can you hear the voice of the great God of the universe? And, how can you know if it is God speaking?

Sometimes I find it's not easy for me to know if it is God's Spirit speaking to me or if it's some other voice. Don't feel like you are alone if you have this same problem. As recorded in the Bible and in the testimonies of people today, for thousands of years, faithful followers of our Father struggled with this important challenge. We all want to be sure we are following the voice of God.

Although discerning the voice of God is difficult, it's not impossible. In some ways, it is like trying to personally discern the symptoms of an illness. "Is that pain in my chest from yesterday's workout? Maybe it's just indigestion? But, could it be the beginning of a heart attack?" When we realize we cannot come to a reliable conclusion on our own, usually we turn for help to a more qualified opinion, our doctor.

For me, it makes good sense to use that same method to help us know how to hear the voice of God and know if it is his voice. Getting help from people who have demonstrated over time that they have been close to our Father, have heard his voice, and helped others, is certainly an humble and worthwhile approach.

No set of guidelines, keys, or principles for discerning the voice of God is perfect. But, over time I have put together some reminders that help me, and I hope you'll also find them helpful. Most of them I've learned from people I highly respect. When you are listening for the voice of God try to remember:

1. *God is spirit and usually speaks to your spirit.* Your Heavenly Father wants to hear your voice, and he wants you to hear his. You don't have to speak out loud for God to hear you. His mind can hear what is on your mind.

    Since God is spirit, he is normally unseen and inaudible. On a few occasions, people have seen and heard him with their physical eyes and ears, but those experiences were exceptions not the rule. You can't always see God at work, but his Spirit is there getting the job done. Usually, you don't hear an audible voice, but his Spirit is present making his message clear and compelling. So how can you, a physical creature, hear, that is, be aware of the voice of God speaking to your conscience?

Your Father built your mind, your conscience, so you would be capable of communicating with him. You are physical, but, remember, you are also spiritual. That means, like the air you breathe, your mind is invisible, but it's able to receive the inaudible messages of God. His voice is as real as he is.

2. *Your Father speaks to you in more than one way.* Your Father is constantly trying to communicate with you through your conscience, but that's not the only way. He also speaks through all of his creation, people's words, music, hymns, and even your God-given instincts. Listen, look, and anticipate your Father communicating with you.

3. *Your Father speaks even to those who don't know him.* Because God built us the way he did, even the person who doesn't believe God exists has a conscience. He doesn't recognize that the inaudible voice he hears is the voice of the living God. The unbeliever interprets the voice of God as a voice from his past or his own thoughts. Although he is not aware of God or his God-given desires and feelings, he may still respond to the voice and make good decisions. Isn't it common for people to take a good idea and follow it without knowing who is behind the idea?

4. *Your seeking conscience hears God's message more.* Your Heavenly Father rarely shouts to your conscience. If you are listening for and wanting to hear his voice, it's more likely you will hear him than if you wait for him to overpower you. That's what happened in the Bible story about the boy Samuel. He spent a night in the Temple with the high priest Eli. Samuel heard a voice in the night calling his name. He assumed the voice was Eli. It never crossed Samuel's mind it might be the voice of God. When he went to Eli's room and asked what Eli wanted, Eli told young Samuel he had not called. Samuel went back to bed and later heard the voice again.

Three times the voice called, "Samuel! Samuel." When Samuel answered, "Speak Lord I'm your servant and I'm ready to listen," he and God connected. Samuel's faith changed when he realized that the voice was from God and not his own thoughts. He started listening to his conscience in a new way and began acting on the messages from God. He became one of God's closest friends and servants.

5. *Your humble mind can hear God better than a prideful one.* When Moses was in crisis in the desert, he heard the voice of God calling him by name. He was afraid to go and do what God told him. He would have preferred to hear something else, but he chose to humble himself and trust that the voice he heard was from God and not his imagination or his personal desires. What if Moses had decided that the voice he heard was just his own thoughts and desires?

   Never be a know-it-all. Never listen for the voice of God with an attitude that you know God's will better than anyone. Never assume everyone should listen to you. Remember, God has many who love him and listen to his voice.

   When you believe you hear the voice of God, in humility, tell at least two people you look up to spiritually. Ask them what they think. If you are about to make an important decision on what you feel God has said, it would be encouraging to hear a spiritual friend say, "Yes, that sounds like something God would say to you."

6. *God's written Word is his clearest voice.* When you hear a voice in your conscience that you think may be God speaking to you, you need to test the message to make sure it is consistent with God's written word, the Bible, and the life and words of his son, our Lord Jesus. If any message your conscience hears is inconsistent with the Bible and Jesus, that message is not the voice of God. If the message is consistent with them, accept it as his voice and respond with all your mind, heart and life.

7. *Silence and waiting are part of hearing and discerning.* Patiently waiting in silence is a good way of discerning God's will and his voice.

8. *The healthier your relationship with God, the clearer his voice.* Your ability to hear God is based more on the health of your relationship with him than anything else. Just as you can hear and understand your loved one's heart better than you can a stranger's, the closer you are to your Father the better you will know it is his voice and what he is saying.

9. *Your motive matters.* Why do you want to hear the voice of God? Having the wrong motive could hinder your communications with your Father. Your loving Father will listen and speak to you whether you come to him as a grateful servant or an arrogant brat, but your attitude and motive will determine what you hear.

10. *Hearing God's voice is a choice.* God doesn't usually force you to hear him. There are many voices seeking to get your attention and will. You will hear them all. They each want to be the primary voice for your conscience, but you will make a conscious or unconscious choice as to which will be your primary or guiding voice. Which one you choose will determine the quality of your mind, faith, relationships and overall life.

We've all heard too many stories of innocent children and adults who listened to misleading voices and swallowed poisonous beliefs only to see their lives deeply wounded or lost. When you summarize the many voices speaking to you, there are actually only three primary voices. Which have you chosen thus far? Which will you choose as you move forward?

Option one: Your own thoughts. You may decide, in spite of all of your mind's limitations and past influences, you will depend on your own mind, your own thoughts, your own inner voice. You cannot think of anyone you trust more or can believe in more than yourself. As the world's most qualified source for making decisions for you, you're willing to wager your life, relationships, and eternity on your thoughts.

Option two: Others' thoughts. If you don't choose your own thoughts, you might choose for your primary source for building your life and relationships someone's or some group's ideas and beliefs. Even though others, and especially groups, have a long list of common human limitations, personal problems, cultural influences, prejudiced backgrounds, and partial experience, you may still put your faith in their voices.

Option three: Your creator's thoughts. The best choice is your creator-savior-best-friend, God himself. Why wouldn't you turn to the highest and most reliable authority? When he created you for a purpose, loves you more than anyone, is available to you anytime, has all the resources you need, and wants to supply you with what's best for you, why wouldn't you choose him?

The Bible says, *"Put your mind on your life with God. The way to life—to God!—is vigorous and requires your total attention."* Luke 13:23. The major idea in that crucial scripture is a central biblical teaching—having a personal relationship with God is the most important thing you can do. Putting your mind on your life *with* God, means concentrating on having a close, moment-by-moment, personal relationship with him. That's the best way to be sure you hear his voice.

EXERCISES TO BUILD AND MAINTAIN YOUR HEALTHY FAITH

You know that God is still speaking to his people, but it is up to us to discern his voice. He speaks to us in many ways, but never will his voice be inconsistent with his Holy Word.

RECORD: Make a list of the different ways that God may speak to you. Put a star by the ones he most often uses to speak to you. Then, write down the three suggestions on discerning the voice of God.

REMEMBER: Memorize the three suggestions on discerning God's voice. These then can become the litmus test for you to know if it is God speaking to you.

REFLECT: In the back of the book, I've listed forty of the Bible's most famous stories, twenty from the Old Testament and twenty from the New Testament.

These character stories are the basis for many of the world's greatest novels, poems, songs and works of art. Reading some of these stories will tell you how other people have heard and responded to God's voice. But now, open your Bible to John 10: 1-18, and listen to the voice of Jesus as he describes himself as a shepherd whose sheep know his voice.

RE-EXAMINE: Have you ever really thought about your ears? You can hear your neighbor's lawn mower, that annoying mosquito buzzing nearby, and recognize the voice of your mother all at the same time. Have you ever noticed how a mother is attuned to her baby's cry above all other sounds? We want to be able to discern God's voice as acutely and accurately as our physical ears can distinguish sounds. Which of the three suggestions on discerning the voice of God is most helpful to you? Why? Think of a time when you were very much aware of God speaking to you. What difference did it make?

RELATE: Discuss with a trusted friend the three ways of discerning God's voice. Share that time when you were aware that God was speaking to you.

Moving to the next Chapter

Keep practicing your exercises; but, it's time to move on to the next chapter. God often speaks to us through the rational part of our mind. When God created the world, he built into his natural world some physical or natural laws that keep it working the way it was intended. When he created humans, he built into his children some Laws of Reason that help us function at our best and accomplish what he for us to do. These God-given rational laws can help you make faith-decisions in the way your Heavenly Father would make them. But how can you recognize and follow his Laws of Reason?

Pray this prayer to your Heavenly Father.

Dear Father, I am talking to you because I love you and need you.
I want to hear your voice and follow your leading. Help me discern your

voice from all the others. You alone are God; and you alone are my Heavenly Father and my hope. I am open to your guidance. You gave me all I am and have. I give all of myself back to you to be used for your purposes. Amen.

CHAPTER 8

How do you RECOGNIZE the laws of reason?

༉

"Life is a battle between faith and reason in which each feeds upon the other, drawing sustenance from it and destroying it."

Reinhold Niebuhr, Theologian, professor, author

"Come now, and let us reason together, saith the Lord."

Isaiah 1:18

Because we have the ability to reason, some people struggling with faith issues have the following kinds of thoughts:

"I don't believe in God because a supernatural God doesn't make sense."

"There are no miracles. Miracles are make-believe, chance mistakes."

"Praying is irrational. Prayers are merely therapeutic wishes."

"I cannot put my faith both in God and reason. So, I choose reason."

Are faith and reason contradictory? Behind all of these statements is one common misconception—for me to put my faith in God, I must give up my intelligence, integrity, and rational thinking. Nothing could be farther from the truth. Some of the world's most intelligent, honest, and rational people have a personal faith in God. For you to have the healthy mind and faith you desire, you need to come to grips with the relationship between your faith in God and your instinct to be honest and reasonable.

Your Reasonable Response. Because we are all made in the image of our personal and thoughtful Creator-God, we will always be incomplete and dissatisfied until we have a personal and thoughtful relationship with him. Just think for a minute about your natural desire for God. What is the source of that basic human desire?

When God created us, he created in us a number of basic human desires. At the same time, he created specific satisfiers for those desires. For example, since our bodies need food to live, he created in us the desire for food and made food available for us. Food is not an option. It's an essential. So, it makes sense to satisfy such an essential desire with good food.

The same is true for love. Although we cannot see love, like food, we all hunger for it. Why? It's one of those built-in, human desires. Like food, God not only gave us the desire to love, he gave us good ways to satisfy that core desire. It is completely reasonable to seek God's ways to satisfy our desire for love.

Your God-hunger is built-in. No one decides to desire God. No one goes through life with no desire for food, then one day stops and says, "I've never wanted food before, but I've decided to desire to eat." That would be absurd. God not only gave us the desire to have a relationship with him, he is available to satisfy that desire. For you to seek to satisfy your desire for a personal relationship with God is completely reasonable. How unreasonable, how thoughtless would it be for you to ignore or avoid satisfying such a strong desire?

See what I mean? Faith and reason are two sides of the same coin. It makes no sense for you to disregard your desire for him, or to try to fill that hunger with inferior substitutes. It's completely reasonable, rational, and good sense for you to seek to satisfy your God-hunger with your personal God.

What an unfathomable, reasonable offer! If it were possible, who wouldn't desire to become a close friend, or better yet an adopted child, of the creator of the universe? Just imagine it. How would you like having a supernatural Father who knows you personally, loves you intimately, stays near you constantly, guides you thoroughly, comforts and helps you compassionately, forgives you mercifully, and, when your body dies, will take you to his eternal home where you can be with him and your loved ones forever? That's the most unfathomable offer I have ever heard. At the same time, accepting such an offer would be the most reasonable decision I could make. That's the very offer God makes time and again throughout the Bible—a generous and rational invitation.

Why would anyone turn down such an amazing offer? Some reject his offer because they say the God-story just does not make sense. For them, it seems blatantly contradictory to the laws of reason to believe in a personal God, miracles, prayer and the whole idea of the supernatural. But let's take a closer look.

Why should you believe in miracles, prayer and the supernatural? Those of us who are rational thinkers, and who place our faith, our lives and our eternities in a personal God, embrace both reason and faith. For us, being reasonable is essential not optional. It's being honest and humble. We are reasonable because our personal God is reasonable and made us to be like him.

Some have a problem with a marriage between faith and reason because they don't understand what it means to be reasonable or rational. Simply put, to be reasonable or rational means you think, believe and make decisions in an orderly, not chaotic way.

Reason says the world operates in a predictable, consistent, or reliable manner. Reason says the world is not out of control, not operating haphazardly. The Laws of Reason are based on the belief that God built order into the fabric of his creation. You can count on billions of invisible and visible activities happening in the world over and over every day in practically the same way.

A healthy faith depends on a dependable God. Since God's creation functions in an extremely orderly fashion, it is reasonable to conclude that the world's creator is orderly. He likes order, not disorder. He chooses dependability over unpredictability. Part of what it means to be healthy is to be dependable and responsible. We cannot have healthy relationships with those we love unless we have beliefs, feelings and behavior that are dependable and responsible.

A healthy faith also depends on healthy beliefs. You can count on your Creator-God to be dependable in what he says and does. How dependable and responsible are your thoughts and beliefs? For you to be able to answer that question you need to compare your beliefs to some standard. It is like asking if your blood pressure (BP) is good. If you don't compare your BP to a standard BP for someone your age, you might think your BP is fine when it is actually at a dangerous level. The same is true for determining your mind's health—your beliefs and way of thinking.

Over the years, I've examined numerous lists of the characteristics used to assess the health of a particular belief, decision or religious position. To help you evaluate your beliefs and way of thinking, I have put together a list of the most commonly-held and biblically-based signs or indicators of healthy thinking. How healthy are your beliefs?

Seven Indicators of a Healthy Belief

1. Your belief is healthy if it is . . .
RELIABLY RESPONSIBLE
A healthy belief is RESPONSIBLE under the best and worst conditions. You can count on a healthy belief like you can count on the sun to rise in the morning. A healthy belief is not one that merely serves your present interests. A responsible belief is consistent and accountable at all times.

Your belief is healthy if it can stand up to the criticisms and doubts of others. It is responsible if it is more concerned with pleasing God than impressing others and with being consistent with God's character than being compared to popular opinion.

Dependable as the Father and his son. Since your heavenly Father is the model of what it means to be responsible, you have a dependable belief if you seek to mirror his way of thinking and his beliefs. The first chapter of the Bible says, "God spoke: Let us make human beings in our image . . . So they can be responsible." Genesis 1:26 CEV. The clearest indicator of a responsible belief is its consistency with the character of God.

The apostle Peter said it clearly, "You call out to God for help and he helps—he's a good Father that way. But don't forget, he's also a responsible Father, and won't let you get by with sloppy living." 1 Peter 1:17

Whether Jesus was teaching his beliefs on a grass-covered hillside to an applauding crowd or hanging nailed to the cross in pain, his beliefs were the same. Like his Father, his actions matched his teachings. He was responsible to his Father.

When you test your belief, to see if it is reliably responsible, stand it up next to Jesus and see how it compares to his way of thinking and acting.

2. Your belief is healthy if it is . . .
PREDICTABLY PURPOSEFUL
A healthy belief has a healthy purpose. If your belief does not help carry out God's purposes, it is unhealthy. Why you believe something can matter more than what you believe. You may believe in prayer, but if your purpose for praying is to convince God to support your evil thoughts or wrong behavior, your belief is far from healthy.

God created the world and us humans with specific purposes in mind. He not only made everything out of nothing, he fashioned everything to carry out specific purposes. The Bible says, "The Lord has made everything for his own purposes." Proverbs 16:4.

Birds were made to fly. If a beautiful bird only walks around with chickens and never flies, it will never fulfill its purpose. You were made for specific purposes. If your beliefs and thinking don't help you accomplish God's purposes for you and others, it's not healthy. You may be lovely and efficient at what you do, but you will always feel dissatisfied.

What are God's primary purposes for you? Before you can seek to grow a healthy mind, you need to know God's primary purposes for you so you can test your beliefs and thoughts. The Bible teaches us that our most important purpose in life is to *bring glory to God*. All the other purposes God has for us are built on this single foundational purpose. What is glory; and what does it mean to bring glory to God?

Paul the great missionary and highly respected Jewish and Christian theologian made it clear, "Everything comes from God alone. Everything lives by his power, and everything is for his glory." Romans 11:36 LB.

The word *glory* literally means *brightest, best* or *highest in value*. For example, when the Bible refers to God's glory in heaven, it says, "The city (heaven) does not need the sun or the moon to shine on it, for the glory of God gives it light." Revelation 21:23. In other words, God's glory is God's best. He is the brightest, finest, and the most valuable Father, friend and savior, you could ever want.

The Bible says, "The Word (God) became flesh and lived among us. We saw his glory . . . a glory full of grace and truth." John 1:14 GVT. If you want to see the glory of God, the best view of the invisible God you can find, the clearest, finest, brightest, most valuable picture of God you can get anywhere, look at his son, Jesus. Jesus was God's glory.

For you to give or bring God glory means you give him your best. You bring him the best you can, all of your mind, heart and actions. He told his Heavenly Father, "I brought glory to you here on earth by doing everything you told me to do." Galatians 6:1-5.

The beliefs that drove Jesus to live the way he did were rooted in these five, God-embedded purposes. He carried out these purposes and brought his Father glory.

* *He loved his Father* in a personal, moment-by-moment relationship.
* *He cared for his Father's family* every way he could.
* *He practiced a moral life* in his relationship to others.
* *He gave himself sacrificially* so others might know his Father.
* *He kept eternity at the center of his life and message.*

If you want to know if your mind, beliefs, way of thinking are healthy, ask yourself these five key questions about your purposes in life.

* *Am I loving my Father* in a personal, moment-by-moment relationship?
* *Am I caring for my Father's family* in whatever ways I can?
* *Am I practicing a moral life* in my relationship to others?
* *Am I giving myself sacrificially* so others might know my Father?
* *Am I keeping eternity at the center of my life and message to others?*

Healthy equals predictable. A healthy belief is more than occasionally or comfortably purposeful. It is predictably purposeful. That is, your belief is healthy if it is consistently, noticeably, and repeatedly carrying out God's purposes.

3. YOUR BELIEF IS HEALTHY IF IT IS . . .
CONSISTENTY LOVING

A healthy belief is unselfish, caring, other-centered, and consistently loving. No matter how many people, arguments or scriptures you may use to support your belief, it is unhealthy if it is egocentric, selfish and self-serving. Love is the acid test of every healthy belief.

The best summary of God's character is "God is love." That's how God thinks, believes and acts. No matter the situation, his love is consistent. To say that God consistently loves does not mean he is some feel-good, sentimental, no-justice kind of Father. His love-based-beliefs and thoughts are a balance of justice and mercy—the two sides of God's love. A belief that does not maintain that balance is not healthy.

A healthy belief causes you to have sympathy, to reach out to others, to be compassionate, caring and forgiving. No matter how much you believe something, if it is unsympathetic, harsh and condemning, it is not healthy.

A healthy belief demonstrates a just kind of love. Our Father loves his children too much to wink at sin and ignore justice. His love does not ultimately allow wrong to go unpunished and evil to be rewarded.

A healthy belief also demonstrates a compassionate kind of love. If your belief over emphasizes God's wrath and justice or his love and mercy, it is not healthy.

4. YOUR BELIEF IS HEALTHY IF IT IS . . .
DEPENDABLY HONEST

The words *healthy* and *honest* are inseparable in faith matters. A healthy belief is not changed by circumstances. Even when surrounded by chaos, confusion and suffering, it will stand strong because it is built on a solid foundation of honesty, truthfulness, and integrity.

A healthy belief is not secretive. It is not characterized by fear, concealment, lies, deceit or control. If your belief is healthy, it is secure, peaceful, pure, and content. It is the same in public as it is in private. What God sees is what others see.

5. YOUR BELIEF IS HEALTHY IF IT IS . . .
REPEATEDLY COMPREHENSIVE

A healthy belief is based on a wide-range of information from a broad-spectrum of sources, including the overall word of God. A belief is not healthy if it is based solely on the beliefs of a small circle of like-minded people or a few carefully chosen scriptures that support your personal opinion.

6. YOUR BELIEF IS HEALTHY IF IT IS . . .
CONTINUALLY CONSTRUCTIVE

A healthy belief or thought has value beyond itself. It's not self-serving. It resists irrational, contradictory, destructive or meaningless thinking. A healthy belief builds, helps, encourages and accomplishes the purposes for which God made us. Your belief is not healthy if it is negative, hurtful, destructive, and discourages you and others from carrying out God's purposes.

A healthy belief enhances your relationship with God and others. It invests in lives and eternity. It openly and unashamedly looks for ways to bring glory to God—to fulfill his purposes.

7. YOUR BELIEF IS HEALTHY IF IT IS . . .
RESPECTFULLY CURIOUS

A healthy belief is not stagnant, lazy or boring. Our rational, analytical and relational sides are never completely satisfied with old answers and solutions. A healthy mind will not depend on other's beliefs but insists on personal investigation and evidence.

A healthy thought or belief is dynamic, searching, reaching and seeking. It's never closed to new insights. It is always open to the *more* in life. It seeks to find and clarify God's will and his desire. It always wants to find more answers, more insights, more clarity and more meaning. It is not afraid to be imaginative, risky, hopeful and curious.

Your belief or thought is healthy if it passes all seven tests, not just two or three. And, to keep the mind healthy, you will need to continually feed it information and images that are responsible, purposeful, loving, honest, comprehensive, constructive, and curious.

EXERCISES TO BUILD AND MAINTAIN YOUR HEALTHY FAITH

God not only gives you life, He gives your life purpose. Let's put some of what you're learning into practice.

RECORD: We're still into list making. Recording these short lists on cards, or in your notebook, or even on your phone keep them near for quick and handy reference. Make a list of the Seven Indicators of a Healthy Belief.

REMEMBER: If you're having trouble memorizing, just choose three of the most important of these seven indicators and repeat them at least three times during your day.

REFLECT: One of the most beautiful stories in the Bible is the story of Queen Esther, who fulfilled her purpose in life and saved her people from annihilation. Perhaps, your purpose in life will never have that much impact, but it will have impact. Read Esther's story in the book of Esther 2-9. Meditate on Esther 4:14. What does that verse say to you about your own purpose in life?

RE-EXAMINE: Make a list of the five primary purposes for your life in your own words. This would be another way of writing your life's mission statement. Frame them, put them on a small easel on your desk or chair-side table, and read them often. Keeping your purposes before you and praying about those purposes will help you develop a healthy mind and will influence your activities.

RELATE: Talk to your trusted friend about the three most important beliefs you have about God's character and your purposes in life. Get your friend's evaluation.

To continue to develop a healthy mind, you need to understand the difference between moral and immoral thinking and why morals are important to your mind. In Chapter Nine, you will learn how to determine what IS right and what IS wrong; and you will get some helpful answers to other popular questions about the relationship between your faith and your morals. A moral mind is fertile soil for a healthy faith.

Pray this prayer to your Heavenly Father.

Dear Father, I come to you because I love you; I am grateful for you; I need you; I want to stay close to you; and, I want your Spirit to speak to my mind so I'll know your will for me. I know you gave me everything that I have. Without you in my life, I would be nothing. I give you my life this day. Use me to carry out your purposes for my life. Thank you for your grace and patience. Amen.

CHAPTER 9

How do you KNOW the laws of right and wrong?

⳨

"Religion needs intelligence to save it from becoming a ruinous curse."

Harry Emerson Fosdick, Pastor and Author

"The Lord says, I will put my laws on their hearts,
and write them on their minds."

Hebrews 10:16 ESV

When Pope Francis took an historic stand against priests who were pe-dophiles and labeled them monsters who were morally sick, he started a fire that ignited thousands of other religious officials around the world. The in-dictment against the church's scandal became an opportunity to once again clarify the historic, biblical conviction about the relationship between faith and morality.

For months following the Pope's condemnation of the priest child-molesters, "Faith without works is dead," (James 2:26) was often used by the religious media around the world. That was nothing new. For centuries that stern scriptural warning served as a battle cry against all forms of fraudulent faith and immorality hidden behind sacred-looking walls and cross-adorned religious robes. The text emphasized a basic biblical truth—no matter how doctrinally sound, religiously-active or emotionally-sincere your beliefs and faith may be, they are worthless unless they are moral.

Since your success in developing a healthy mind and faith is greatly dependent on your morals, you must understand what morals are and why they matter. How can you know what's right and wrong, good and bad?

1. *What are morals?* Like the three legs of a tripod, there are three primary morals that hold up all personal and societal relationships: *humility, responsibility* and *honesty*. If you want a healthy relationship, you must have all three moral legs. I found that most people who have a weak, troubled, or broken faith also have problems with their morals and don't understand what morals are.

   Too often people are confused about morals, thinking they are a matter of opinion or up-bringing. They're not. *A moral is a God-given, God-like attitude that produces a God-like behavior.* Cultures, traditions and other human influences produce different socially acceptable behaviors we call customs, mores, or appetites. Don't confuse them with God-given moral laws. Customs continually change. Moral laws do not change. They are absolute, fixed God-made-laws built into your mind.

   Just as there are fixed laws of nature and reason, there are unchanging laws of right and wrong, good and bad. *Physical laws* keep our physical world from being chaotic and self-destructive. *Moral laws* keep our relationships and minds from being unhealthy and in constant conflict.

   Whether you were born in 2015 BC or 2015 AD, live in Bangladesh or Bar Harbor, were educated at Harvard or have no formal education, are a sheltered eight-year-old or a highly experienced eighty-year-old, you know it's wrong to be selfish, lazy, or dishonest. Without being taught, you know there's something right about being unselfish, responsible, and honest.

2. *Are moral laws really that important?* Morals are extremely important for developing a healthy mind and faith. Don't kid yourself. You can't have a healthy mind and faith and continue to hold on to the poison of immoral thoughts and behavior. Like your body's immune system, which protects your body from outside harmful elements, morals are your mind's immune system. God-given morals help protect you from harmful and destructive attitudes that will eventually weaken and destroy your healthy relationships with others and your Lord.

Jorge came for counseling because his wife wanted a divorce. After eighteen years of being happily married, he and Rosa started arguing most of the time. Jorge didn't want to lose Rosa; but he was so angry at her he didn't know what to do. She got angry at him for being so angry at her. It was a vicious angry cycle they couldn't stop.

After a short time, Jorge admitted to me that he had a secret life of immoral thoughts that started about the same time as their fighting. He hated himself and felt extremely guilty for his covert life. Unfortunately, to hide his guilt, he took his anger out on Rosa, who had no idea about his secrets. The morning Jorge came to my office, looked into her face and through tears of sorrow confessed his secret life, the wall between them came down. It was painful for Jorge. But, when Rosa saw the new humble, responsible and honest way he related to her, she embraced him and in a short time their love was restored.

The words *laws* and *morals* are not popular in a day when tolerance is valued more than truth, personal choice more than personal obedience, and individual rights more than family values. It's fashionable to say, "What's true for you may not be true for me. What's right for you may not be right for me. Truth, right and good are not absolute. They are not the same for everyone. They are a matter of opinion."

The truth is, our opinions do matter when it comes to man-made laws and customs. Some opinions need to change. For society and relationships to work like God designed them, man-made laws need to be tested and made to conform to God's moral laws.

When it comes to God-given laws, our opinions don't matter. What matters is our willingness and commitment to conform to what is right and best for us and others. Moral laws are like physical laws, you may choose to disobey them; but you don't break them. They break you. If you follow them, they help you reach your full potential as designed by your creator.

You're reading this book to help you develop a healthy faith, not to justify your ideas about right and wrong. Now is the time to exercise your free-will and choose to build your faith on what God says is right and wrong.

Our world struggles with many moral crises such as substance abuse, human trafficking, racial prejudice, human indignity, financial inequality, hate-crimes, rape, injustice and corrosion of the family. You and I may disagree over the extent and importance of these issues, but no informed person denies that the underlying dilemma with our society and our individual relationships is not merely intellectual but moral. Your morals matter.

3. *How can you know what is right and wrong?* When I was a pastoral counselor, people often came to me for advice at important intersections in their lives. They asked questions like, "Is this the right career-choice, the right marriage partner, the right medical decision, the right way to believe?"

When it comes to important and difficult decisions, you don't want to flip a coin and take your chances, or ask around and hope you get good advice. On things that matter most, you want to be sure your choice is right. The best way to be sure you're traveling the right road to get you to your desired destination is to follow the right person, the one who made the road and traveled it many times before you.

Go to the source of truth to find the truth. When you read in the Bible and observe how the Father related to his children throughout history, it is obvious that he is all-loving, all-powerful, all-knowing, and all-present. He alone knows what is best and how we can find the best in our relationships with others and him. With God as your source, you can tell who else is telling you the truth.

On November18, 1978 in the smoldering jungle of Guyana, Jim Jones, a Baptist preacher, led 1,000 of his followers to commit suicide. I remember the front-page headlines of the *Atlanta Constitution*, "The Children Died First." Over two-hundred babies and children and more than seven-hundred adults drank poison and died because Reverend Jones said it was the right thing to do. How could they do that to their children? Why couldn't they see through Jones' insane beliefs? A broader question that tragedy leads me to ask is, how can you tell who is telling the truth about right and wrong?

You may believe that God's laws are right and still wonder how you can make the right decision in specific situations. Since you will face too many different situations to deal with each individually, it is best for you to learn the key biblical criteria that can help you know what's right or wrong in any situation.

I suggest you use the historic criteria found throughout the Bible and used consistently by Bible-teachers over time. Sometimes these timeless tests are most helpful when they come in the form of questions. When you try to determine what is right or wrong, before you make your decision, remember these five Tests for How Can You Know the Truth.

First, the test of CHARACTER

Ask yourself, if I make this decision, what will it do to my character? Will my conscience be clear? Will my Heavenly Father be proud of me? A choice is right, good and moral if it builds the primary character qualities found in our Lord. A decision is wrong, bad and immoral if it compromises or harms my character or the character of others.

Second, the test of AUTHORITY

Ask yourself, if I make this decision, who am I following? Who is my authority? Is this taught throughout the Bible or is it just something I accept as truth to justify my behavior. Am I simply looking for a few scriptures and other people who believe like I do so I can convince my mind that I'm right? Paul warned God's children to be careful about whom they followed, "Watch out unless you are taken captive by hollow philosophy." Colossians 2:6-9. Some teachings may sound right, but end up leaving you with empty, destructive promises. A thing is right because it is repeatedly considered right in God's word.

Third, the test of PURPOSE

Ask yourself, if I make this decision, what is my purpose? What do I really want? What am I trying to accomplish? Who will benefit most from this choice? Will this decision be consistent with God's purposes for my life and the lives of those for whom I care? If a thing is right, good and moral, it brings glory to God and helps others. Right decisions are not usually easy to make. Following the right way generally costs a great deal in the short term but pays off in the long run.

Fourth, the test of RELATIONSHIP

Ask yourself, if I make this decision, how will it affect my personal relationship with my Lord? Will your choice draw you closer to him? Will it please him? You know that you can't please everyone. Making decisions is primarily about choosing the one you want to please most. If your decision pleases your Lord, it's right and good. Therefore, it will build relationships, will draw you closer to your Lord, and will keep your heart and conscience at peace.

Fifth, the test of ETERNITY

Ask yourself, if I make this decision, where will it take me? What are the probable long term results? What are the eternal consequences for me and others?

You were born with eternal value. Right and good decisions support God's investment in you. Immoral decisions and acts keep you from being and doing all your Lord has in store for you.

First published in London in 1805 in the book "Songs for the Nursery," the English Tudor satirical nursery rhyme, *Pussycat, Pussycat*, was about a cat that went to London to visit the Queen but missed its opportunity.

> "Pussycat pussycat, where have you been?"
> "I've been up to London to visit the Queen."
> "Pussycat pussycat, what did you there?"
> "I frightened a little mouse under her chair"
> "MEOWW!"

A profound lesson is found in the final question, "You mean, you were given the privilege and opportunity to go on a noble mission to visit the queen of the most influential country in the world and you spent your time chasing mice?"

Doing what is right is not wasting your eternal opportunities. It is doing what brings honor, valuable and eternal benefits to your Lord, you and others.

4. *What are the three parents of all morals?* For you to seek to have a moral mind and make moral decisions, it will help you to know what the three primary morals are and to know the three enemies of moral thinking and behavior. For centuries, religious scholars, philosophers and psychologists have recognized the power and importance of morals and have put together many lists of morals.

I've examined a good number of those lists and consolidated them into a short, easy-to-remember version. You will readily recognize each of the three primary morals in the character of God and throughout the Bible. They are also the most common and respected morals in all of the major world religions.

PRIMARY MORALS   Forms of Primary Morals

1. HUMILITY: Being unselfish, loving, thankful, kind, gracious, generous, joyful, courteous, patient, encouraging peaceful, compassionate, sympathetic, or understanding

2. RESPONSIBILITY: Being faithful, accountable, courageous, attentive, sacrificial, dependable, loyal, reliable, purposeful, trustworthy, consistent, diligent, self-controlled, or just

3. HONESTY: Being truthful, authentic, sincere, clean, pure, straightforward, open, confessional, genuine, honorable, respectful, or respectable

PRIMARY IMMORAL
ATTITUDES   Forms of Primary Immoral Ways

1. PRIDE: Being selfish, critical, ungrateful, mean-spirited, gluttonous, vain, self-absorbed, unforgiving, greedy, hateful, inconsiderate, discourteous, impatient, discouraging, unconcerned, narcissistic, insensitive, or judgmental

2. IRRESPONSIBILITY: Being lazy, unfaithful, unaccountable, unstable, cowardly, inattentive, undependable, disloyal, unreliable, untrustworthy, two-faced, inconsistent, careless,

uncontrolled, adulterous, untrue, sloppy, unjust, disrespectful, or meaningless

3. DISHONESTY: Being untruthful, inauthentic, fake, insincere, counterfeit, false, deceitful, unfair, insincere, unclean, untrustworthy, secretive, hypocritical, fraudulent, dishonorable, or disrespectful

You were born with God's three primary morals embedded in your mind and in your conscience: humility, responsibility, and honesty. They were put there to guide you in making and maintaining healthy attitudes, decisions and relationships. If you are aware of them, use them as your personal measuring stick, and moment-by-moment seek your Lord's help in keeping them, then your relationships with God and others are more likely to work the way they were designed. If you don't, you're likely to deteriorate into a broken life of pride, irresponsibility, and dishonesty. The choice is not easy, but it is clear and critical. You can do this.

EXERCISES TO BUILD AND MAINTAIN YOUR HEALTHY FAITH

Knowing right from wrong and what is truthful are necessary for living out a healthy faith.

RECORD: List the three primary moral attitudes and at least three characteristics of each. Then list the three primary immoral attitudes with three characteristics of each. Keep this list readily available to you for the next few days.

REMEMBER: Memorize the three primary moral attitudes and the three primary immoral attitudes. Remember, all attitudes and behaviors will come under these six.

REFLECT: Open your Bible and read the Parable of the Lost Son found in Luke 15: 11-31. Look at the lost son, the loving father, and the older brother.

What morals were driving each of the characters in this story? Which one of these characters would you be in this story?

RE-EXAMINE: Remember that pride, irresponsibility, and dishonesty are enemies of your faith and your relationships. Is there someone in your life with whom you have a relationship that is not healthy? Examine how your own attitudes and behaviors are negatively influencing that relationship. Pray and ask God to direct you to change your attitudes and behaviors, then go to that person. Ask for forgiveness for your part in creating an unhealthy relationship, and explain what you're going to do to be more humble, responsible, and honest in this relationship.

RELATE: Be honest with yourself, responsible to your Lord, and humble before your friend. Talk to your trusted friend about your attitudes and behaviors that are not healthy and do not contribute to the development of your healthy faith and peaceful life. Be specific in describing your issues and which one of the three primary immoral attitudes they fit under. Discuss with your friend which ones of the primary moral attitudes you'll use to replace the immoral ones.

Moving to the next Chapter

Don't let your doubts and life's crises harm your faith. If handled properly, they can actually help build your mind and faith. Chapter Ten is designed to teach you how to turn your doubts and troubles into your best friends.

Pray this prayer to your Heavenly Father

Dear Father, Thank you for caring about me and wanting to be close to me. I need your help, Father. I am grateful for the morals you've built into my mind to guide me. Speak to me through those morals. I give you my mind to be attentive to your voice. I give you every part of me to be used any way you wish. I am your humble servant. Amen.

CHAPTER 10

How do you TEST your doubts?

✂

"Doubts are the ants in the pants of faith; they keep faith alive and moving."

FREDERICK BUECHNER

*"The faith that does not come from reason is to be doubted,
and reason that does not lead to faith is to be feared."*

G. CAMPBELL MORGAN

*"The important thing is not to stop questioning,
but to never lose a holy curiosity."*

ALBERT EINSTEIN

WHILE I ATTENDED FLORIDA STATE University, I enjoyed spelunking, sometimes called caving. It's classified an extreme sport because it is ridiculously dangerous. Climbing, crawling, squeezing through small passageways under the earth's surface was certainly an adventure of faith. Take my first exploration with my buddy, Allen.

We had crawled for over three hours when we saw a magnificent cavern just ten feet away. I stopped. The soggy wall above us was quivering and about to cave in. I warned Allen, "Hey Buddy, we've got to turn back." "Have you lost your mind?" Allen scowled. "We're almost there." I insisted, "If we don't back out now, I think we're going to get crushed to death." Allen argued, "Stop thinking so much, Nichols. Just have faith. Everything will be all right." About that time, a huge slab of the dripping clay ceiling splashed to the ground in our path. We both screamed and hurriedly wiggled backward to safety.

Over the years I've thought about that near-death moment when Allen urged me to *stop thinking and just have faith.* Even at his young age, Allen's way of handling our crisis was a clear picture of how too many people see faith. Faith is not a hopeful wish or positive thinking.

Faith is good. Doubt is bad. Wrong! A healthy mind never discourages tough questions or constructive doubt. When you doubt constructively, you question for the purpose of building and growing, and doubt can become one of faith's bet friends. Destructive doubt tries to tear-down and destroy.

In his unprecedented book, *The Language of God*, Francis Collins, the world's foremost geneticist and leader of one of history's greatest scientific achievements, explains how he used doubt to help him support his faith. He describes his personal pilgrimage from a self-described, obnoxious atheist to a respected scientist committed to faith in God and his son, Jesus. Collins, head of the Human Genome Project, along with his team of over a hundred leading scientists from around the globe, accomplished the remarkable task of being the first to map the human DNA, the code of life. His journey through this mammoth project taught him that faith and doubt are not enemies but perfect complements of each other.

Great believers are great doubters, too. If you're going to grow a strong, resilient, healthy mind and faith, you're going to stop accepting ideas as true just because your family, peers, religious leaders, recognized professionals or anyone else tells you so. Faith by proxy doesn't work. You're going to start testing ideas, beliefs, theory or practice.

Too often, being hesitant, cautious, curious, thoughtful or doubtful is equated with being evil, sinful, rebellious or even faithless. That's not the case with the great people of faith in Bible history. They were considered great moral and spiritual leaders because they refused to passively, blindly, mindlessly or cowardly go along with the falsehoods around them.

Jesus is the world's most well-known faith figure. But, in his day, he was known more for questioning commonly-accepted beliefs than he was for being a quiet believer. Can't you just hear Jesus questioning the religious leaders who said God demands justice and requires all sinners be punished?

How shocking it must have been to hear this great man of faith say, "I doubt that. That's not the Heavenly Father I know." God's son was history's greatest believer and its greatest doubter. Many other Bible characters like Abraham, Esther, David, Mary, Peter, John and Paul were outstanding people of faith and outstanding doubters too.

Go prepared or don't go. For years, Phyllis and I have led short-term medical mission teams to work in orphanages in Guatemala. Most of our first-time team members had never experienced poverty, substance abuse, ignorance, rampant crime, sickness and sexual exploitation like they witnessed on this venture. So we did our best to prepare them for unfamiliar customs and difficult questions they would face from the orphans, their families and other team members. Experience shows that unprepared volunteers actually do more harm than good. In-country leaders often say, "Short-term volunteers have only two choices either get prepared or stay home."

You have no choice. You can't stay home. When it comes to short-term mission trips, you can choose to stay home. But, when it comes to your mission trip through life, you have no choice. You're already on a mission trip. God sent you to carry out his mission for your life and others. You're going to get prepared for the most common and difficult questions people ask about faith, or you will have faith-related problems.

What-How and Who-Why Questions. Developing a healthy mind and faith is not for the lazy-minded. The more you're engaged in growing your faith, the more you'll be challenged by two groups of questions from your family, friends and enemies. Getting prepared to answer these questions will strengthen your mind, build your faith, and help eliminate your destructive doubts. It will also help you help others.

What-how questions. The first group of questions is the easier to handle. I call this category of questions the *what-how group.* At some time, you'll ask or be asked, "*What* caused this problem, this evil, this suffering? What is the reason for this? Am I being punished for something I did? I don't understand what's going on. This doesn't make any sense."

You may assume every problem has a cause and the secret to finding out how to fix or answer your problem is to locate the cause. That's good when you're working on a car that won't start, but it's not always the way things work when you're trying to help someone with a serious personal problem or question about God. There's more to helping than simply knowing about the problem.

Why-who questions. As you develop a healthy mind and faith, you're going to find, as important as quality thinking is, you will never be content with having answers to just these two mechanical or analytical questions. We faith-oriented people also want to handle the harder questions, the second group of questions you'll often face. I call this group the *why-who* questions.

We should never minimize the importance of the logical, descriptive, scientific, functional questions, but we should also be prepared to find meaning, purpose and value in what's happening to us and others, especially those we love.

As I mentioned earlier, when Viktor Frankl observed that hundreds of Holocaust victims committed suicide while others survived and maintained their dignity and hope, he concluded that people can live with any *what or how* if they only have a simple *why or who* to live for. My experience in working with hurting people is that the *why-who* questions require a tougher, more committed mind and faith than the *what-how* questions.

I was the chaplain-on-call during the late shift at Harris Methodist Hospital in Fort Worth, Texas when a nurse paged me to go immediately to the room of a twenty-five-year-old male who had just died. When I arrived, his wife was alone in his room. Earlier, the young man's wife checked him into the hospital because he was experiencing some muscle spasms in his lower back. Other than his muscle-contractions, it appeared that the young man was a picture of health. Sadly, he had a more serious problem, an untreatable form of cancer that took his life during his hospital stay.

Shortly after I got to the room, a hospital surgeon came by. In shock and desperation the young wife asked the surgeon, "Why did my husband have to die?" The *what-how* trained doctor answered her *why* question with a complicated medical description about *how* cancer works and *what* part of his body shut down that ultimately caused his death. After he left, I could tell his *what-how* answer wasn't what she was really wanting or what she needed. She needed caring support more than cold facts.

If you're unprepared for the *why-who* kinds of questions, you'll feel confused and maybe threatened by sincere inquiries and agonizing requests for help. And, if you're not prepared for the *why-who* questions your own mind is asking, you'll move from destructive doubt to painful depression. You may respond like that surgeon by avoiding the real question and moving to an easier *what-how* answer. But, with a little preparation, you can be ready to respond with confidence. In the process of listening to others' reservations, evaluating their doubts, feeling their pain and developing more meaningful answers to their questions, you'll sharpen your own thoughts and beliefs while being helpful at the same time.

Get ready for questions from all directions. The more you work on developing your own healthy mind and faith, the more you're going to find that your loved ones and friends will turn to you for answers to their faith-questions. Some will be looking for help. Others will be looking for an argument. Every challenge will be an opportunity to give your mind a healthy workout. Whatever their motive for asking you questions, it's best if you decide ahead of time how you'll respond. You have four primary options. You can choose to compete, hide, join or invite them. What will you do?

First, you may choose to compete. You may take the contest-approach. You can see every question as a contest in which you will either win or lose a debate. Arguing about emotionally-loaded faith issues is completely unproductive and insensitive. Even if you score more points and *win*, you lose. The compete-choice is an insecure, thoughtless choice.

Second, you may decide to hide. You can hide by avoiding questions, changing the subject, or trying to talk only with those who agree with you. Being quiet when you could help is irresponsible. The hide-choice may appear gracious, but it's really a cowardly choice.

Third, you may choose to join. In your attempt to be tolerant and accommodating, you may choose to agree with whatever the questioner says by positioning yourself as an accepting, sympathetic friend who puts harmony above everything. Offering genuine compassion and understanding is a good place to begin, but eventually it's no more than flavored dishonesty. If you were physically sick and needed answers to get well, you'd want more than sympathy. You'd want practical, substantive help. Don't rob your questioners of the medicine they need. The join-choice is deceitful.

Fourth, you may choose to invite. When someone asks you a faith-related question, that's your opportunity to *invite* them to share with you what they think and feel before you tell them what you think and feel. A good way to test your own beliefs is to see how well you listen sincerely and compassionately.

Help others' doubt while helping yours. Try to discern where the questioners are coming from and the source of their questions. Do your best to earn their respect as a fellow human being and to gain the right to speak. Before you ever offer a word of information, let them know you are genuinely interested in them and want to be helpful, not just give some clever text-book answer. When you take this approach, you're not arguing, pressuring, or shaming the questioner. You're being respectful and courteous, and asking for the same. The invite-choice is the healthiest choice. This approach will help others and will help you evaluate your own doubts, attitudes and motives.

Short answers and memorable answers. It was nearly midnight when Phyllis and I arrived at the ER at the University Hospital in San Antonio. The pain in my abdomen was excruciating. After seeing the CAT scan, the trauma team decided I needed surgery.

Although Phyllis and I knew my surgeon came highly recommended, we still wanted some answers before we agreed to such a serious procedure. I asked, "What exactly is wrong with me and what are you going to do?" The lead surgeon could have given me a long, thorough, highly-technical answer. Instead, in just a couple of statements, he summarized my problem, described what they would do to fix it, told me that he had done this procedure hundreds of times and assured me that he expected no problems. What a great, concise, clear, all-we-needed-to-know answer. We were completely satisfied.

My experience with people looking for long, complicated answers to serious why-questions is that they don't actually want help. They want ammunition to help them win their debate or argument. It's my experience that hurting, inquiring people want brief, honest, uncomplicated answers and comfort. But, you've got to be careful with brief answers. They can easily mislead people.

Be brief. Not trite. Brevity is no excuse for trite platitudes that sound true but are false and hurtful. Remember these old favorites:

- *Good things come to those who wait.* Not most of the time.
- *Whatever happens was meant to be.* Not usually.
- *Time heals all wounds.* Not if you've lost your limb.
- *Everything happens for a reason.* That's cruel and wrong.

Get to the essence and the helpful. Although we have to be careful about short answers, if you stay alert to their limitations, concise answers can still be the most practical, helpful and appreciated way of addressing difficult and complicated questions. When you prepare short answers to difficult and complicated questions, it helps you get to the essence of the problem and construct answers that you and other find most helpful.

Over the years, I've heard dozens of faith-related questions from both skeptics and believers. Such questions point to doubts that often become stumbling-blocks to those who want faith. Probably you have asked God or others some of these questions. I encourage you to prepare answers to as many of the popular faith-questions as you can.

EXERCISES TO BUILD AND MAINTAIN YOUR HEALTHY FAITH

Exercising your body is intentional. You don't accidentally stumble into an exercise facility. The same is true with your faith. No doubt, life's tests, pressures, and suffering will come, so get ready. Use the in-between times to intentionally test your beliefs, examine your doubts, and ask the hard questions. Below are some exercises that will help develop those faith muscles.

RECORD: Write down the four options you have when someone asks you the hard questions. Circle the option you'd most likely choose this moment. Then in a few sentences, record your answers to the following questions:

1. Why would a loving God allow evil and suffering?
2. Why would a loving God command soldiers to kill people?
3. How can you say the Bible is better than other religious books?

REMEMBER: Memorize the four primary options you have in dealing with doubt and serious questions.

REFLECT: Close your eyes and try to imagine yourself as one of the followers of Jesus when he was on earth. You had given up all to follow him because you expected great things, but the Crucifixion destroyed your hopes and dreams. Now open your Bible and read Mark 16: 1-8. What are your thoughts about the empty tomb and the Risen Christ?

RE-EXAMINE: If you could rationally understand it all, and I mean everything, you'd have no need of faith. Our faith takes over in that mysterious region where there is little understanding. You've been asked to record your answers to three very tough questions in this exercise. Which one of these questions causes you the most doubt? How has that doubt influenced your faith? Think of ways that doubting can be helpful to your faith. Also, think of some ways it can be destructive. Then ask God to help you doubt your doubts and demonstrate your faith.

RELATE: Choose one of these difficult questions and have a conversation with your trusted friend. Examine where you agree and where you disagree. Discuss faith's role and doubt's role in coming to these answers.

In the next step you will see some sample answers to what I think are the four toughest and most frequently asked faith-questions. I challenge you to let these serve as examples for you to construct your own answers to these and other questions.

Pray this prayer to your Heavenly Father.

Dear Father, I am grateful for your patience and understanding. You know everything in my mind, heart and activities. You already know that I have doubts and questions that bother me. Help me recognize the difference between my constructive and destructive doubts. More than answers, I want you as my closest friend. I give you my doubts and ask you to use them to make me a better servant of yours. Amen.

CHAPTER 11

How do you PREPARE for life's toughest questions?

"At the end of the day, the questions we ask of ourselves determine the type of people that we will become."

LEO BABAUTA, AUTHOR, *THE POWER OF LESS*

"Always be prepared to give an answer to everyone who asks you to give the reason for the hope that you have."

1 PETER 3:15

WE'RE ABOUT TO TACKLE WHAT I think are four of the most frequently asked and toughest faith-questions you'll ever face. An important part of growing a healthy mind is getting your mind ready to handle faith-shattering questions. Your faith's stability and practical value will greatly depend on how you answer these critical questions. Your answers will also determine how much help you can give to others who are seeking faith in the face of crises.

Being honest and clear about these answers. Before I offer my answers to these four tough faith-questions, I must confess that all of my answers have been written, torn up, and rewritten many times. For years I've studied, contemplated, prayed, and had numerous conversations about each of these questions.

After years of comforting people in the darkness of loss and pain, I know a little about what it's like to wait and wish for just some light to break through the darkness of fear and confusion. I too have felt the sting and sometimes throbbing agony of personal loss and the lonely misery of long periods of unanswered questions.

Often, it's during our darkest days that hard faith-questions and doubts seem to block the light of God and the hope of tomorrow. I wish I could throw open the windows to all human and divine knowledge. I wish I could give you all the light you want, but honestly, that's not going to happen. Like you, I have a long list of my limitations. No matter how much I want to have all the answers, I've discovered, none of us can do that.

But, what I can do is offer you are some rays of light that have helped me and many others see a little further and more clearly through the darkness. I can offer you this hope-filled truth. Many of those I counseled through their worst times came out on the other side saying, "God used this situation to turn me around and get me going in the right direction." Your most difficult question or most painful experience may be just what you needed to get you to where you need to be.

Change my starter-answers into your own answers. To help you begin, I want you to see these starter-answers as guides that can help you with other questions with which we all struggle at different times in our lives. My first attempt at constructing good answers to the difficult questions before us was far from satisfactory. No doubt your first stab will not be your best either. But, don't wait until you get the perfect answer before you begin sharing your answers. If you do, you'll never get started. In the days ahead, I hope you'll do additional study on these issues. The bibliography at the back of the book provides a number of excellent works by respected authors who more thoroughly address these questions. What I'm doing is basically giving you a few samples.

The most important part of your answer is your attitude, your mind-set. As I pointed out earlier, how you see yourself will determine how you answer any question. Keep working on your answers until you feel they've become your own. But, for now, put on your mental seat-belt and take a look at my concise starter-answers to these four faith-threatening questions. I will take more time with the first two questions than with the others because much of what I say about these two applies to the others.

1. Why would a loving God allow evil and suffering?
2. Why would a loving God kill people and send some to hell?
3. Is the Bible the word of God and can you depend on it?
4. Is the Bible or science right?

QUESTION 1: WHY WOULD A LOVING GOD ALLOW EVIL AND SUFFERING?

For generations, this has been the toughest and most frequently asked faith-related question. For some, it's a roadblock to faith in God. For many, it's a plea for help. For others it's an attack against the God of the Bible and its four basic convictions about God: God is all-loving, all-powerful, all-knowing, and all-present in our lives.

On their way home from an away-game, three high school cheerleaders were killed in a head on collision with a drunken driver. One of the mothers asked me, "How could God let something like this happen?" As a minister and counselor and a person who has grieved, I shared in the pain of those three families. This subject gets real and personal, but perhaps the main task in dealing with this crucial question is not to construct clever answers, but to help broken lives. A God-like answer does just that. The primary way God's son dealt with evil and suffering is the way I choose. It's the model I use in every situation; and I invite you to examine it and use it yourself. The essence of Jesus' helpful answer to this question has three parts.

1. WE ARE GOD'S CHILDREN AND HIS SERVANTS.

Jesus hurts when his family hurt. He wants us to have more than answers when we suffer.

Jesus was on a temporary mission. He was sent by his Father to face and overcome evil and suffering before he went back to heaven. Just like our master, Jesus, we don't see ourselves as people who are here to serve ourselves. Even when we don't understand the evil and suffering that we and others experience, we view those encounters as opportunities for us to be faithful in our mission. We want others to see God at work in us.

2. We are God's OVERCOMERS.
Jesus overcame suffering and death. Because of what God did in the death and resurrection of Jesus, we, his followers, are able to overcome any evil and suffering. We are given the ability not only to survive but actually to thrive no matter what. Since we have the mind of Jesus, the same point-of-view that he had about heaven and suffering, we may not see all before us now, but we anticipate the homecoming.

3. We are SAFE SOJOURNERS.
Evil tried, but it could not conquer Jesus. Because of who God is, evil never wins. God is always just and loving. Sometimes things don't appear fair, but in his timing, evil will be judged and good will be rewarded.

The Jesus-answer to evil and suffering is far better than any other. Our answer always includes the safe place of God's all-loving, all-powerful, all-knowing and always present Spirit. What could be better than knowing that God's Spirit is with us, going before us, and all around us at all times? We are certainly *Safe Sojourners* on our way home.

The most common answers to this tough question all fall far short of the Jesus-answer. Below are the most popular of those types of answers:

* *The Fatalist's answer* says, "God has his reasons. Everything that happens is God's will."
* *The Perfectionist's answer* says, "It just seems bad now. All is good. You need to look for the good in it. Good will come from this."
* *The Humanist's answer* says, "God is not involved. Evil and suffering make people stronger or eliminate the weak."

- *The Dualist's answer* says, "The devil made me do it. It's not up to us. We struggle between good and evil spirits."
- *The Optimist's answer* says, "Suffering purifies your mind. You will become what you think. God is using this to help you grow."
- *The Pessimist's*, "Everything physical is evil. Life is the prison-house of the soul. Suffering is punishment for desiring to live in this world. Focus on the eternal."

In their search for understanding evil and suffering, some Christians replace the strong pillars of the Jesus-answer with one or more of these other answers. Not every part of these other answers is contradictory to the Jesus-answer. But, if you overemphasize any one of these other answers, you will find that you and the people you are trying to help will become confused, fearful, angry and defeated. Those who follow the Jesus-answer experience the opposite.

Because evil and suffering are so real and rampant in the world, some conclude that the four basic Bible convictions about God are false and utterly contradictory to real life. Others, like me, observe the same evil and suffering and come to the opposite conclusion.

For us, the confusion around this question doesn't persuade us to reject our convictions but to admit our limitations, question our own questions and seek God's help to serve him better in the midst of such challenges. Sure, we have questions. We also have a God and a faith that are bigger than our questions. We're like the puzzled father in the Bible story.

The father's son, in a Bible narrative, had seizures since he was an infant. The father went to Jesus for help. Jesus asked him, *"Do you have faith that God can heal your son?"* The father answered, *"Yes, Lord, I do have faith, but help me with my doubts."* Mark 9:24. When someone asks you why your loving God allows evil and suffering, see yourself as this troubled father did. Express your child-like faith, but seek God's help with your human lack of understanding.

When you see yourself as God's child, Jesus' servant and an eternal person, you will be able to find meaning in suffering that comes in different forms.

What are some ways God's faithful servants view their suffering?

1. *Enlightenment.* Often suffering is viewed as enlightening. Many of us have discovered that suffering, at times, provides us unexpected and deeper insights into what really counts in life. It helps us stop focusing on trivia and start concentrating on more important matters including life after death.

2. *Preparation.* Suffering can strengthen us. Some have said their suffering helped them build character or sharpened their abilities. It prepared them for their future tasks. Jesus was led into the desert for forty days to get ready for his public work and his painful death. A father allowed his son to endure hardships so he'd be better prepared for adulthood. Proverbs 3:11-12.

3. *Revelation.* Suffering can be a gift. Many interpret their personal suffering as a gift to be cherished, not a problem to be solved. Dr. Sam Cannata, a missionary doctor who served in Kenya and Ethiopia for thirty-five years, lost his eye from an infection he got while performing surgery. Years later, I heard him say, "As a one-eyed doctor, I can now see far better with one eye than I ever could with two." He explained that he wasn't referring to his physical vision but new found ability to be a more effective and caring physician than before. Some suffering is eye-opening.

4. *Hope-building.* Sometimes suffering is hope-building. We often witness courageous and unselfish acts that come from suffering. Such acts give some a new sense of hope for the future. For Christians, ultimately our hope is based on Jesus suffering, death and resurrection. Suffering can produce hope.

5. *Protection.* Suffering can rescue us. One gentleman told me how suffering saved his life, "If it hadn't been for a horrible chest pain that caused me to get help, I'd be dead today." Sometimes pain and suffering are gifts. They serve as warnings, protections that save us from worse harm. At times, suffering alerts us to physical, moral and

relational problems that need attention before they cause far more dangerous problems.

6. *Reasonable.* Some suffering is natural. Many events of nature that cause human suffering, such as floods, hurricanes and earthquakes are a result of the physical laws that are part of the way the earth operates. The world was created with certain uniform natural laws that make it possible for vegetation to grow, rivers to flow, rain to fall and humans to survive. At times, God's laws of nature, such as gravity, may appear rigid, harsh and painful, but the alternative would not only be unreasonable and irrational but horrific, chaotic and more painful. Sometimes, suffering is part of the price of living in the natural splendor and order of God's amazing creation.

7. *Sacrificial.* Often suffering is a sacrificial choice. We admire those who suffer sacrificially. When a soldier courageously and voluntarily suffers for his country, he's a hero. Because Jesus died a sacrificial death for those who mistreated him, he's respected by people of all faiths around the world. Sometimes, suffering is a consequence of love, caring more about others than one's self.

8. *Irresponsibility.* Some suffering is a result of immorality. Too many women and children suffer emotionally and physically because men abuse and neglect them. Behind much suffering is irresponsible behavior. Often those who are poor, hungry, sick, and without God suffer because those with resources do not act responsibly. Some floods, famine, and pestilence happen because of our irresponsible use of our forests, rivers, and farmlands.

9. *Evidential.* Some suffering is proof of faith. Some view suffering as evidence that they are not fair-weather but loyal followers of their suffering savior. The imprisoned apostle John wrote these words on God's behalf, "Do not be afraid of what you are about to suffer. . . Be faithful, even to the point of death, and I (God) will give you life as your victor's crown." Revelation 2:10. Many Christians around the world are forced to choose between godless practices and persecution.

Those who choose persecution interpret their suffering as evidence that their faith is authentic and they will be rewarded in time.

10. *Probational.* Many see suffering as a temporary. It's considered a necessary part of God's gift of having a free will. To benefit from the joyful privileges that come from being part of the family of God, Christians are willing to suffer for a short time. Like their Lord, they willingly suffer during this probational part of their journey that will end in heaven and be worth it all.

11. *Punishment.* Some suffering is judgment on evil. God told Moses to tell Pharaoh, "This is what the Lord, the God of the Hebrews says, 'Let my people go . . . or I will send the full force of my plagues against you.'" Exodus 9:13-14. When Pharaoh would not change, God punished him and his people by sending plagues that caused suffering. Because evil can damage what God made and loves, he hates it and will not ignore it. Out of love for his people, he doesn't just feel for victims, he acts on their behalf.

  The Bible's dominant theme is not punishment but grace. It's not a story of an angry, hate-filled God who enjoys punishing people. It is the opposite. It is a story of a God who is actively involved in his peoples' lives, knows the details of what's going on, and loves his children so much that he gets angry when someone hurts them.

  It's also a record about that loving father's rebellious children, who, time and again, responded to their father's bounteousness by being arrogantly ungrateful, cruel to others, irresponsible, and dishonest. Yet, the gracious father was not quick to punish but was continually forgiving, offering many chances to start over. But, there came those rare times when the father decided to use suffering to try to bring them back to him. There were even rarer times when he knew, like only God can know, that the horrible effects of their evil actions required judgment. Out of love, he took actions to protect his other children and generations to follow.

12. *Mystery.* Some suffering is simply a mystery beyond our understanding. Although we can see many values and reasons for suffering,

ultimately I see suffering as a mysterious contrast to our future life with God where we will have no suffering. For those of us who take this position, suffering is not a problem to solve but a mystery to encounter, and endure. We can strengthened by our suffering, grow from it, and eventually overcome and be rewarded for it.

QUESTION 2. WHY WOULD A LOVING GOD KILL PEOPLE AND SEND SOME TO HELL?

Can the God who loved his enemies, forgave sinners, and wanted everyone to go to heaven be the same God who commanded Israel's soldiers to kill men, women, and children? Does a caring God bring judgment on people with floods, earthquakes and hell?

For centuries scholars and ordinary people have wrestled with this highly-emotional and personal faith-question. Several answers have helped but none have put the struggle to rest. While on this earth, we can have the mind of Jesus, but we're still clothed in our human bodies and limitations.

This difficult question is fueled by scriptures in both the Old and New Testaments. Both describe God as a God of love and judgment. Even Jesus, God in flesh, said both, "Love your enemies, do good to those who hate you." Luke 6:27. And he said, "You snakes! You brood of vipers! How will you escape being condemned to hell? Matthew 23:33.

WHAT ARE SOME HELPFUL ANSWERS TO THIS TOUGH QUESTION?

No one answer is completely satisfying to everyone. But, many people have found pieces of all these answers helpful.

1. *The Mechanical Answer.* The mechanical answer to the God-loves-and-judges question says, "The Bible says it. I believe it. That settles it." The mechanical-answer-approach to God's wrath is that God's word says God ordered or did these drastic acts himself. They are accurate accounts in

an accurate Bible. This answer emphasizes a flawless Bible and absolute obedience. From this perspective, nothing more needs to be said.

2. *The Cultural Answer* says, "The Bible is the voice of culture, not God." Biblical references to God's wrath are not God's will. God never told people to do those horrible things. The Bible's authors wrote out of their cultural experience. They simply made a mistake. They justified their harsh actions and understandings by saying God told them to do what they did. God is not a God of wrath, but only a God of love. Not all of the Bible is accurate.

3. *The Rational Answer* says, "God has his reasons that reason cannot know." Our tiny brains cannot begin to understand God's thinking. He knows best. Wrath is a reasonable, logical and natural response to evil. This approach emphasizes the importance of justice and order in the world.

4. *The Liberation Answer* says, "God's priority is to help his people individually and collectively find freedom (salvation)." Freedom is God's highest good. God's wrath is necessary for purifying and building a free life or nation.

5. *The Dispensational Answer* says, "God has a sovereign plan and his wrath was for that dispensation or stage in his plan." The wrath-dispensation has passed, and God is dealing with people in a different way during our dispensation. With the coming of Jesus, we are living in the grace and forgiveness stage.

6. *The Progressive Answer* says, "God has in the past and does now deal with people at their level or ability to handle things." During the Old Testament times, people did not have the benefit of all the teachings of the prophets and Jesus. Their understanding of God had not progressed yet. This approach says that God's revelation of himself is progressive.

7. *The Situational Answer* says, "God does what's most loving for each situation." This approach contends that God's wrath was the most loving thing he could do for the most people in that situation. It may seem cruel to let a person drown. But, if a lifeboat is full of people and

the one overboard cannot be brought on board because he will sink the boat, the most loving decision is to let him drown.

8. *The Incarnational Answer* says, "God's love is a tough-love. God is not a supernatural Santa Claus. His kind of love is unselfish, responsible and honest." When I read and study the Bible, it's clear to me that it was penned by men who wrote through their own individual personalities but were inspired by God. Their reports were guided by God and were reliable accounts of God's acts of love and judgment in actual events. When the Bible says God sent plagues on Egypt as punishment, that's exactly what God did. He acted in love for his children. His was a tough-love. When the Bible says Jesus told the religious leaders of his day that they would go to hell for misleading God's children, his was a tough-love.

For me, the *Incarnational Answer* is the most comprehensive and best way to answer this question. The more I understand God's character and the biblical meaning of God's love, the more satisfied I am with the idea of a God of love and wrath.

The most concise description of God in the Bible is, "God is love." I John 1:3. But, don't get confused by that word love. This statement does not mean God is so loving and so nice that he overlooks evil. It doesn't mean he is so affectionate that he requires nothing from anyone and forgives everyone for anything. It doesn't mean there are no consequences for those who hurt people, cause suffering, break trust, destroy life and inflict pain on others. Genuine love is responsible.

The Bible statement, "God is love," is a succinct summary of God's core characteristic or primary personality trait. It's more like a conclusion I would make if I followed God around for a several hundred years and watched him interact with his people, observed his thinking, examined the way he felt for his children, scrutinized his every act, then wrote one sentence to summarize all of my first-hand observations. His love was *unselfish, responsible* and *honest.* That's why God's love includes judgment and mercy, punishment and forgiveness.

Love without responsibility is not genuine love. The God I know and see described in the Bible repeatedly responded to evil with a responsible kind of love. His love does not ignore evil against his children. He will not treat wrong, hurt and hatred lightly.

If someone breaks into a home and rapes and murders a young girl, you can be sure your heavenly Father gets angry because he knows his children personally and loves them intimately. He doesn't just get angry. He responds with an accountable kind of love. That is, he judges with a thoughtful decision and in his own time takes the wisest action. Only he knows what's right and best for all involved.

In God's moral economy, all wrongs will be made right and all right will be rewarded. Because of God's love, he came to earth, became a man and died in the place of the guilty. He paid for our sins so that we don't have to pay. If we accept his payment for our sins, he forgives us and removes our judgment. The way we can accept his payment is to act in faith. We give him our whole lives in gratitude and service. God's Incarnational-love included allowing humans to crucify him on their behalf. But, you might ask, "What about hell? Can a loving God send people to hell?"

WHAT ARE SOME HELPFUL ANSWERS TO THE QUESTION OF HELL?

1. *Hell is a choice.* God doesn't send anyone to hell. He doesn't want anyone to go to hell. Jesus died so no one would have to go to hell. Hell is where we end up if we choose to turn our backs on God and walk away from him and his way of life. One of the reasons he created humans was because he wanted to have a loving relationship with us. Since a relationship is a choice, it requires a free will. So, God created each of us with a free will to choose or refuse to enter into a relationship. If we choose to have a loving relationship with him (a heavenly way of living) or choose to live without him (a hellish way of living), the choice is ours.

2. *Hell is a place.* Hell is the eternal home of the self-absorbed. The choice to be self-centered and self-directed, rather than God-centered and God-directed, leads to bitterness, anxiety, envy, greed and various kinds of self-destructive thoughts and actions. To choose to reject God's love, his friendship and his way for our lives, is to choose to live in a hellish way now and for eternity. Hell is living in the prison we create. It's not what or where God desires. But, because of our free will, the scripture says, "God gave them up to their own desires." Romans 1:24.

God's love and wrath make sense to me because of his character, his quality of love, the free-will he gave us and because of the integrity of the Bible.

QUESTION 3. IS THE BIBLE THE WORD OF GOD AND CAN YOU DEPEND ON IT?

Christians say that the Bible is a record of God's revelation of himself to us. It is his way of informing of the best way to live and the way to eternal life with him. It's our authority for what's true and good.

The Bible's authors were a diverse group from a number of different countries, backgrounds, cultures, ages and educational levels. The Bible asserts that God's Holy Spirit (His presence) guided and protected each of the authors as well as the gathering of its many writings into one Book that we can trust. 2 Timothy 3:16.

Other religions make similar claims about their sacred writings. How is the Bible different from other religious writings? What evidence and reasons cause Christians to believe that people in every language, generation, and culture should depend on the Hebrew-Christian Bible above all other writings?

Why Believe the Bible and Depend on it?

1. *It is dependable.* You should depend on the Bible above all others because it has authority like no other book. Deciding on what's right and wrong, good and bad comes down to *who says so.* The Bible is

called God's Word because God guided all of its writers in what they wrote. The authors all claimed that the God of creation and all eternity himself was the author behind their authorship. How could you find a more dependable source to tell you about God and the best way for his creation to live than to get it from God himself?

With all of the writers' personal human limitations, and with the many different translations, interpretations and compilations over time, the Bible has been and continues to be a satisfying source of truth, comfort, hope and guidance for billions of people all over the world for hundreds of years. Like many others, I've studied the sacred writings of all of the other major world religions and personally found the Hebrew-Christian Bible to be my most dependable resource for guidance, comfort, inspiration and truth more than any other writing on earth.

2. *It is truthful.* You should depend on the Bible because it is truthful like no other book. *Truth* is a vague word to some people, but it basically means something you can count on. For generations, believers and unbelievers have tested its validity, sought to understand its teachings and wrestled with its morals. At the end of it all, the overwhelming conclusion is that you can count on it. You will never completely understand all of it or its full meaning, but it is completely honest and trustworthy; and you can count on it more than anything thing else.

3. *It is credible.* You should depend on the Bible because it's historically credible like no other. Since this amazing book was put together, historians, scientists, and archeologists have examined the people, places, events and two-thousand prophecies of the Bible, and the overwhelming majority have concluded that it is a book of historical facts and truth, not a book of myths, fantasies, and fairytales about imaginary people and places.

4. *It is consistent.* You should depend on the Bible more than any other because all of its teachings and stories are consistent with its basic message. Although the Bible is a collection of sixty-six writings written by many authors, from many cultures, over many centuries, facing

many different crises and political powers, its timeless teachings and stories never contradict each other. Some teachings, like the requirement to not eat certain foods, were obviously designed for a specific time and culture. But, the great moral and spiritual reasons behind those teachings were consistent with the other great moral teachings of the Bible. The character that you see in the God that created the world and saved his children from slavery in Egypt is the same character of the God who came to earth in the form of the man, Jesus, who saved his children from their sins. How could such a diverse collection be completely consistent and compatible in its message, beliefs and descriptions of God? Simple. Our God was over and under and behind it all.

5. *It is transforming.* Another reason you should depend on the Bible more than any other book is because its message has radically and positively transformed more people and groups than any other writing in history. Throughout generations, and still today, it transforming message has led its believers to remove ignorance, fear, hatred, dishonesty, injustice, irresponsibility and self-centeredness like no other writing. It has motivated people to build more hospitals, orphanages, schools, shelters, research centers, rehabilitation clinics, counseling facilities and many other transformational communities for hurting people than all other religious, philosophical and educational books in the world combined.

6. *It is relevant.* Another reason you should depend on the Bible more any other book is because its stories, morals, truths and main characters, like Jesus, are relevant, timeless, and applicable for every time, person, and culture. With the help of God's Spirit speaking to your conscience, you can apply its teachings and stories to every part of your life and relationships. The more you make the Bible *your* personal guidebook, the more you will sense that it speaks directly to your needs and desires. It will become your manual for life and not just a good history or religious book. I guarantee you, it works for me and it will work for you.

8. *It's Purposeful.* Another reason you should depend on the Bible more than any other book is because it will give meaning and purpose to your life like no other book. Its stories are about real people in real places with real problems like yours. Those people found real life-changing, meaningful solutions just like you can. It seriously addresses life's most difficult issues and will help you find purpose in everything that may happen to you in this life. It will also prepare you for your life after death and help you have purpose beyond your life on earth.

QUESTION 4. IS THE BIBLE OR SCIENCE RIGHT?

False assumptions always cause serious consequences. Both the Bible and science begin with a few basic assumptions. Your assumptions always determine how you interpret everything you believe and experience. For example, if you believe in science and have the false assumption that the Bible should be consistent with science, you will find places in the Bible that you consider inaccurate and misleading. If you believe in the Bible and have the false assumption that science should be consistent with our belief in the supernatural, you will consider science an enemy of faith.

I was eight-years-old the summer I visited my grandfather on his farm in Virginia. He was a member of a local independent Christian congregation. That summer I came down with mumps which is an extremely contagious, viral infection. I got up one morning and my cheeks looked like a chipmunk. Both of my salivary glands were swollen and throbbed with pain. My head hurt. I was nauseous and had a burning fever. When I told my grandfather I had mumps and couldn't eat the pancakes and maple syrup my grandmother had prepared for breakfast, he got angry. He said, "Sickness is all in your head. There's no such thing as being sick."

I'll never forget how my grandfather made me stand facing a mirror and repeat over and over again, "I'm not sick. It's all in my mind." He told me I'd have to stand there and say it until I stopped thinking and feeling sick. I felt so miserable and didn't want to stand there any longer so I repeated those words for a short time then lied. I told him what he wanted then went to my room sicker and more angry.

Based on the belief that God and all the material world are completely spiritual and perfect, my grandfather's religion taught that it's never God's will for anyone to suffer, be sick, or die. That kind of belief system assumes that the physical world is not real. It's is only an illusion. Suffering is part of our imagination like unicorns and flying dragons. They believe we are only subject to the laws of this physical world and all of its problems to the extent we think those things are real.

Usually those who are dedicated to this false assumption will not visit doctors or take medicine. To do so would mean they accept sickness as physical not imaginary. They use the many Bible-references to prayer as proof that genuine, godly people don't turn to physical medicine to help solve spiritual problems. They explain that Jesus prayed, the sick were healed, the dead were raised to life, and that's exactly what we should do. False biblical assumptions and interpretations have serious consequences.

Be careful of ignorance and poor communications. I've found that most misunderstandings between Bible-believers and science-oriented people are rooted in ignorance or poor communications. Those committed to science, hold false assumptions about the Bible and its purposes. Too often, the skepticism, and sometimes anger, found in the hearts and minds of some science-oriented people come from a personal experience with an ignorant or mean-spirited religious-fanatic. It is not the Bible they reject, but some irrational, bigoted, religious egotist that they falsely assume represents all Bible-believers.

On the other hand, people committed to the Bible sometimes have false assumptions about science and its purpose. They often judge science by the views of a few anti-religion scientists.

When I try to answer questions about science and the Bible, I like to begin by clearing up some of the most common misunderstandings about the two. One way to do that is to examine the main assumptions or foundation-stones of the Bible and science. With those basic assumptions in hand, I like to compare the two to find out how they are different and how they are alike.

WHAT ARE THE BASIC ASSUMPTIONS OF THE BIBLE?

The Bible, the word for book, is primarily a story book. It is full of stories about God, the world, his people and his activities with his people. Some of the stories are *factual accounts,* like the stories of Moses and the exodus from Egypt and the life of Jesus. Those were factual records of what actually happened in the lives of real people in real places.

Others stories in the Bible were designed intentionally as *symbolic narratives,* not factual accounts. For example, the parable of the Prodigal Son was a symbolic story like many parables Jesus used. Whether Jesus knew an actual boy who took his inheritance, ran away from home, ate with the hogs, then later came home to be welcomed by his father, was not the point. The story was told, not to recall historical facts, but to proclaim basic truths, to paint lasting mental pictures, and to teach foundational beliefs or morals.

Among the many biblical stories are forty that noticeably standout to me. I listed them in the back of the book. When you read them for the first time or read them again, I hope God will speak to you through them as he does to me every time I read them. In all of these classic stories, I notice some common assumptions about God, his creation, and his relationship to his children.

1. *Creation:* God created everything out of nothing and it was good, orderly, and purposeful.
2. *Laws:* God made physical and moral laws for his creation to follow and use for good.
3. *God's Character:* God is all-loving, all-powerful, all-knowing and all-present with his creation and especially with his children.
4. *Humans are the crown of God's creation.* Unique in all of his creation, we were given a free-will and are more than physical. We are made in the image of God and have the ability to be in a loving relationship with him and others. We were chosen to use our built-in morals to be unselfish, responsible and honest in managing the rest of God's creation and relating to one another.

5. *Pride is our primary problem:* From the first human being until today, we have all made bad choices. We have used God's gift of a free-will to turn our backs on God. Our pride, irresponsibility and dishonesty are the sources of our problems.

6. *God's Responses to Our Rebellion:* No matter how hard we try, we can't set ourselves free from making decisions that hurt us and others. We need help to free us from our pride and for greater and more ultimate purposes in life and eternity. Without taking over our free will, God does everything he can to save us from self-destruction and self-isolation. He wants us to have a personal relationship with him.

7. *God's Clearest Revelation of Himself:* Throughout the first part of the Bible, God promises that a Messiah (savior) will come to set us free. In the second part of the Bible, we read about the promised Messiah, Jesus. Although it's beyond our ability to understand, God did what only God could do. In Jesus, the Messiah (Christ) took on the form of a human.

God came to earth, cared for people, died on the cross for our sins, rose from the dead so his Holy Spirit could be with us all the times. He taught us by example how to live life at its fullest, gave us an ultimate purpose for living, and promised to take us to be with him and those we love for eternity to receive the rewards for our faithfulness and full benefits of being his children.

Now that you know the basic assumptions of the Bible, let's look at science.

WHAT ARE THE BASIC *ASSUMPTIONS OF SCIENCE?*

Simply defined, science is a way of getting reliable answers to our questions about the physical world and a way of making decisions and solving problems based on those answers. Science relies on our human abilities to ask questions, do research, construct theories, test theories, observe evidence and make tentative conclusions. Like the Bible, science has some basic assumptions.

1. *The physical world is real.* Science assumes that the world is knowable. It's not an illusion. Science is not for or against the idea that God

created the earth. It doesn't attempt to prove or disprove anything about God. Its task is to work with the physical, material, natural world, not the spiritual world.

2. *Faith is basic to science.* Science assumes that the world is orderly, predictable and reasonable. Science has faith that the natural world will continue to function in an orderly manner. Much about the physical world is taken on faith by science; and it seeks to find evidence and reasons why the visible and invisible world operates that way. The reason for the world's predictability is not known to the scientist. It's taken on faith.

3. *Searching for truth is important.* Science assumes knowledge is good and truth can be found. Science is a search for truth. It wants to overcome superstition, dispel myths, find cures, conquer problems, explain mysteries and answers all questions about the visible and invisible world.

4. *Everything that happens has a cause.* Science assumes there are physical causes for everything that happens. For example, if a rock falls to the ground, science assumes that there must be a physical explanation as to why it fell. If something happens and the explanation is not obvious, science does not assume God or some supernatural force caused it to happen. Causes are determined by finding hard evidence. Science assumes any explanation that is not physical is fantasy.

Now that you have a brief understanding of the basic assumptions of the Bible and science, can you see how they have some things in common?

WHAT DO *FAITH AND SCIENCE HAVE IN COMMON?*

1. *Both depend on truth not superstition.* Both the Bible and science are committed to finding truth, seeking to help, acting responsibly, being honest and making decisions based on truth not feelings. Both look

for truthful not wishful answers. Both assume truth is rooted in reality not ideas, emotions, personal experiences or fantasy.

2. *Both rely on reason and research.* Both the Bible and science depend a great deal on human abilities to make rational decisions and do research, construct theories, test theories, observe evidence and make conclusions. Both believe in the value of rational thinking and hard evidence, not irrational thinking, prejudiced-judgments, superstitious myths or emotion-based conclusions.

3. *Both have meaningful purposes.* Both the Bible and science are designed to help people and make life better for all. The conviction that we have a responsibility to be good stewards of the physical world is rooted in the Bible and science.

4. *Both have Bible-believing leaders.* Most of the early scientists were Christians, and it's not surprising that many of today's most famous scientists are Bible-believers. Many scientists do not see the Bible and science as enemies but partners.

WHAT ARE THE DIFFERENCES BETWEEN FAITH AND SCIENCE?

Although the basic assumptions of the Bible and science have much in common, they also have some important differences. What are the main differences?

1. *A different view of what's real.* Both the Bible-believer and the scientist seek truth and look for it in that which is real not fantasy. However, one of the main differences between science and the Bible is that science only deals with the physical world. To be true to its task, science doesn't look beyond the physical for evidence. The responsible scientist says if there is something real beyond the physical, something that causes things to happen that are not physical, that's not my job to investigate or use as an explanation. My tools only fit the physical world.

The Bible, or faith-perspective, says that part of what's real is made up of the physical world; but, there's more to what's real than the physical. Bible-believers should appreciate the work of science, but not expect science to give up the methods and tools that help us in the physical world.

The Bible teaches us that we humans are more than physical or natural (part of the natural creation). We are physical, mental, emotional and super-natural (more-than natural) creatures. Bible-believers should not expect science to answer questions and solve problems about the super-natural with answers from the natural world. And scientists should not expect Bible-believers to answer questions and solve problems about science with super-natural answers. When a Bible-believing scientist assumes the natural and super-natural are real, he or she sees the values both can contribute to both worlds.

2. *A different view of evidence.* Both science and the Bible are evidence-based. Scientists separate truth from fantasy by testing evidence over and over to decide what is real and what is mere myth (make-believe). For the scientist, there is only one kind of evidence, physical evidence. For the Bible-believer, there are other forms of evidence that are just as real but not explained physically. For example, below is a list of just a few forms of evidence that are not based on science:

    * Evidence of many answers to prayer with no medical explanation
    * Physician-reported healings that they can't explain by science
    * Evidence of millions of people whose immoral lives became moral and productive because of an experience with God
    * Evidence of highly respected people who report experiencing God's still, small voice and presence
    * Evidence of lives changed by love—no scientific explanation
    * Reports from thousands, including respected scientists and physicians, of near-death experiences and out-of-body experiences with God and heaven
    * Reports by respected, reasonable and science-oriented people about miracles in their lives that are beyond natural laws

3. *A different view as to their purpose.* Science limits itself to the kinds of questions it can answer. And that's why we look to God and his Bible to give us answers to question beyond the realm of science.

   Science helps us learn how things work in the physical world, how to fix things that get broken, how to heal disease, and how to prevent problems. It can't and doesn't try to explain why we are here and who is behind what's happening. Science's purpose is to find cures to problems; but it needs God to find an ultimate purpose for doing the work and for what happens after we die. That's the Bible's job. We need science and the Bible.

4. *A different view of what is right and wrong?* Science seeks answers through studying cause and effect. It's good at finding physical solutions to physical problems, but it needs the Bible to decide what to do with its solutions. Science can use physical laws to make powerful instruments, but it's the Bible's moral laws that help scientists decide how its powerful instruments should or should not be used, what's good or bad, right or wrong, ethical or unethical. Science and the Bible need each other.

WHAT SHOULD YOU DO WHEN THE BIBLE AND SCIENCE CONFLICT?

What should you think when the Bible seems to contradict science or when science is in conflict with the Bible? I'm both a Bible-believer and science-believer, and I appreciate and respect both when I'm faced with this question.

When the Bible says the earth and everything in it, including humans, were created in six days, what can I say? It's obvious that the Bible language and science don't agree here. The way I and many others resolve the difference is to recall the basic assumptions of the Bible and science then seek to explain the seeming contradictions in light of those assumptions.

I believe the Bible was written by humans with their limited abilities and interests in science. Those writers were inspired by God to accomplish what he wanted in telling the story. It's obvious to me that our Lord's purpose for the Bible was not to give us an early scientific explanation of the origin of the earth. God's purpose was to provide all of us his basic assumptions and instructions that would guide us in life.

Our Lord gave us some simple, down-to-earth accounts of real people that we could relate to and use as positive and negative models for our lives. It seems obvious to me that he wanted to communicate that he is a God who *loves* us. He's *able* to do anything he wants, like creating the world and humans. He *knows* everything and what's best for us. He will always be *present and involved* in our lives no matter what happens in his orderly, somewhat predictable creation.

For me, the Bible's creation story does not disagree with science any more than love disagrees with mathematics or peace disagrees with the laws of physics. Since they are not trying to do the same thing, their differences are not contradictory but complementary. Let's appreciate them both for their unique contributions to our lives.

EXERCISES TO BUILD AND MAINTAIN YOUR HEALTHY FAITH

If you decide to take a trip, you make preparation. You're on life's journey, and you need to be prepared. Your preparation will not only benefit you, God will use your preparation to help someone else.

The four questions detailed in this chapter are critical factors in your preparation. The world's finest minds have been dealing with these same questions for centuries. Hundreds, perhaps thousands, of books have been written on each question. They are important questions because they are most often the most serious barriers to faith.

RECORD: Choose one of the questions detailed in this chapter. Re-read my answer to that question, and then in just a few sentences, summarize your answer to that question. You might find it helpful in your re-reading to make some notes or jot down an outline that would help you distill and formulate your answer.

REMEMBER: Relief—there is not list for you to memorize in these exercises. Now would be a good time to pull out the lists you've made before and tried to commit to memory and review them to see how you're doing.

REFLECT: There is the beautiful story of Jesus' taking Peter, James, and John up on the mountain. It was there Jesus' appearance changed, and the three disciples with him witnessed Jesus conversation with Elijah and Moses. They were all engulfed in a cloud and heard God's voice. My, what an exhilarating experience, and then they had to leave the mountaintop and come back to the city streets. Now, open your Bible to Mark 9: 14-24 and read the story where it picks up. After reading, sit quietly and close your eyes, and try to put yourself there on the cobblestone streets. See the crowd, hear the arguments going on between the disciples and the religious teachers, and feel the desperation of a loving father. Read verse 24 again and meditate upon each phrase. Make that your prayer to your Heavenly Father.

RE-EXAMINE: I invite you to look at what other authors have to say about these questions. You may choose one to two books from the annotated bibliography in the back of this book, or you may choose to check out some really helpful blogs or articles on the internet. This can be an on-going study for you as you examine others' insights.

RELATE: Ask your trusted friend to read and evaluate your answer to the tough question you chose in the RECORD section of these exercises. Discuss the value your answer might have with someone who has serious faith questions.

You probably noticed this chapter's exercises were a bit different in that I asked you to focus on one of the questions. But that was just for now. You've read this chapter, and you recognized it was difficult. My hope is that even when you've finished this book you will continue to read and study this chapter, and do for the other three questions what I've asked you to do with this one. Continue reading what other writers have to say on these topics. When you've done that, then you'll be prepared to answer some of life's toughest questions, and you'll be prepared for life's toughest situations.

As you continue in the process of developing your healthy mind, you not only need to feed, test and prepare it, you also need to protect it from information and images that can harm it. Chapter Twelve: How do you PROTECT your mind? is designed to do just that.

Pray this prayer to your Heavenly Father.

Dear Father, I come to you as your humble servant. I want to be useful to you and to make you proud of me. Lead me to prepare my mind to be help to people when they have questions about you and your way of living and dying. As I prepare to help others, teach me. Shape my mind to think like you think and value what you value. You are my source of all that's good. Draw me close to you. I love you Lord Jesus and a so grateful for what you did for me on that Cross. Amen.

CHAPTER 12

How do you PROTECT
your mind?

"Sickness may be the solemn occasion of God's intervention in a person's life."

PAUL TOURNIER, MD, CHRISTIAN AUTHOR AND PSYCHIATRIST

*"Consider it a sheer gift, friends, when tests and challenges
come at you from all sides. . . Let it do its work so you become
mature and well- developed, not deficient in any way."*

JAMES 1:1-3

IMPURE WATER IS A MAJOR cause of sickness and death throughout the world. Fortunately, many people who live in regions where all the water around them is contaminated by pollution and human waste are getting help from Christian organizations. Many of these caring groups use a two-part, proven solution to this dangerous health problem. First, they teach the people to *stop drinking impure water.* Second, they train them to *drill for clean water and only drink it.* What an excellent and effective approach for protecting your mind.

First, avoid impure images and information. Don't fill your mind with impure images and information. If you've been doing it, stop now. At first glance just like the impure water, the images may look harmless. But those hidden impurities you're allowing into your mind will unquestionably harm your mind and prevent you from reaching your goal of having a healthy mind and faith.

You may think, "A small, periodic sip of impure images won't bother my mind. I'm tough-minded. I can handle them." Wrong. If that's what you're thinking, no doubt you've already gulped down too much pollution, and it's negatively affecting your judgment. Unclean images in your mind are not inactive. Like hungry, invading microorganisms, they're always working inside your mind. They're fighting against your healthy elements, and over time those enemy-invaders will always do harm.

Second, look for healthy images. To effectively protect your mind, you need not only to stop allowing impure images into your mind, but you must intentionally look for the healthy images for which your mind was designed. When you find them, feast on them. They're not only good for your mind and faith; you'll enjoy them more in the long run.

If you look for clean, refreshing and wholesome images and information in books, movies, programs, music, art, people, the Bible and other sources, you can find them.

Those who are committed to healthy food and drink for a long while eventually find unhealthy food and drinks distasteful. The same is true for the well nourished mind. Over time, a healthy mind thirsts for and enjoys the kinds of stories, movies, art, music and relationships that are nourishing. It desires wholesome love, unselfish pleasures, and forms of communication and entertainment that emphasize the great, timeless morals.

So, let's talk about what I consider the most effective way you can protect your mind from such impurities. It will help you discern the difference between healthy and unhealthy information and images. It will also help you stop swallowing impurities and only desire pure content.

In case you haven't thought about it in a while, just take a look at a few of the most common mind-invaders that infect and harm people's beliefs and morals. From time to time, mental-healthcare and spiritual-healthcare professionals put together lists of common dangers to our minds. I included the list below to remind you of the sheer volume of possible threats our minds have to face. Hopefully this list will encourage you to be serious about the work of protecting your mind.

Primary Enemies of the Mind
Influences that often harm a healthy mind

1. Biological Causes:	Brain infections, injuries, substance abuse, poor nutrition, toxins, heredity
2. Emotional Causes:	Childhood traumas, sexual abuse, emotional abuse, loss of loved ones, neglect, loneliness, lack of purpose, lack of community, perversions, violence
3. Environmental Causes:	Dysfunctional family life, severe community crises, natural disasters, dramatic cultural changes, serious social pressures
4. Moral Causes:	Being self-centered, irresponsible, guilty, purposeless, hopeless, greedy, revengeful, unsympathetic, angry, addicted

One thing cannot be taken from you. You can't change your past or control your future, but you can control one thing that no one and nothing can take from you. You're probably thinking, "That's an over-statement, if I ever heard one." Actually, it's not. Remember, I'm the cautious type and am totally opposed to exaggerations or over-statements. Viktor Frankl discovered the one thing no one and no circumstance could take from him.

Earlier in the book I described how Frankl was brutally tortured in the Nazi concentration camps but never gave up like so many of his fellow inmates. He reported that most of the prisoners, who were not murdered, eventually lost hope, cursed God and committed suicide. Yet, he was able to overcome everything his enemies threw at him. Neither his torturers nor his circumstances were able to take away his hope. And, during some of his most painful experiences, he was even able to find inner peace and meaning for what he went through.

There were actually times in the middle of agonizing suffering when Frankl turned to pleasant memories of his beloved wife and of his sweet family. He would picture her lovely face and envision the two of them going places where they enjoyed being together. In his mind he reflected on how it would be when he got home again and how he could use this horrible experience for good. How did he do it? What did he do to protect his mind from going insane, turning from God or choosing to commit suicide?

After Frankl's release from the camps, he came to this profound and helpful conclusion that everything, except one thing, can be taken from us. He called that one critical, unyielding, immovable thing that could not be moved by any situation, our *human freedom*. Sometimes he referred to it as our *ability to choose* or our *capacity to determine* our own *attitude* towards any set of circumstances.

That's the kind of freedom and attitude we want and need. It's a special point-of-view, a pre-determined choice or mind-set that is not some flimsy sort of positive thinking technique. It's a rock-solid, peace-producing, fixed way of looking at everything in a way that changes everything.

Like Frankl, my friend, Frank Short had it. And, it worked for him, too. When Frank was only days away from death, I heard one of his nurses ask him how he was able to be so other-centered and never complain. For months they'd watched my dearest friend strain from the excruciating pain caused by his cancer; yet he never lost his big smile or attitude. He learned the names of all the nurses and most of the patients on his floor at the hospital. Every day, he checked on those he was allowed to visit, inquired about their condition and prayed for them. He continually expressed gratitude for his caretakers and the Lord's presence.

One morning during his rounds, Frank's primary physician questioned him about his unusual selfless attitude. I'll never forget Frank's answers. It may be the clearest and most Jesus-like attitude I've ever witnessed. "This cancer may kill me, but it will never get me down." It never did.

When you're faced with any kind of difficult situation or tough faith-question, like Viktor Frankl and my friend Frank faced, you can be prepared to handle them or, as I like to put it, thrive, no matter what. If you already have in your mind an easy-to-remember, simple-to-state, well-rehearsed and biblically-grounded attitude or point-of-view, you are ready.

What does this special kind of attitude or point-of-view look like? We all have a *view* about everything we encounter. It's our way of looking at, interpreting, and responding to every situation. Two people often look at the same problem and *view* it in two completely different ways. We also have a *point* in our life from which we got our view. That point usually started with some significant person, like a parent or close friend, who made a major impression on us. Our point-of-view may be one we didn't choose or one we deliberately chose. In either case, our point-of-view sticks with us or, you might say, it sticks in our mind. It never goes away unless some other, more powerful point-of-view takes its place.

For you to get the healthy faith and mind you want, you must make a calculated choice. You have to take into your mind the attitude or point-of-view you were designed to have—the attitude that God created you to have. Jesus had that kind of attitude.

The Bible describes the mind of Jesus as "*one* with his Father (God)." His mind was in sync with his Father's mind. Nothing ever changed Jesus' special kind of mind-set. Not his enemies. Not arguments from learned religious lawyers. Not beatings. Not even being crucified. Because Jesus' mind was so in-tune with his Father's mind, he often said that he looked at things the same way his Father looked at them. It was as if their minds operated like one mind. Jesus pictured himself the same way his Father saw him.

That's the kind of mind or attitude he offers and wants for all of his followers including you. Regardless of what you have faced in the past or will face in the future, you can have this new point-of-view or attitude. If you haven't already begun, you can begin today.

How did early Christians thrive in spite of persecution? After Jesus' resurrection and return to heaven, early Christians and their family members faced all kinds of persecution, including such atrocious acts as watching their family members being fed to lions. Even under such torture, historians and the writers of the Bible recorded how many followers of Jesus were able to overcome their gruesome trials. How did they do it?

The answer was always the same. "We understand these things, for we have the mind of Christ." I Corinthians 2:16 NLT. "Let this mind be in you which was also in Christ Jesus." Philippians 2:5 KJV. "Fix this picture firmly in your mind." Timothy 8-13. It was a call to make a mind-change. It was an invitation to take on a new self-image, attitude or point-of-view. It was and is today an offer to permanently engrave into your mind a new way of seeing yourself.

A way to protect your mind. To protect your mind and prepare you for a healthy faith, I invite you to begin picturing yourself in three ways. These three, easy-to-remember pictures come from the activities of our Heavenly Father and his son as those acts were recorded in the Bible. Practice picturing yourself in these three ways and see the difference it will begin to make in the way you see everything around you. The Bible says, "You're blessed when you get your inside world – your mind and heart – put right. Then you can see God in the outside world." Matthew 5:8. How does your Heavenly Father want you to see yourself?

1. Humble CHILD vs. Arrogant ADULT

First, when you start picturing yourself, begin from the position of one who is a humble CHILD requesting help, not an arrogant, demanding ADULT requiring explanations. When you take this posture, you'll find a new peace of mind in the face of troubles. It will give you the ability to help others like you've never had before. You'll begin to take on the mind of Jesus.

In our more analytical and narcissistic culture, when we suffer or face anything uncomfortable, our primary interest is relief from pain, not strength to endure or overcome.

As I've traveled to countries where Christian persecution is intense and Christians are martyred daily, I've noticed a distinct difference in the prayers of suffering believers. Many of them don't focus on asking God to help them *escape from suffering* but to help them be faithful *in their suffering*. How do they picture themselves? They look at themselves as children of their Heavenly Father. They picture Jesus with them in all situations and at all times like he promised, *"Be content with what you have, because God has said, 'Never will I leave you; never will I forsake you.'"* Hebrews 13:5.

A perfect mixture of suffering, mystery and commitment. In the Bible, God is often called *Father* and his followers called *children*. When Jesus was dying on the cross in severe agony, he asked this mysterious question, *"My God, My God, why have you forsaken me?"* Matthew 27:46. No one understands all he was communicating. But, for me and many others, in part, God's Son saw himself, as he usually did, in the uninterrupted presence of God, "My God." He saw himself as his Father's child, his boy, who was reaching out for help from his Daddy. He could see his tortured-self on the cross, but he would at the same time see his Father there with him.

In that unimaginable moment of suffering, Jesus cried out to God, *Abba*. He chose that tender, child-like word that, if spoken today in English, would be translated something like *Papa* or *Daddy*. And, just before "he breathed his last," he used that same last breath of air by which he asked his last question to make his last statement of faith, *"Father, into your hands I commit my spirit."* Luke 23:46.

When you attempt to answer tough questions or thrive in difficult situations, begin today practicing seeing yourself in a new position. Picture yourself as his humble little child with his arms around you. Then say to him, "I am your child. Thank you, Father, for being all-loving, all-powerful, all-knowing and always present with me."

2. Grateful SERVANT vs. Entitled SKEPTIC

No matter what happens to you, good or bad, try to picture yourself as a grateful SERVANT committed to following him completely, not an entitled SKEPTIC committed to understanding completely. In our entitlement-oriented and impression-driven culture, being a servant is probably somewhere near the bottom of our list of how we want others to see us. Yet, the most famous and successful man in history, chose to be and be known as a servant of others. When his followers asked him to take on the role of a king, he answered by getting on his knees and washing their feet.

To his disciples' question, "Who is the greatest of all?" He answered, "The one who is the servant of all." One of the main reasons people listened to him, committed their lives to him, and believed his answers was his unselfish, other-centered attitude. He had a noticeable humility that was different from the religious answer-makers. When we read the Bible stories about how he related to all kinds of people and situations, he was the perfect picture of a true grateful servant.

Although the word servant may seem out-of-date in our sophisticated society, the root-concept is timeless and admired by all cultures in all times. Putting the well-being of others before yours, taking less that others might have more, giving your life for someone because you are grateful for all they have done for you are all grateful-servant-concepts that are never out-of-date or out-of-place. It's an attitude that is the height of integrity.

It wasn't the first time our two teenaged daughters' questioned our judgment, "Why do we have to be home on the weekends by 11:00 PM? All the other girls get to stay out until midnight." Their *why* was not really *why*. Their question was not actually a question. It was a teenaged-attempt to make a statement, not so diplomatically, in the form of a question. They were really making a declaration, "Mom and Dad, we think you are wrong. Your decision and reasons are old-fashioned and need to change. We know more than you about such matters and have the right to decide for ourselves what time we come home." Their question was far from an humble, trusting, faith-seeking-understanding request for help.

Often when hard times come and hard issues confront us, we questioners act like our teenagers. Our questions are really arrogant statements. They are loaded with hidden questionable assumptions. We assume we have abilities and knowledge we don't have. We're certain we are entitled to do whatever we want even if it will hurt us and others. But we don't have that right.

I've noticed that many pseudo-God-questions and anti-God-statements are in reality personal, egocentric declarations. The questioner is actually saying, "I don't like the way God is handling things. If he wants to be fortunate enough for someone as wonderful as me to follow him, he'll have to change the way he's doing things. If I were God, I'd fix everything so everyone would be happy and no one would ever be unhappy. I have the right and ability to understand the mind of God. If I can't understand why God does what he does, I'll just refuse to believe he exists. That'll show him." Really?

I've found that more questioners find more satisfaction from better relationships than they do from better explanations. Practice being in his presence at all times. See yourself as being with him and he with you. In every circumstance you find yourself, whether pleasant or distasteful, practice seeing yourself as his grateful servant. Under your breath, not for anyone else to hear, talk to him intimately like you would someone you love most. Tell him something like, "I am your grateful servant, Father, and I thank you for being all-loving, all-powerful, all-knowing and always present with me. Thank you Father."

3. Eternal-SOUL vs. Physical BODY

When something hard comes crashing into your life or into the life of someone you love, picture yourself as an eternal SOUL not just a physical BODY. I don't want to appear overly spiritual or highly religious. My wife and best friends will tell you, I'm not either. But, as I explained before, we should never overlook that fact that we are more than physical beings. We are primarily eternal, and when we see ourselves that way, it changes everything.

As I said earlier, you are the sum of your mind, emotions, and actions. The total of your three parts is called self, personality, person or soul. So remember this and repeat often, "I don't have a soul. I am a soul." You aren't a body that's going to die and evaporate. You are an *eternal person*. Your physical body will die like the rest of the physical world, but your soul—the combination of your mind, emotions, and actions will live forever.

Don't be short-sighted on your long trip. You and those you are trying to help through hard situations and questions need help with both parts of their lives—physical and eternal. How you picture your relationship with your Lord and your eternal-future greatly determines the way you will view and deal with your struggles along the way.

Frankl said he was able to endure any form of suffering his concentration-camp tormentors inflicted on him because his mind and heart were focused on a day in the future when he would be back with his wife, the love of his life. He had an eternal focus. He saw himself as an eternal-person not just a tortured body. They couldn't take that from him. And, nothing can take that from you either.

EXERCISES TO BUILD AND MAINTAIN YOUR HEALTHY FAITH

Being aware of the diseases and contaminants that can harm your body does not mean that you are protected against them. Knowing is the first step, but protection demands action. You still need to do things like getting required vaccinations or keeping your hands clean in order to stay healthy. The same is true for your mind, especially related to your beliefs and morals. These exercises will help you establish and maintain a healthy attitude or point-of-view and will keep you resolute when hardships come.

RECORD: Write down the three descriptions of how God wants you to see yourself. Also write down the enemies of the mind listed in this chapter. Circle the five which are your biggest enemies.

REMEMBER: Memorize this sentence: "I am a humble child, a grateful servant and an eternal soul." Repeat this sentence at least five times to yourself today.

REFLECT: Open your Bible and read the parable of the Good Samaritan recorded in Luke 10: 25-37. From this story, how do you think the priest, Levite, and Samaritan saw themselves? How did the way the Samaritan thought of himself influence they way he viewed the injured man on the roadside?

RE-EXAMINE: In this chapter, you read about Viktor Frankl and his experience as a prisoner of war during World War II. Thinking about the horror of his experience, how do you think he was able to maintain inner peace and hope? What was his point of view? How was his mind similar to the mind of Jesus when he was under persecution? Perhaps you won't experience the trauma that Jesus and Frankl did in your lifetime, but how you view yourself will determine your attitude and behavior when tough times come. How is your mind like the mind of Christ?

RELATE: Discuss with your trusted friend some of the ways you are leaving your mind unprotected. Talk about replacing some of your habits with new practices that will help protect your mind.

Moving on to the next chapter

Now that you've completed the first two steps in your faith-development-plan, you know that a healthy faith is built on more than healthy knowledge, reasoning, beliefs, morals and a good attitude. It also must include a healthy heart.

As you recall, your heart is one of the three essential parts of you. In Step Three you will learn how it works, how powerful it is, and how it can be your best friend or your worst enemy. This step will give you five requirements for strengthening your heart to fortify instead of fracture your faith.

Pray this prayer to your Heavenly Father.

Dear Father, when I think of all you've done for me and continue to do, I am humbled and feel like a little child. I am so very dependent on you. Forgive me for ever acting in pride or giving the impression that I deserve anything. I am your humble child and grateful servant. Forgive me for any time I have taken you for granted or acted like I knew more than you. I love you with all my mind and heart and want to be just like your son, my Lord Jesus. Amen.

Reclaim Your Heart

Four heart-healthy requirements

"The heart has reasons which reason cannot understand."

BLAISE PASCAL, PHYSICIST, AUTHOR, AND CHRISTIAN PHILOSOPHER

"The essential difference between emotions and reason is that
emotions lead to action while reason leads to conclusions."

DONALD CALNE, CANADIAN NEUROLOGIST AND AUTHOR

"A heart at peace gives life to the body."

PROVERBS 14:30

BRANDI WAS ONLY SEVENTEEN WHEN she attempted suicide. I listened to her story and was saddened by her pain, embarrassment, anger and guilt. On her first date, Brandi was so infatuated by the overly sweet words of an older boy that she gave him her heart. He manipulated her by telling her he loved her and wanted to marry her. The day after she told him she was pregnant, he disappeared. She was brokenhearted and kept saying to me, "How could I have been such a fool?"

You might wonder how such a bright, respected, family-oriented, Christian girl could be so easily deceived and make such bad, life-altering decisions. That was just not at all like Brandi. At one time or another, we've all watched our hearts take over our reasoning and faith. Who hasn't made heartfelt and heart-driven choices that brought painful consequences?

Although your life and faith are dependent on your mind, heart and behavior, your heart is the most volatile. Unless you get your heart under control, it generally takes control of the other two. In the next chapter you will read about the functions of your physical heart and the parallels with your invisible heart. This chapter deals with six key questions on that invisible heart of yours, how it works, and how its three parts influence your faith: your emotions, desires, and will-power.

CHAPTER 13
How do you UNDERSTAND your heart?

"The best and most beautiful things in the world cannot be seen or even touched. They must be felt with the heart."

HELEN KELLER, CHRISTIAN POLITICAL ACTIVIST, AUTHOR

"The heart wants what it wants - or else it does not care."

EMILY DICKINSON, POET

"You will seek me and find me when you seek me with all your heart."

JEREMIAH 29:13

IN ONE SENSE, WE CAN never understand our hearts. After all, the heart is not a *thing* we study with our eyes or hands. It's such a mystery the prophet Jeremiah asked this about the heart, "Who can understand it?" Jeremiah 17:9. Although we'll never completely understand our hearts any more than we will fully understand love, we mindful-types will not rest until we have at least a sliver of understanding.

Have you noticed the word *heart* pops up nearly everywhere? As Americans, we put our hands on our hearts when we pledge allegiance to our flag. We send heart-shaped cards to people we love. We talk about our friend's heart surgery. When we refer to how we feel about ourselves and others, we use words like: kindhearted, openhearted, heartless, heartsick, softhearted, sweetheart, tenderhearted, warmhearted, bighearted, chickenhearted, cold-hearted, fainthearted and halfhearted.

When I ask a group to define faith, someone will say something like, "Faith is the heart in action." Or, "Faith is doing something with all your heart." In many people's minds the words faith and heart are inseparable. In all this heart-talk, it's useful to remember how your heart and faith work together and why we use the word heart in the first place.

We can't deal with all of the perplexing questions about this puzzling part of us, but to build our faith we must tackle a few of them.

1. *Why call it your heart?*

When you say the word *heart*, what comes to mind? When I learned where the word came from, it helped me better understand how important my heart is to God and should be to me.

The Bible may be the oldest record of our ancient ancestors' use of the word heart when they talked about the physical heart and invisible heart. The Old Testament writers named the organ located at the center of the body, *lebab*, which is the Hebrew word for center or core. Therefore, the word *lebab* (translated heart in English) sometimes points to our souls, other times to our emotions or inner-self.

When the New Testament writers referred to that most important, life-enriching, emotionally-powerful, center part of our inner-spiritual-lives, they use the Greek word *kardia* (heart in English). *Cardiology* is the study or treatment of the heart. The Latin word for heart was *cor* (core or heart in English).

Both the Old and New Testament writers believed God considered the physical heart the most important part of the body. So, in creating the human body, he gave the heart a special (holy) place. To protect it from dangers, he placed it at the center of the body, behind a defensive wall of ribs.

The writers also viewed the heart's blood as the source of life. Without it we die. So naturally, when they referred to the invisible heart, they believed it was the central and core part of us that supplies every part of us with life-giving elements. If our hearts get sick, our minds, behavior and relationships get sick. And, when our hearts are healthy, every part of us has a better chance of being healthy.

In Bibles that have around one-thousand pages, you may be surprised that the word *heart* is used over one thousand times. That makes it one of the most frequently used nouns in the entire Bible; and it's the Scripture's most common anthropological word. An anthropological word is one that uses man-like things (physical and visible things) to describe God-like things (spiritual and invisible things).

When we say, "That's the heart of the matter," we mean it's the most important part of that subject. That's why the Bible says, "Man looks at the outward appearance, but the Lord looks at the heart." 1 Sam 16:7. To God, your heart is the central, core, life-giving part of you. If God considers your invisible heart that important, obviously it's important for you to get to know it better.

2. *What makes your heart so amazing?*

Your physical heart is amazing. This grapefruit-size powerhouse beats 100,000 times per day, pumping five or six quarts of blood each minute or about 2,000 gallons per day. It carries life-giving oxygen and nutrients through some 60,000 miles of blood vessels. Your body can live without some of its parts, but it cannot live without a heart.

Your invisible heart is more amazing. Your other heart, the non-physical, invisible one, also works 24/7. It, too, supplies you with life-enriching nourishment of a different kind for every part of your life. That nutrition comes in the form of emotions, desires, and will-power. Your invisible heart is amazingly mysterious yet powerfully practical in the way it influences how you believe, act, and relate to God and others. Just like your physical heart, if you feed, exercise and discipline it to work the way it was made to work; your heart will be healthy and useful for your entire life.

Don't define it. Describe it. Have you ever tried to define the wind or explain what joy looks like? Do you find it difficult to define the heart? I do. My brain gets confused trying to picture something I cannot see. To make matters worse, I've read over ninety different definitions of the heart from different psychologists, philosophers and theologians, and they don't agree. The reason definitions and explanations are so inadequate is that the heart is invisible, and our language requires us to use visible things to describe it. For you to think and talk more clearly and comfortably about your heart, focus on *describing* what it does, not on *explaining or defining* what it is.

Your heart serves as your secret place. Often we use the word heart to refer to our most private, secret, inner self. I like to think of my heart as my private-personality inside my public-personality. I can't explain where my heart is, but I can describe how it's portrayed in the Bible and in my life. Have there been times when you've said something like this to yourself, "I haven't told anyone yet, but in my heart I've decided to . . ." Isn't it true?

Your heart is where the real you lives. It's the inner-you, not the outward-you. The outward-you smiles when you don't feel like smiling, plays happy when your heart is sad, and acts peaceful when you're about to explode on the inside. Your heart is where the inner-you, the genuine, honest you lives.

Only you and God can be there. No one else enters without your invitation. The scripture says, "You (God) alone know every human heart." 1 Kings 8:39 NIV. The scriptures also refer to your heart as the authentic you, "As a person thinks in his heart, so is he." Proverbs 23:7. Your heart is where you alone, and sometimes you and God, make your faith decisions.

Your heart's parts. Without your heart, you would be machine-like. You wouldn't be human, much less made in the image of God. Because of your heart, you have a full-range of *emotions and desires* that make life worth living, and a *will* that gives you the ability to make personal choices. You can get a much better understanding of your heart by dissecting it, so to speak, into its three main parts or functions: Emotions – how you feel; Desires – what you want; and Will – what you choose

3. *ARE YOU AWARE OF YOUR HEART'S EMOTIONS?*

Your heart contains a wide range of emotions, sometimes called feelings, such as love, happiness, surprise, fear, hate, anger and a long list of others. I've found that most of us are not aware of our emotions.

I'll never forget a highly emotional husband who came to me for help. He looked like he was about to explode, his face red with anger and his hands and voice quivering. He explained that his wife was angry all the time, and she needed my help. When I asked him why *he* was so angry, he was stunned. "What? No, you didn't understand me. I'm not the one who's angry. It's my wife."

Can you call them by name? The angry man couldn't. We're much better at recognizing and naming other people's emotions than we are our own. We pay about as much attention to our feelings as we do the air we breathe, and yet, these feelings quietly go on controlling our minds, decisions, and faith without our knowing they're doing it. But don't forget, you'll never be able to control your emotions until you first become so aware of them that you can call them by name and admit they are yours. Remember, if you don't have control of your emotions, you will not have a healthy faith.

When I refer to our emotions, I am not only talking about our momentary, natural, animal, instinctual emotions, like the fear we feel when we are standing on a dangerous precipice and the rocks underneath us are slipping. It's difficult to control our natural instincts. But it is important to be aware of them and our other emotions, especially those we experience when we are under pressure.

Let's see just how well you know your emotions. You may be able to name the Mega-emotions, our two most powerful emotions, but I'm guessing you might need assistance to list our six primary emotions and our secondary emotions.

Over the years, numerous experts have made lists and charts of human emotions. Since no one has a definitive list, I've combined and simplified a few of the most respected lists. As we continue to learn more about the heart, you can use this simplified list. As for now, review these emotions and think about which you deal with the most.

Mega-Emotions. One way to categorize your emotions is to consider love and fear your *Mega-Emotions.* Think of them as your most powerful emotions and the parents of all of your other emotions, which are forms or variations of these two. When your mind, body, or conscience is provoked or in some way stimulated, you will feel love or fear or some form of them. Below is a list of examples.

Mega-Emotion	Secondary Forms of Mega-Emotions
Love	Joy, happiness, caring, tenderness, trust, compassion, truth, contentment, satisfaction, affection, adoration, liking, tenderness, passion, infatuation, awe, pride, excitement, pleasure, hope, peace, surprise, expectation, wonder.
Fear	Anger, anxiety, control, sadness, depression, inadequacy, confusion, hurt, grief, guilt, shame, Irritability, aggravation, agitation, frustration, rage, wrath, hostility, bitterness, hatred, vengefulness, dislike, resentment, disgust, revulsion, envy, jealousy, agony, anguish, hurt, despair, unhappiness, loneliness.

Primary-Emotions and Secondary Forms. Another way of listing emotions is to consider some primary emotions and their secondary forms. This is the most useful approach because it provides you with a more detailed and comparative list so that you can better differentiate your emotions from one another. As you read them, think about which ones you notice most often.

Primary Positive Emotions	Secondary Positive Emotions
1. Love	Affection, adoration, liking, hope caring, tenderness, compassion, lust, desire, passion, infatuation, obsession, zeal, delight, gladness, esteem, respect, value, meaning, cherished
2. Joy	Cheerfulness, peace, delight, enjoyment, gladness, happiness, satisfaction, euphoria, enthusiasm, zeal, excitement, thrill, pleasure, pride, optimism, hope,
3. Wonder	Surprise, anticipation, amazement, shock, awe, alarm, astonishment, revelation, expectation

Primary Negative Emotions	Secondary Negative Emotions
1. Anger	Irritability, aggravation, agitation, annoyance, complaining, exasperation, frustration, rage, fury, wrath, hostility, bitterness, hatred, spite, vengefulness, dislike, resentment, disgust, revulsion, envy, jealousy.
2. Fear	Alarm, anxiety, shock, fright, horror, terror, panic, hysteria, nervousness,

	uneasiness, apprehension, worry, distress, dread, distrust, suspicion
3. Sadness	Agony, anguish, hurt, depression. despair, gloom, unhappiness, grief, sorrow, misery, melancholy, disappointment, dismay, displeasure, shame, guilt, regret, remorse, alienation, defeat, dejection, embarrassment, humiliation, insecurity, insult, isolation, loneliness, rejection, pity

Surprise. All emotions are good. That statement may puzzle you, and you may be asking how can negative emotions like anger, grief and fear be good? We all prefer positive emotions like love, affection, passion and tenderness. But, negative and positive emotions can be used for good or bad.

In the Bible we read about God's emotions:

"My heart is changed within me; all my compassion is aroused." Hosea 11: 8.

"He looked around them in anger." Mark 3: 5.

"The Lord was grieved that he had made man on the earth, and his heart was filled with pain." Genesis 6: 6.

"I, the Lord your God, am a jealous God." Exodus 20: 5.

"I have loved you with an everlasting love." Jeremiah 31: 3.

"My soul is overwhelmed with sorrow to the point of death." Matthew 26:37–38.

Our Lord is a very emotional Father, and everything he does is ultimately good. He created us to be emotional like him. In a way, emotions are like medicine. Various medicines are created by good-hearted scientists for the purpose of healing or relieving suffering. For example, morphine is good. When it is used properly, I can't tell you how many times I've seen it relieve horrific suffering. Unfortunately, I've also witnessed dreadful suffering and even death caused by the misuse of morphine. In the same way, God created emotions to be used for good, but he gave us the freedom to choose how to use them.

Anger is good. Fear is a gift. How can negative emotions like anger, bitterness and fear be positive? After all, they *are* labeled negative emotions. The reason they are categorized as negative is because our basic human or animal instincts resist any emotion that does not bring immediate pleasure. However, those of us who value something more than instant gratification and physical pleasure know it usually takes work, some pain, and uncomfortable effort to reach our goal. If want more than instant gratification, in faith your negative emotions must be used for good.

For example, think about anger. Anger can be used for good or bad. If you see innocent people suffering in war, it's normal to feel anger. The important question is what will you do with your anger? You can choose to use your anger to speak hatefully, take revenge, and inflict pain on those who caused the suffering. Or, by faith, you can make the decision to use your anger as fuel for good.

Some of the world's greatest non-profit, caring organizations were created by people who were enraged from witnessing their families and neighbors suffer from disease or violence; but, they made a faith-decision to use their anger to motivate them to do amazingly good deeds.

4. *What are your heart's basic DESIRES?*

Your heart is not only filled with emotions, it also houses your five basic human desires: safety, love, respect, purpose, and eternity. Everything we think, do, and feel is our attempt to satisfy one or more of our basic desires—sometimes called, needs, drives, wants or motives. Your desires are important because faith is a commitment to someone or something you desire. Being aware of your desires and knowing how you manage them is critical to your faith's health.

If any one of your basic desires is not properly satisfied, your heart will get upset and will send out emotions letting the rest of you know that your heart is not happy. Sometimes your heart will react in extreme ways. If your desire to be safe is threatened, your heart will send out emotions like fear, anxiety or stress. If a number of your heart's basic desires or needs are not satisfied, you can imagine how such strong, negative emotions would influence your faith.

An important part of managing your desires, emotions and their affect on your faith is becoming keenly aware of your basic desires.

FIVE BASIC DESIRES

We want or need:
Safety - healthy, sexually-satisfied, secure, protected, structure, predictability
Love - family, cherished, special, affection, belonging, community
Respect - worth, importance, competence, confidence, prestige, value
Purpose - fulfillment, faith, meaning, mission, confidence
Eternity - forever, heaven, reward, justice, relationship with God

5. IS YOUR *WILL-POWER* THAT POWERFUL?

The third part of your heart, which makes choices, decisions, and faith-commitments is your *will*, sometimes called your *free-will* or *will-power*. Your will is a critical part of any faith-decision because it gives you the power to choose. Because of your will, you can make a choice to be more than a puppet of your cultural, biological, psychological, or sociological influences. When you engage your will, you have the ability to over-ride your natural instincts that are primarily selfish, irresponsible and short-term appetites. Your will gives you control of which desire you will seek to satisfy.

Do you use your God-given control? Nothing and no one can control your will except you. You alone can make the decisions of your heart for you. You may choose to turn over your will and your control of your heart to someone or something else, but it's still your decision. You cannot blame anyone for your decision. Whether you respond to something with feelings of love or fear, joy or sadness, forgiveness or hate, is a choice only your free-will can make.

6. HOW DOES YOUR HEART WORK?

Because you have a better understanding now of the function of your emotions, desires, and will, let's take a look at how to get a better grip on monitoring, guarding, and controlling your heart.

Why do your emotions get out-of-control? Have you ever shocked yourself with something you thought, or worse, something you said out loud that was completely out of character for you, some emotional volcano that erupted to your surprise? It happens to all of us. We wonder, "Where in the world did that come from? That's not at all like me." You may have passed it off as a simple blip on your screen that meant nothing, but it did mean something. Actually, it meant a great deal. Those kinds of emotional explosions are important warning signals.

We all understand that sudden, shocking, out-of-the-ordinary changes to our physical heart should never be dismissed or minimized. Any heartache could be a warning-sign about some serious, deeper problem in your heart.

On the way to work, my friend Carlos had a surprising shooting-pain in his chest. Hoping it was indigestion and would go away, he tried to ignore it. By the time he got to his office, his pain was worse. His secretary convinced him to call his doctor, who told him to go immediately to the nearby ER. You guessed it. Carlos' shooting pain was a symptom. A heart attack was prevented. As painful and frightening as his symptom was, it turned out to be a blessing. It probably saved his life.

Heartaches to your inner-heart. When our physical hearts have trouble, they send out signals to the entire body. In the same way when our inner-hearts have problems, they too send out signals. We should always take those emotional signals seriously because they are the flashing red-lights that point to our deeper, more severe heart-problems.

For example, someone said something hateful and false about Bob in front of his friends. Bob felt angry. Why? For you to understand what made Bob so angry, first you must interpret his anger as a symptom not the problem. View his anger as an indicator pointing to the problem in Bob's heart. The problem was there before the person was hateful to him. When Bob's deeper heart-condition was aroused, his heart sent out a flashing red light, emotions, saying "There's something wrong inside. It needs attention."

When emotions appear, like they did with Bob, most of us get distracted by asking the wrong kinds of questions like, "Who made Bob angry? What caused him to get so upset? What did someone do to Bob that made him so explosive?" Those kinds of questions only lead us away from recognizing the source of our emotions. Playing the blame-game sidetracks us. No one can "make" Bob's heart feel angry but Bob. His outer circumstance just aroused the anger already in him. The anger was not caused by the circumstances. It was a reaction to one of his unsatisfied basic needs or desires. Bob allowed his animal instincts to take control and respond with anger.

Josh experiences the same hateful treatment from the same mean-spirited person that confronted Bob. But, Josh felt compassion, not anger. What's going on here? We see two emotions that are symptoms: *anger* and *compassion*. Both hearts have the feelings of anger and compassion available to send out as signals. The same painful outside attack strikes their hearts. Two different emotional responses (symptoms) show up. Why? It's the *condition inside the heart* that arouses different responses.

The condition of your heart always makes the difference. Jesus' response from the cross is a good example of how his heart worked. He was tortured, shamed, ridiculed and finally murdered in a brutal way. Moments before he died, we get a glimpse of the condition of his heart by what he was feeling and his response to all his suffering. His words indicate he felt compassion. "Father, forgive them, for they do not know what they are doing." Luke 23: 34 NIV. Jesus' heart was healthy. It was a snapshot of his relationship to his Father and what he wanted most. Even in his humanity, his heart was like the heart of God.

In summary, here's how your heart works:

* Your heart is a responder, not an initiator.
* Your heart's desires are put on alert when hard times hit.
* Your emotions react to your mind, heart and body.
* Your emotions are symptoms of what's going on inside your heart.
* Your heart's response is not determined by outward circumstances.
* Your heart's response is determined by the condition of your inner-heart.
* Your heart's free-will decides what response you will make.
* Your free-will makes a choice alone or in cooperation with your Lord.
* Your heart's response is an important part of your faith-decisions.

Exercises to Build and Maintain your Healthy Faith

It truly does come down to where your heart is. That's where your thoughts and feelings begin. Your emotions are the best barometer of your faith's health.

RECORD: Make a list of the five reasons your heart is so important to your healthy faith. List the three parts of your "heart" and how they function. In the same place, record your three primary positive and negative emotions. Keep this list close by and review it throughout today.

REMEMBER: Review several times a day for the next few days the list of positive and negative emotions. Memorize the three parts of your heart and how they function. If you don't know what they are and can recognize them, you're not likely to be able to do anything about them.

REFLECT: The Bible is filled with "heart" stories, but the one I chose for you is the story of Jesus' friends, Mary, Martha, and Lazarus. Read thoughtfully the story found in John 11: 1-43. Think about the emotions displayed by each of the characters in this story. What emotions drove each of their behaviors? What does this story tell you about the heart of Jesus?

RE-EXAMINE: In your home or on your job, begin to pay closer attention to the emotional responses from the people around you. See if you can name that emotion. Begin to look beyond the emotion to see if you can recognize which desire, want, or need is not being satisfied.

RELATE: Talk to your trusted friend about how the heart works. If you have needs or desires that are not being fulfilled, discuss with your friend how your faith can help satisfy those needs.

Moving on to Chapter Fourteen: How do you MONITOR your heart?

It's time to get to the heart-of-the-matter. Now that you know a little more about your heart and how it works in relationship to your faith, let's look again at the inside-condition of your heart. Since you cannot see your invisible heart, you must learn to recognize the signs of serious heart issues and the signs of a healthy heart. In the next chapter, you will learn how to monitor your heart and notice the seven most serious signs of an unhealthy heart.

Pray this prayer to your Heavenly Father.

Dear Father, Thank you so much for caring about me. It doesn't seem possible that I could be talking with you, the creator of the whole universe and everything in it. But your Word and my heart tell me you love me and even died for me on a cross. I give you my emotions, the deepest desires of my heart, and my will. I love you with all my mind and heart and want to be just like your son, my Lord Jesus. Amen.

CHAPTER 14

How do you MONITOR your heart?

*"Examine your heart and put away any distraction
so you can worship God freely."*

JIM GEORGE, AMERICAN AUTHOR

*"Examine your heart often to see if it is such toward your neighbor
as you would like his to be toward you were you in his place."*

FRANCIS DE SALES, BISHOP OF GENEVA

"Above all else, guard your heart, for it is the wellspring of life."

PROVERBS 4:23, NIV

WHEN TWENTY-YEAR-OLD, INTERNATIONALLY-RECOGNIZED, DANISH BAS-
KETBALL player, Rasmus Larsen, was found dead in his home from a heart
attack, his family recalled that a few days before he had noticed some symptoms but didn't give them much attention. After all, he was a healthy, young,
world-class athlete. Nothing could be wrong with his heart.

Are you about to have heart attack? You're thinking "No, I'm in pretty good condition." Heart attacks take the lives of thousands each year because the victim never noticed any symptoms.

Cardiologists use technologies such as the arteriogram, cardiogram and heart-monitors to observe our hearts. Their findings enable them to possibly prevent and treat serious heart problems.

Like your physical heart, your spiritual heart (emotions, desires and will) needs monitoring. Unless detected early, most of us don't even notice the subtle, problematic symptoms until our faith doesn't work or our relationships with God and others are in crisis.

Can you see your own spiritual-heart problems? Most of us can't and wouldn't if we could. We've lived with our spiritual heart problems so long they have become our unhealthy normal.

When the symptoms of our physical heart problems are mild, sometimes physicians use a treadmill stress-test to make them more recognizable. While being monitored, the treadmill puts the heart under added stress so that it magnifies possible negative heart-related symptoms such as chest pain, shortness of breath, or lightheadedness.

Once the diagnostician observes your various symptomatic responses to the stress-test and compares them to the symptoms of a healthy heart, the physician can determine just how healthy or unhealthy your heart is and how to proceed.

Why not take a spiritual-stress-test? We don't need to go to a medical facility to take a spiritual-stress-test. Spiritual treadmills are all around us, but we routinely pay no attention to them, much less make use of them to examine our emotional responses. If we paid attention, we would continually identify them, compare them to the symptoms of a healthy heart, and be aware of the conditions of our heart.

If you're serious about developing a healthy heart, you must learn a simple way to continually monitor your heart and make a commitment to do it throughout each day. How can you do that? Develop some specific habits.

The only new practices that last are those that become serious habits. Most people who begin diets, exercise programs and other new routines quit before these become habits. If you're going to be consistent and faithful in making new habits, you must make them part of your routine-essentials. The question becomes—is having a new spiritual heart worth it?

Modern science has given people with ailing hearts the chance at new life with the heart transplant. Even with a new heart, the recipient still must take anti-rejection drugs. The body's immune system is designed to attack foreign invaders and recognizes that the new heart does not have the same DNA as the patient. If this heart recipient does not take his medication seriously and as the doctor ordered, he places his life in jeopardy.

If you want the healthy emotion, desires and will-power that come with a new spiritual heart, you will need to approach this heart-trans-formation with the same seriousness and discipline of a heart-transplant patient. Here are the elements to which you need to be committed. You will need to daily:

1. Watch for any strong feeling you have and call it by name.
2. Use any emotional experience you have as a spiritual-stress-test.
3. Decide which of your desires was unmet that triggered your feelings.
4. Compare your emotional response to the response of a healthy heart.
5. Avoid rationalizing, excusing, or minimizing any unhealthy response.
6. Immediately turn any unhealthy response into a healthy one.

For you to be able to compare your emotional response to a healthy response, you need a list of the indicators of a healthy heart; or better yet, you need a real person you can use as a model for any situation. You need someone who faced negative situations like you do and responded with healthy emotions and actions.

What are the basic indicators of a healthy heart? The best example of a healthy heart under pressure is Jesus, the model-human. While he faced rejection, humiliation, torture and death on the cross, he revealed his honest emotions and deepest desires—a perfect picture of a healthy heart.

Dr. Luke, in Chapter twenty-three of his Gospel narrative, gives us a brief look at how Jesus responded to his enemies and how he felt on the cross. Picture what happened. He and two other men were nailed to crosses. Their bodies were racked with pain, bloody from beatings, and close to death.

While the butchers who tortured and crucified Jesus were playing games, laughing and mocking him, he gasped for enough air to speak. His lips quivered and everyone wondered what he would say. Who could blame him if he used his last words to curse his torturers for their cruelty, denounce his disciples for their disloyalty, and spew out anger towards his God for allowing all this to happen?

For centuries, Jesus' last seven statements from the cross have been called the Seven Last Words of Christ. They highlight seven significant principals that summarize his key life-values and most significant teachings. They reveal his true *feelings*, his primary *desires*, and his healthy *choices* in responding to some of life's hardest challenges, including death.

Observing a real person, in a real situation, expressing his real feelings and commitments, helps me visualize the real options I have when hard times crash into my life. I've never seen a more comprehensive and easy-to-understand list of symptoms of a healthy heart than I see in the famous Seven Last Words of Jesus. I use them as a model by which I evaluate my symptoms and determine the real condition of my heart.

Before I ask you to compare your heart's health to Jesus' heart, I must make a confession and clarification. When I compare my emotional-responses to those of Jesus, I always fall far short. I know my heart will never be perfectly healthy, but I also know that the way Jesus responded to difficult situations is my goal and his way is the only way I can keep heading in the right direction.

If your emotional responses are not as healthy as Jesus', don't give up and don't think, "It's impossible for me to respond that way." You can improve. Your heart can get healthier. You can get closer to having new kind of heart, one that has desires, feelings and makes choices like his. Join me in taking this stress-test for your heart. It will be a major tool in helping you develop a healthy heart and faith.

The Seven Signs of a Healthy Heart

1. When pain comes, a healthy heart feels
COMPASSION not ANGER

> Jesus' first word from the cross:
> "Father, forgive them, for they do not know
> what they are doing." John 23:34

A healthy heart is full of compassion and forgiveness in the face of pain.

Jesus' first word from the cross had to shock his onlookers. After all his pain, no doubt they expected anger, bitterness and hatred. To their amazement, he didn't react with hateful anger. He responded with deep compassion. "Father" was his first word because his Father was the source of his strength, self-image, point-of-view, and his attitude in the face of all circumstances.

His first statement from the cross was filled with compassion flavored with forgiveness. Jesus looked beyond the hateful, brutal actions of his accusers and murderers and saw their deeper heart problem. He had pity for his enemies, asking his Father to forgive them instead of giving them what they deserved. He was understanding, not unsympathetic and mean-spirited. He wanted the best for them, not the worst.

A person with a healthy heart does not react to painful situations with feelings of revenge, rage, hostility, bitterness, or hatred. Instead, he responds with compassion, care, tenderness, kindness, hope, and sympathy. Jesus taught his followers, "You have heard that it was said, Love your neighbor and hate your enemy. But I tell you, love your enemies and pray for those who persecute you." Matthew 5:43 NIV.

If you emotionally punch the center of a healthy heart, forgiveness will pour out because it is full of compassion not anger.

2. When harm comes, a healthy heart feels
MERCIFUL not REVENGEFUL

Jesus' second word from the cross:
"Today you will be with me in paradise." Luke 23:43

A healthy heart is full of mercy in the face of personal harm.

His second word was just as much a surprise as his first. With all the physical brutality, emotional misery, public humiliation, and personal rejection, you might expect Jesus to be revengeful. After all, doesn't evil deserve evil? Not if you have a healthy heart. To the crucified criminal next to him who cried out for mercy, Jesus offered mercy. He gave paradise to one who deserved hell. He was generous, kind, and tender-hearted to one who deserved judgment, punishment, and retribution. That's the way of a healthy heart.

3. When danger comes, a healthy heart feels
PEACEFUL not FEARFUL

Jesus' third word from the cross:
"Dear woman, here is your son." John 19:26

A healthy heart is full of peace in the face of danger.

According to His Father's plan, the cross was always in the shadow of the star of Bethlehem. As the son of God conceived by the Spirit of God, he knew he was born to die for all. When he looked from the cross to his mother, Jesus recalled why he was born and how. "Dear woman, here is your son," was a word of reassurance, gratitude, security and peace. It was as if he were assuring Mary, "Look, Mother, it is all happening just like you said and just as my Father designed. People don't understand now. But, they will later. It's been worth it all, and now I feel completely at peace for completing his will."

A healthy heart is a heart at peace no matter what comes. Peace is not the absence of danger; it is the presence of God. Where his Spirit (his presence) is, there is peace.

While he was preparing for his cross, he knew his followers would face some dangerous days. He gave them the secret to a peaceful heart in the face of danger, "I am leaving you with a gift—peace of mind and heart! And the peace I give isn't fragile like the peace the world gives. So don't be troubled or afraid." John 14:27. When you have him and his peace in the center of your heart, there's no room for fear.

An unhealthy heart is only at peace when external circumstances are peaceful. A healthy heart is at peace no matter what. Its peace does not come from an external tranquility but from an internal contentment. When your heavenly Father is your peace, you always have peace because he is always with you.

When you face a heartbreaking relationship, a confusing crisis, the loss of a loved one, the threat of a serious health problem and other hurts, initially you will have a mixture of negative and positive feelings. But after your inner heart looks at the situation and then looks to your Lord, you will feel peace, inner joy, and satisfaction. You have those emotions because your peace depends on the one who is all-loving, all-powerful, all-knowing, and all-present and resident in your heart. Why should you not be at peace?

When difficult or dangerous times come, I like to silently sing to myself the old hymn "It Is Well" that Horatio G. Spafford wrote as a testimony to the peace found in God after he lost his family at sea.

When peace like a river attendeth my way,
When sorrows like sea billows roll,
Whatever my lot, Thou has taught me to say,
It is well, it is well with my soul.

When dangers come, do you have this kind of peace?

4. WHEN PROBLEMS COME, A HEALTHY HEART FEELS
HUMBLE NOT PRIDEFUL

Jesus' fourth word from the cross:
"My God, my God, why have you forsaken me?" Mark 15:34

A healthy heart is humble not prideful in the face of problems.

Jesus' fourth word from the cross was a sign of humility, not a symptom of pride. "My God, my God, why have you forsaken me?" was not a son's arrogant indictment against his father because he felt unfairly treated. His *why* was not an angry question from a know-it-all, spoiled, I-deserve-better-than-this son. It was no cry from a confused, complaining, defeated servant who felt he deserved much more for his faithful service.

Jesus' fourth word was a perfect picture of faithful humility, a clear symptom of an unselfish heart. This word is one of the greatest confessions of faith of all times. With all his human limitations, his pain, his life slipping away, he still proclaimed, "No matter what, you are *My God*." Faith can never understand all of the present or see all of the future. Faith says, "My God" and "why" in the same sentence. It's a powerful statement of humble faithfulness.

This famous fourth word was not a declaration of *independence,* but a bold declaration of *dependence.* "Why have you forsaken me?" was his signature attitude. When his voice spoke the words "why" and "forsaken," Jesus heart sang, "I am weak, but you are strong. I don't know, but you do know. I feel like I am alone with darkness all around me, but I trust you more than my feelings. In this darkness, you are still my light. In my weakness you are the hand that guides me. No matter what, I depend on you alone. You are still 'My God.'"

Unhealthy pride is the parent of all sins. It is a symptom of a dishonest, unrealistic, selfish, independent, unhealthy heart. If our hearts are full of pride, we deceive ourselves into feeling entitled. When we face any problem, we feel God and everyone owes us, so we say to ourselves, "This is so unfair and wrong. I'm not perfect, but I'm better than most people. I should never have problems, pain or discomfort. I should always be happy, healthy and wealthy. Why did God let this happen to me? He's supposed to take care of me."

When problems come, if you have a healthy heart, you feel humble, honest, grateful, and unselfish. You feel so thankful for all God has already done for you and promises to do for you in eternity that you do not feel he owes you anything. Out of gratitude, you want to use your blessings and problems to help others and show your Father how much you appreciate all he means to you.

5. When disappointments come, a healthy heart feels
CONTENTED not CONTROLLING

Jesus' fifth word from the cross:
"I thirst." John 19:28

A healthy heart is full of contentment in the face of any disappointment.

Jesus' fifth word from the cross was a display of patient restraint, an expression of purposeful contentment. Since early that day, he had no water, food or rest. He had lost so much blood from his brutal flogging he was dehydrated and exhausted. By the time he carried his heavy cross through the scorching stone streets of Jerusalem and up the mountainside that led outside of town to the skull-like rock hill where he was crucified, it's no wonder he said, "I thirst."

However, his fifth word was not what you might first think. It was not a request for relief but a statement of contentment. No doubt he was thirsty but he put his mission and his faithfulness to his Father above his physical needs. When his persecutors offered him something to drink, he refused it. What they did not know was that they had not crucified an ordinary man. They had made a momentous mistake when they tortured and crucified the very son of the living God.

This is the same one who, a short time before, told his inner-circle what everyone would soon know, "All power (authority) in heaven and on earth has been given to me." Matthew 28:18 ESV. "Don't you realize that I could ask my Father for thousands of angels to protect us, and he would send them instantly?" Matthew 26:53 NLT. He had the authority, the ability and the power to take control and get anything he wanted, but he didn't. He was content in pleasing his Father and his will. That was his heart's greatest desire.

A healthy heart is a submissive and contented heart. What we see in this fifth word is power under control, the choice to be content with temporary suffering for the sake of higher purposes. It's the sign of a heart that waits on God to do his work behind the scene.

An unhealthy heart is a controlling heart. It snatches the reigns of control out of the hands of God and says, "I'm taking over. I'll do it my way. I know best. I'm going to make things happen. If I thirst, I get what I want at any cost." When disappointments and difficulties come, the symptomatic differences between a healthy and unhealthy heart are easy to spot. The healthy heart patiently invites, calmly waits, gently encourages, while the unhealthy heart anxiously demands, manipulates, pressures and forces.

6. WHEN DISCOURAGEMENT COMES, A HEALTHY HEART FEELS FULFILLED NOT DEPRESSED

Jesus' sixth word from the cross:
"It is finished." John 19:30

A healthy heart is full of satisfaction in the face of discouragements.

When Jesus spoke his sixth word from the cross, "It is finished," the spectators thought he was referring to his suffering. It was finished. But the *It* in that sentence did not refer to his suffering. It referred to his mission, his purpose in life. He finished the job he came to do.

Many times before, Jesus explained that he came to complete a specific job—to give his life for the sins of the world. "It is finished" could be translated "Mission accomplished." With all the discouraging words and pessimistic feelings around him, the heart of the Lord felt satisfied. That's how you feel when you carry out the job your Father gives you and you know it pleases him.

By the time Jesus spoke that sixth word, the hope the bystanders' once felt had drained out of their weary, now empty hearts. The discouragement all around them quickly filled that void. And, as usual, the contamination of discouragement left untreated became a toxic resentment. Their resentment grew into a poisonous bitterness which later turned into wide-spread anger, presenting itself as a pessimistic, negative, hateful, critical spirit—all symptoms of an unhealthy heart.

When the angry, critical crowd heard Jesus say "It is finished," some said, "He is finished for sure. And we are finished with him. We had hoped he was our savior; but, he could not even save himself. Look at him. He was no holy man. He was a fraud, a fake. He got what he deserved. He is finished."

Jesus did not become discouraged by their discouragement. He was fulfilling his Father's mission and felt the satisfaction of finishing his purpose in life. A healthy heart does not let outside discouragements determine its purpose or disposition. It is motivated by the presence of the Lord within and by the satisfaction of doing the will of the Father. There is no greater joy.

7. WHEN DEATH COMES, A HEALTHY HEART FEELS CONFIIDENT NOT FRIGHTENED

Jesus' seventh word from the cross:
"Father, I entrust my spirit into your hands." Luke 22:46

A healthy heart feels confidence in the face of death.

When he was about to die, no doubt his skeptics wondered, "In the face of death, will he say anything more?" He did not leave them or anyone forever wondering how he felt about such an important subject as death.

Did you notice the smallest two words of his last words? "Father, *I* entrust *my* spirit into your hands." These two words are small in size but massive in meaning. *I* and *my* represent our free-will, our God-given right to choose. Jesus made a willful, intentional, confident choice to put his Spirit in his Father's hands. He felt a longing for the eternal because he had a long, loving relationship with his Father.

Jesus wasn't hoping for eternity. Eternity was in him. He and the Eternal One were one. The words, eternity, eternal, and heaven are best understood as being with the Heavenly Father. When you are with him, you already have eternity. When he lives in you, your spirit is already eternal. Confidence is knowing you are secure in your eternal relationship with God.

When Jesus experienced pain, harm, danger, problems, disappointment, discouragement and even death, he consistently responded with compassion, mercy, peace, humility, contentment, satisfaction and confidence—all symptoms of a healthy heart.

You'll probably never experience what Jesus experienced as he was crucified, but you will face serious difficulties in your life. When you do, if you have a healthy heart, you will respond like he did. Use these seven symptoms to monitor your heart.

A Summary of the Seven Signs of a Healthy Heart

When faced with difficult situations, a healthy heart feels:

1. COMPASSION not ANGER in the face of PAIN
2. MERCIFUL not REVENGEFUL in the face of HARM
3. PEACEFUL not FEARFUL in the face of DANGER
4. HUMBLE not PRIDEFUL in the face of PROBLEMS
5. CONTENTED not CONTROLLING in the face of DISAPPOINTMENT
6. FULFILLED not DEPRESSED in the face of DISCOURAGEMENT
7. CONFIIDENT not FRIGHTENED in the face of DEATH

Exercises to Build and Maintain your Healthy Faith

I have a friend who was diagnosed with diabetes when he was very young. Don understood that he must monitor the sugar level in his body in order to stay healthy, so he got the necessary equipment to do that and made it a part of his daily schedule. Monitoring his blood sugar became very important to him because he understood what the consequences would be if he didn't. The same holds true for monitoring your heart. Make a prayerful, passionate, serious decision today to follow the "doctor's orders" to monitor your invisible heart and keep it healthy.

RECORD: On a note card, in your journal, or on your phone, record the Six Steps to Monitoring Your Heart and the Seven Signs of a Healthy Heart. Keep this list accessible.

REMEMBER: Review often and memorize the Seven Signs of a Healthy Heart. If you don't know what they are, you won't be able to recognize them.

REFLECT: We all enjoy a good story with a happy ending, but I wonder how much we learn from stories like that. There is a story in the Bible that doesn't have a happy ending, but it certainly illustrates the importance of monitoring your heart. Read the story of Ananias and Sapphira in Acts 5: 1-11. What was it in the hearts of Ananias and Sapphira that dictated their behavior?

RE-EXAMINE: Doctors who regularly treat people with heart problems easily recognize symptoms of an unhealthy heart. For a few days, take on the role of a spiritual heart specialist. Observe the people around you, looking for heart indicators. See how many emotional responses you can recognize, and try to discern what unmet desires may be triggering emotional responses.

RELATE: Now that you have been practicing and observing others' emotional behaviors, turn your watchful mind to your own. Once you have identified them, talk over your observations with your trusted friend.

It's time to move to Chapter Fifteen: How do you CONTROL your heart?
     Now that you have a better *understanding* of your heart and how to *monitor* your heart, it's time to learn how to *control* your heart. One of the most important and challenging parts of developing a health faith is learning how to control your heart—your desires, feelings and behavior. So, let's dive right into this key question.

Pray this prayer to your Heavenly Father.

Dear Father, I am especially grateful that you care about me. I don't understand how you could when you have billions of children. Your greatness far exceeds my small mind. My heart longs to know you better and be drawn closer to you. Help me develop a heart like your heart. I give you my heart to cleanse and renew so that I might be what you made me to be. Fill my heart with your Spirit and speak to my heart so I'll do all you want me to do. I do love you with all my heart. Amen.

CHAPTER 15

How do you CONTROL
your heart?

"All my life, my heart has yearned for a thing I cannot name."

ANDRE BRETON, ENGLISH POET

"Don't drink too much wine, for many evils lie along that path;
be filled instead with the Holy Spirit and controlled by him."

EPHESIANS 5:18

YOU DON'T HAVE TO LISTEN to the radio long to hear one major theme running through hundreds of country songs. It's found in the title of one of Joni
Bishop's classic country hits, *Heart Out of Control*. Each year that same theme
is the subject of thousands of new books, movies, articles, blogs, sermons,
lectures and research papers. At one time or another, we all feel like our hearts
are out of control, and we want to get them under control.

Unfortunately, getting control of our emotions, feelings, and wills is not
going to happen for most of us. Sound pessimistic? It's not. It's simply realistic. It takes more than *want to* for us to get control of something as powerful
and important as our hearts. After all, to some degree, our hearts are products
of our out-of-control culture.

Your culture wants control of your heart. We live in a culture where our hearts are immersed in a media-ocean of unbridled violence, shameless entertainment, unrestrained perversions, unclear morals, an ambiguous view of God, and a no-belief-is-wrong approach to the family, marriage, abortion, self-medication, suicide, and other traditional values and issues. These potent influencers dramatically affect what we desire, feel and decide. For many, they control the heart.

Although your heart is significantly shaped by your family and culture, it is possible for you to get it under control like God originally designed. There is no easy solution, and it will take hard work. Some areas of your heart are broken, others are infected, and some have become highly resistant to change. That means you will need more than a little heart-to-heart advice. You need heart surgery—spiritual-heart surgery. If done properly, it works.

First, you need a proven protocol. If you want the best chance of having a good outcome, you can't proceed just any way you want. A proper protocol must be followed. No heart surgeon would simply crack open someone's chest and hope for the best. A heart surgeon follows a surgical protocol, a standard, historically-proven series of steps used in a particular procedure, that when followed, produces the highest probability of success.

A protocol that works for spiritual-heart surgery, and gives you a healthy kind of control over your heart, includes four practical steps: (1) REMOVE the unhealthy myths about control. (2) REPAIR the broken meaning of control. (3) REPLACE the popular attempts to control, and (4) GUARD your heart with five proven practices.

1. REMOVE THE UNHEALTHY MYTHS ABOUT CONTROL.

An important part of physical heart surgery is careful preparation. If the surgeon takes the necessary steps to eliminate potential problems at the outset, the rest of the procedure has a better chance at success. If you want control of your unhealthy desires, emotions, and behavior, you need to begin by removing a few of the major myths about control.

First, get rid of the myth that YOUR HEART IS OUT-OF-CONTROL. Your heart is never out-of-control. It may be out of your control, but someone else or something else has control of your heart at all times. If you don't understand that, you are living in denial. It's another way of saying, "My unhealthy responses are not my fault. I will not take responsibility for my heart's condition, my explosive feelings, my mean-spirit, my outbursts, my mood-swings, my addiction, my hateful responses or anything else that comes out of my heart."

Denial prevents healing. Healing always begins with honesty. To get on the road to healthy control, you're going to have to take personal responsibility for every emotion, desire, and decision that comes from your heart. Every time your heart responds to a situation in an unhealthy way, stop immediately, take a deep breath, and say to yourself, "My heart is one of the three main parts of me. How I just responded is my fault. I take full responsibility. In the past, I let my circumstances control my heart. Not anymore. I'm taking back control. My culture-shaped-self, my false-self no longer has control. My original, God-given, birth-given, the-way-it-was-designed-self, my true-self is taking back control of my heart."

Second, remove the myth that A SINCERE HEART IS A HEALTHY HEART. For decades, I've listened with deep sorrow to many people who sincerely wanted to get control over some runaway personal attitude, feeling, craving, compulsion or addiction. Unfortunately, few got what they wanted mainly because they thought being sincere would eventually produce control.

A sincere heart is one of the indicators of a healthy heart, but alone it will not get the job done. You can have extremely sincere desires, wishes, prayers, and even public commitments to take back control of your heart and stop letting your past control, but it takes more than feelings and desires alone to get you the control that's healthy and produces joy and peace in your life. Your feelings are controlled by your desires. And your desires are controlled by your circumstances until you make a radical change.

Third, remove the myth that a LACK OF CONTROL IS DUE TO A LACK OF WILL POWER. "If she put her mind to it, she could get control of her terrible temper." That's sounds reasonable, but it's not true. If you think you can control your heart by sheer self-discipline, hard work and self-determination, you're fooling yourself. Many people struggling with anger, pride, addictions and other dependencies lose their battle because they believe in that old, and all too popular, will-power lie. Although the will-power myth works for a few, most of the time it leads to relapse or worse.

Fourth, remove the myth that CONTROL IS ALWAYS GOOD. It's important to have your heart under control, but not all forms of control are healthy. They can be extremely self-destructive and hurtful to you and others. The desire to control your heart can be a sign of a sickness—a controlling personality.

2. Repair the Broken Meaning of Control

Let's take a look at the difference between healthy and unhealthy forms of control. Since we're talking about your invisible heart, I thought it best to give you a picture of unhealthy control that you can visualize.

When Bonnie came to see me, she wanted to leave her husband Vick but was afraid to chance it. They had four children. How could she leave him? How would she survive? Vick traveled nearly every week for his work. While he was gone, Bonnie and the children felt like they could breathe and get a little relief. But, when he returned, they held their breath and tip-toed around the house in fear of his next explosion. Vick was extremely critical, highly demanding, distrustful, dishonest, and controlling. He found fault in everyone and everything around him and was volatile anytime he didn't get his way. Vick did have control of his family; but his kind of control was sick, hurtful and self-destructive.

Whether you are trying to help someone get control of their harmful behavior or trying to get control of your own troubled heart, make sure you're going about it in a healthy way. There are two main approaches to understanding and getting control: (1) OVERPOWER or (2) EMPOWER. Which are you trying to do?

First, the unhealthy way to get control of your heart is to OVERPOWER it. Vick's control was overpowering. He told his family that everything he did was because he loved them and just wanted to help them. He probably believed that, but his control was destructive to his family and to himself. It produced what an overpowering approach always does—seriously unhealthy consequences. Vick was spiritually and emotionally sick and didn't know it, and this sickness spilled over into his family relationships.

Like any improperly treated bacterial infection, an improperly treated spiritual sickness takes hold and spreads with a vengeance. With the best of intentions, you may use threats, fear, shame, guilt or other self-imposed forms of power to try to help change someone's attitude or behavior. But no matter how sincere or hard you work at it, those approaches ultimately aggravate the problem and defeat your purpose. If you use that unhealthy approach, it will only heighten your negative feelings, desires and behavior.

Second, the healthy way to get control of your heart is to seek to EMPOWER it. Your heart can be controlled by negative, unhealthy influences from your past. These past experiences can cause your heart to respond with negative feelings, rebellious desires, and destructive behavior. Your heart is held captive by old tapes that won't let it function unselfishly, enjoyably, openly and freely, the way God intended. It needs to be set free from whatever is holding it back. Vick's family dynamics would have been encouragingly different if he had empowered rather than overpowered his wife and children.

How does our Heavenly Father control his children? He doesn't over-power them. He empowers them. He offers them the opportunity to partner with him and take back their ability to live the way they were created. If you read about our Father's way of relating to his children throughout biblical history, you will come to the conclusion that he sought to empower, not overpower even his most rebellious children. He brought healing, direction, and strength to the most broken, mean-spirited, and rebellious hearts. And that's the way his son, Jesus, practiced control when he changed the hearts of people he met.

Jesus offers us self-control. When people were confused, discouraged, sick, broken or rebellious, Jesus taught them how to become enabled, empowered to overcome such problems. He didn't manipulate, pressure, or force them to accept his way. He invited them to become his close friends and watch him along the journey so they could develop the same kind of self-control he had. The Bible has numerous references to the importance of self-control, but self-control may not be what you think it is.

> "The fruit of the Spirit is love, joy, peace, patience, kindness, goodness, faithfulness, gentleness and *self-control*." Galatians 5:22-23 ESV

> "Make every effort to supplement your faith with . . . *self-control*." 2 Peter 1:5-7 ESV

> "God gave us a spirit not of fear but of power and love and *self-control*." 2 Timothy 1:7 ESV

> "Stop getting drunk with wine, which leads to wild living, but keep on being *filled with (being under the control of)* the Spirit." Ephesians 5:18 ISV

The Bible-word *FILLED* is synonymous with *SELF-CONTROL* and *HEALTHY CONTROL*. When God's word says we should have *self-control*, it is not the contemporary view of making our SELF (mind, heart and behavior) take control of a situation. Rather, it is instructing us to allow our SELF (our minds, hearts, and behaviors) to come under the control or influence of God's presence.

The Apostle Paul clarified the concept of self-control when he described it to the new Christians at Ephesus. "Don't get drunk with wine, because it makes you lose control. Instead, keep on being filled with the Spirit." Ephesians 5:18 CJB. The key point in Paul's illustration about self-control is found in the particular word he chose to use for *filled*. It was not the word that referred to a glass that is so full it's about to run over. He used a different Greek word for *filled* that referred to being *under the influence of* something other than the self. For you to be *filled* with God's Spirit is to let your inner *self* be so influenced or affected by God that your heart is changed and working in cooperation with God's Spirit. The heart still participates, but it's not alone. It's under the influence.

Your Father's greatest desire for you is to help you so that your heart will thrive—love, enjoy and work the way it was originally designed. He doesn't want to take over. He wants to partner with you so that his Spirit and your spirit have such an intimately-close relationship that your desires, emotions and will are one with his.

As a boy, I grew up in a house with two sisters and a mother who picked up after me. Mama was from that era when housework was not something boys or men did. Boys had our *man-chores* and girls had their *women-chores*. Cleaning and picking up were definitely women-chores.

At an early age I developed some sloppy habits that I unconsciously practiced as an adult. When Phyllis and I got married, I discovered she loved a neat, clean house. I wanted to make her happy so I tried to break my old, careless, throw-it-on-the-floor habits. At first, I kept forgetting. Breaking old habits is not easy. I asked her to help me remember. She loved me, encouraged me, and reminded me when I forgot. Under her loving influence, I changed my old ways.

After years of enjoying a happy marriage and a close personal relationship with her, I continue to tell Phyllis how grateful I am to be *under her influence*. The feeling is mutual, and we help and empower each other in different areas of our lives. That's the biblical, healthy approach to self-control, being filled, being under the influence, being empowered not over-powered by the Spirit of our Living God.

3. Replace the Popular Attempts to Control.

If you are going to get your heart under control by having an intimately-close relationship with your heavenly Father, it will not happen automatically. You must get rid of some old ways and replace them with the one way we know works.

In our hearts we all want to do what's good. We also want to do what feels good. The battle between our desire for self-control and self-indulgence is nothing new. People in every culture and every generation have struggled with this universal and personal conflict.

We all struggle with self-control. The Apostle Paul knew what self-control was and how to get it, yet he still had an on-going tug-of-war between his self-indulgence and his self-control. "I have the desire to do what is right, but not the ability to carry it out. For I do not do the good I want, but the evil I do not want is what I keep on doing." Romans 7:18-19 ESV.

If you take a giant step back in history and take a panoramic view of cultures around the world, you'll quickly discover that historians, philosophers, psychologists, and all the major religions offer three main ways to get control of your desires, emotions and behavior, and to get close to God.

First, ELIMINATE your desires. One of the oldest and most popular ways people attempt to control their undesirable desires is to eliminate them. This approach is rooted in the religious belief that the physical world is evil and the spiritual world is good. So, the best way to control your desires is to stop craving anything physical. Seek those things that are spiritual and avoid those that are non-spiritual.

The elimination-denial-answer to controlling your heart has four main problems. It's narcissistic, dishonest, irresponsible, and doesn't work. It's a self-centered, false humility that avoids personal duty and compassion by placing all responsibility on the shoulders of others. Pushing your desires into the background will not eliminate them. It only elevates them. An infection must not be ignored or denied or it will continue to spread. It must be faced and controlled.

Second, MANAGE your desires. The second most popular way some people use to try to control their undesirable desires, emotions and actions is to attempt to manage them by themselves or with other's help. This approach appeals to our technologically-oriented mind because it's the scientific or business way we deal with most of our problems.

When our heart-problems get to the point that they are disrupting the other parts of our lives, at first glance the management-approach is especially helpful. It's a responsible and important first step towards controlling your heart. It's a form of personal confession, a way of admitting your need and accepting outside help.

The management-approach is not a means to a cure. It's a way to cope. It teaches you ways to get some control by practicing habits, managing symptoms, making adjustments, and learning skills to respond more successfully when you are in difficult situations. Management-methods such as counseling, therapy, and support groups are practical and highly effective, but limited. They generally lack an essential ingredient for lasting, healthy control—a personal, intimately-close relationship with your first-love. This approach does not satisfy the greatest desire of your heart and your God-designed life—an intimate relationship with the Eternal One.

Since you are a spiritual being made in the image of the eternal Spirit, you have a built-in desire and need for an intimately-close relationship with him. You cannot neglect that primary desire without experiencing many negative consequences. Nothing but God can satisfy your built-in God-shaped desire. All the self-denial and therapy you do will not fill that ultimate desire and need.

Some management techniques can be especially helpful when they serve as tools God and you use as you work together to develop your self-control. More important than a mechanical technique is a personal live-in-Lord. More than an occasional-counselor, on-call-coach, or intermittent-trainer you can run to when trouble comes, you need an in-your-heart, always-there Lord.

Meeting your five basic desires is an inside job. As you remember, we're all built with five basic human desires or needs—the desire to feel *safe, loved, respected, purposeful* and *eternal.* The strongest, most powerful of the five is our desire for an intimately-close relationship with our Eternal-Father. When that desire is satisfied, all of the other four desires can be satisfied. And when our basic desires are satisfied, healthy emotions and choices naturally follow.

For example, if you have that intimate kind of relationship with your Eternal-Father, your desire to feel safe will be completely satisfied under any circumstances. Since he is all-powerful, as your relationship with him grows closer, you can overcome any fear about anything. You will be secure in knowing he can handle any problem.

Since he is all-loving, you will begin to learn that he wants the best for you. He cares for you more than you care for yourself. Eventually, as it becomes clearer to you that he is able to handle anything and care for every detail in your life, you won't feel insecure about anything.

If you believe that your Father is all-knowing, you won't be afraid of the future or what you can't understand because he understands everything. He knows what's going on behind the scene. He's doing what's best for now and for the long-haul.

Since he is all-present, which means he never leaves you and is with you at all times and in all situations, you will feel secure and peaceful. In the same way, your intimate relationship with Him will bring satisfaction to your other three desires.

So, how do you get into such an intimate, transforming relationship with your living-Lord? In this chapter you've learned three of the four practical steps in the protocol: (1) REMOVE the unhealthy myths about control. (2) REPAIR the broken meaning of control, and (3) REPLACE the popular attempts to control.

In the next chapter you will study the fourth and most critical step in getting control of your heart—GUARD your heart with five proven practices. These five practices work. And, the task of guarding, defending, securing our hearts is so important that God's word warns to, *"Guard your heart above all else, for it determines the course of your life."* Proverbs 4:23 NLT. Before you move to Chapter Sixteen, practice these exercises.

Exercises to Build and Maintain your Healthy Faith

The ironic part of controlling your heart is giving your control up. The idea of self-control from a Biblical perspective is putting yourself under the influence and control of the One who made you. Getting control of your heart and emotions means giving them to Him.

RECORD: In just two or three sentences, record your understanding of overpowering control and empowering control. Write down ten words that would describe your life.

REMEMBER: Developing a healthy faith will make a difference in your life because a healthy faith implies that you have healthy relationships. You have put yourself under the influence of God's spirit living in you, and his spirit brings with it those things that make for a productive, satisfying life. Memorize this verse which reminds you of the empowering qualities of the life lived under God's control. "But the fruit of the Spirit is love, joy, peace, patience, kindness, goodness, faithfulness, gentleness and self-control." Galatians 5: 22-23 NIV.

REFLECT: Turn in your Bible to Romans 8: 5-11. Read the entire passage, and then read it again, stopping to meditate on each phrase.

RE-EXAMINE: The two scriptures used in these exercises are measuring sticks. Think again of those qualities of life that come from God's spirit living in you. Earlier you were asked to write down ten words that described your life. How do those qualities compare with the qualities of the kind of life described in Galatians 5:22-23? Who or what controls your desires and what you set your mind on?

RECALL: Get real honest with that friend you trust. Discuss those ten words that best describe your quality of life. Perhaps one or two stand out that you'd really like to see changed. Talk about ways to make a positive change, and ask your friend to hold you accountable in your commitment to make the change.

Pray this prayer to your Heavenly Father.

Dear Father, You are amazingly patient with me, and I'm so grateful. When I think of how many times I've disappointed my family, friends, and you, I am embarrassed and sorry. But I know your grace and forgiveness are greater than my sin. So I thank you for your love and interest in my life. I want you to fill my heart with your Spirit and empower me to be all that you made me to be. Partner with me to do all you want me to do. Give me the strength to do my part. I do love you with all my heart. Amen.

CHAPTER 16

How do you GUARD your heart?

"His Holy Spirit, moving and breathing in you, is the most intimate part of your life, making you fit for himself. Don't take such a gift for granted."

EPHESIANS 4:30 MSG

"Guard your heart above all else, for it determines the course of your life."

PROVERBS 4:23 NLT

LEONARDO DA VINCI'S PAINTING, *THE Mona Lisa*, is valued at one billion dollars, making it by far the world's most valuable painting. Can you imagine the kind of security system and extreme protective measures the Louvre Museum in Paris uses to guard this matchless piece of art? As valuable as *The Mona Lisa* is, it is just a painting, and your heart is far more valuable to God and you.

The greatest desire/need of the heart is for intimacy. It is the most powerful and influential part of the human personality. That is why it is critically important for us to guard our hearts from anything that would separate us from our heavenly Father and those closest to us.

We crave human-intimacy more than safety, community, respect or purpose. When we don't find it, we try to substitute something for it and are always discontented. Throughout history, people have willingly given up anything for it—their security, families, positions, fame and fortunes. But, perhaps spiritual-intimacy is even more powerful than human-intimacy.

Pop-culture would have you think that human-intimacy is a momentary physical or emotional high. It's not. True human-intimacy, intimacy at its best and deepest, is far more dynamic, meaningful, joyful, lasting, transforming and all-consuming. It's much more than physical. It's an inexplicable connection or closeness that happens over time between two people and involves their minds, hearts and actions. One woman said, "We've been married for forty-five years. I can't explain it, but we think and feel like one person with two bodies." Spiritual-intimacy between a person and God has those same characteristics.

The Apostle Paul knew the importance of guarding his heart so that nothing would come between him and his Lord. He described the importance of his intimacy with the Lord in this way, "I count everything as loss compared to the possession of the priceless privilege of knowing Christ Jesus my Lord and of progressively becoming more deeply and *intimately acquainted* with Him." Philippians 3:8 AMP.

Before he left his friends to return to heaven, Jesus told his heavenly Father about his greatest desire for his followers. Above everything else he wanted them to have the same kind of relationship with the Father that he had.

When I examined Jesus' habits, words and practices, I've discovered *five extraordinary practices* Jesus constantly repeated to stay close to his Father. If you conscientiously follow those same practices, over time you, too, can develop an intimate relationship with your heavenly-Father and be able to guard your heart. Listen. Thank. Touch. Pause. Simplify.

Five Practices for Developing an Intimate Relationship with God

1. LISTEN to His Heart
Be silent more. Talk less. Listen attentively. Learn all you can.
Couples who have an intimate relationship with each other guard their hearts from being self-centered. They enjoy listening to one another. They want to know everything they can about their loved one's heart and life. They are more interested in learning about the other's thoughts, feelings and

experiences than taking about themselves. They don't half-way listen while thinking about what they want to say. Intimacy is the reward we get for listening when we would prefer to talk.

Healthy listening is more than hearing. Intimacy-building listening is more of an attitude than an action. It's being other-centered. It's choosing to be patiently quiet, while your ego says, "Interrupt. You have something much better to say." Healthy listening gives the one you love all the time he or she wants to think out loud, tell every detail, or share every feeling. It's sympathetically asking and expressing interest more than impatiently telling and expressing frustration. Intimate-producing listening is the result of a passionate, humble desire to know everything possible about the one you love.

Like human-intimacy, spiritual-intimacy is all-consuming. An important part of having an intimate relationship with your Lord is guarding your heart from only caring about yourself. You can develop and protect your intimacy by passionately attempting to find out all you can about him. The more you listen to him and learn about him, the closer you will feel to him. But how can you listen to him when he doesn't generally speak audibly? He does something much better than simply talk.

He wants to speak to you through his word, his writers, and others. Jesus practiced listening to his Father from his childhood until his last breath on the cross. Jesus quoted his Father's words he learned from his Father's Bible. He didn't just talk about his Father and to his Father; he stayed in touch with his Father throughout each day. He meditated on the scriptures he had learned and listened to his Father's inaudible voice.

The best kind of Bible-reading is Bible-listening. For centuries, people have read the Father's holy words in the Bible, pausing to quietly meditate on its stories, instructions, and encouragements. They desired to hear his voice, to feel his heart, to sense his desires for their lives, to know his truth, and to hear his voice. Those kinds of seekers were never disappointed.

He speaks through others. Your Father wants to speak to you not only through his Bible, but also through his ancient and contemporary writers and others who have had an intimate relationship with him. As you read and listen to godly men and women, your Father speaks to you through them. If you take time daily, make room intentionally, stop asking incessantly, and sincerely listen, you will hear him pour out his heart to you softly, clearly and personally. As you do, you will begin to feel a new, growing and vibrant intimacy.

2. *THANK HIM WITH ALL YOUR HEART*
BE GRATEFUL IN ALL. SHOW THANKFUL MERCY. MELT A HEART WITH THANKS.
When a couple has an intimately-close relationship, they have an inner, private kind of joy no matter what's happening around them. They guard their hearts from ingratitude and bitterness. Intimate joy is more than a passing pleasure. It's a slowly-developed, deep feeling of satisfaction, contentment or happiness. It happens when our basic human desires are met. And the primary way to get such a comprehensive satisfaction is to practice the discipline of gratitude in all circumstances.

Gratitude unlocks the door to intimacy. Gratitude has been the core virtue in practically every culture and religion throughout time. It is central to the overall message of the Bible. It's the most basic, appropriate, and natural response to all that our heavenly Father has done for his children. Anything less than unselfish gratitude is self-centered ingratitude. Healthy, intimacy-building gratitude is the all-consuming attitude of people with deeply satisfying relationships.

Gratitude is more than saying thank you. People with a close human-intimacy constantly communicate their gratitude to one another. For them, it's like breathing. It's their normal. They don't take anything the other does or says for granted. When they express their gratitude, they are doing more than merely acknowledging an act of kindness. For them, being grateful is being accepting, kind-hearted, reminiscent, forgiving and active.

ACCEPTING. People who practice intimacy-building gratitude accept others even when they don't deserve it. Genuine gratitude creates an atmosphere of loving-reception not rival-rejection.

KIND-HEARTED. People who practice intimacy-building gratitude are kind-hearted, not hardhearted. If you want to get closer to the one you love, at all times be kind, gentle and tender with your words and actions. As the sun melts a block of ice, kindness melts a cold, callous, wounded, and mistrustful heart.

REMEMBERING. People who practice intimacy-building gratitude recall blessings from their past and talk about them. When you gratefully retell the sweet stories, fun times, painful experiences, surprising victories, and special joys you shared in the past, you reveal a grateful heart for your underserved blessings from God and others.

FORGIVENESS. People who practice intimacy-building gratitude are forgiving, merciful, and gracious. Even the best of relationships have conflicts, disappointments and sorrows. But, couples with a healthy, intimate relationship remember how others and God forgave them and offer the same gracious not judgmental response.

ACTIVE. One of the best ways to guard your heart from losing intimacy is to demonstrate your gratitude. People who practice intimacy-building gratitude are more than talk. They continually look for small, thoughtful and surprising ways to demonstrate their appreciation.

As a father and grandfather, I can assure you I'm like all dads and granddads, I love to hear my children and grandchildren tell me thank you. But what warms my heart more than words of thanks is to see them or hear about how they are living lives of gratitude.

Our God is a far more gracious and grateful Father than I could ever be or imagine. He wants our gratitude for him to spill out into our gratitude for his other children. Through his servant Paul, he says to all of his children, "Be joyful always; pray continually; give thanks in all circumstances, for this is God's will for you in Christ Jesus." 1 Thessalonians 5:18 NIV.

Gratitude during suffering is the highest level of gratitude. When you respond to a pleasant experience with gratitude, it's thoughtful. But when you respond to a personal heartache, crisis or loss with gratitude, you reveal a much deeper, unshakable, trusting intimacy with your Father.

Intimate gratitude is expressing thanks *in* all circumstance, not *for* all circumstance. That kind of gratitude is a display of humility, dependence and honest faith. It's the acid-test of authentic, tough faith versus fair-weather faith. On the night before he was crucified, Jesus thanked his heavenly Father for the bread and wine he served his disciples. He dreaded the cross but was grateful in the face of torture and death because he knew his Father would be with him.

3. TOUCH HIS HEART
EMBRACE THE POOR. TOUCH PAIN. SEE CHRIST IN THE LEAST OF THESE.

You can guard your heart from losing intimacy and develop a deeper intimacy by touching. Do you know how important touching is to intimacy? Some researchers, like the internationally-renowned neuroscientist Saul M Schanberg, MD, said that touching is ten times more powerful than talking or listening. For example, one study found that regularly-touched premature infants became far healthier than those untouched by human hands. Those that were touched regularly matured more rapidly, were more responsive, were released from the hospital sooner and months later were physically, emotionally and socially healthier. It's a proven fact, touch is vital to the overall well-being of children. It's also critical to developing intimacy between adults and our heavenly Father.

Jesus did more than talk. When he healed the leper, deaf man, elderly woman, blind man and dead little girl, he didn't just speak to them or pray for them from a distance. He went to them personally and touched them individually with his loving, caring presence.

Jesus' relationship-building touches did more than give good feelings and physical health. His touches were acts of compassion, friendship, acceptance, care, love and humility. He participated in their suffering. He experienced their woundedness. He felt their misery. He wept with them. And, when he did, former strangers became close friends. Former observers became life-long followers.

The invisible food that nourishes human-intimacy. Sharing physical pleasures and expensive gifts can never produce intimacy like physically and emotionally participating in someone's pain. When your spouse, child, or other loved one is wounded by a sense of failure, disappointment, embarrassment, sorrow, loneliness, loss, or any other heartbreaking experience, the touch of your presence is more meaningful than your words. Shared-suffering is the invisible food that nourishes human-intimacy.

Spiritual-intimacy works the same way. Too many people sincerely love God, passionately tell him of their love, generously give him gifts, and earnestly want to feel close to him; but they never get there. They don't because, like human-intimacy, spiritual-intimacy takes more than words, gifts and desires. It takes sharing the heart of God. It requires participating in the Father's hurts. If you reach out and take part in his pain, you experience an unexplainable personal intimacy with him that happens in no other way. That's one of the important ways Jesus stayed close to the Father.

When Jesus touched wounded people, those no one else wanted to touch, an unexplainable, life-altering bond began between him and those he touched. But, something else significant happened. By tenderly touching his Father's hurting children, Jesus also touched his Father's hurting-heart. By sharing in their pain, he shared in his Father's pain.

Before Jesus left the earth, he explained to his followers that, if they would touch those who were poor, hungry, thirsty, and homeless, without clothes, sick, in prison or alone, they would be touching God. He told them to do more than just speak to them as they passed by them, or only pray for them, or send money to them. He insisted that they personally touch them personally with their lives. "If you do it *to* the least of these, you do it *to* me." Matthew 5:46.

Mother Teresa interpreted those words of Jesus by saying, "Christ is crying out to us in the lives of the poor." I've seen it over and over again. When we follow the example of Jesus and touch the lives of the poor with loving care, something mysterious and meaningful happens to our hearts and relationship to the Lord.

4. PAUSE
BE PRIVATE IN PUBLIC. STAY CONNECTED OR YOU'LL GET DISCONNECTED. BE INTENTIONAL.

Another way you can deepen your intimacy with your heavenly Father and guard your heart from losing that intimacy is to pause. That is, you can intentionally and privately take a spiritual-breather. You can decide to momentarily give your mind and heart a brief break from whatever has your attention. You can reconnect with your Lord.

Intimacy is hard to find and even harder to keep. Our compulsive-driven-culture is the enemy of intimacy. Whether you have a paid job or are retired, you're probably like the rest of us. You are compulsive about your time. You are a slave of your demanding lists, phone, internet, projects and overall lifestyle. At the end of the day, you probably ask yourself, "Where did all my time go?" After being disconnected from your loved one day after day for a good while, eventually one of you looks at the other and asks, "Why aren't we close like we used to be? What happened?"

Swim against the raging current. Couples, who have an intimately-close relationship, make plans and work at staying connected. It's not easy. They have to swim against the raging current of their culture, other responsibilities, and routine. Although they are separated physically, they do whatever they can to get reconnected as often as they can because their hearts crave being close. They leave love notes, make short phone calls, send brief text messages, and do other creative gestures. The same is true for those who want to be close to their heavenly Father.

A rich, young man asked Jesus how he could find God. Jesus told him to sell all he had and follow Jesus. The young businessman was shocked. But Jesus knew that the wealthy fellow's heart and life were controlled by his work. He also knew the young inquirer would never connect with his heavenly Father until he was willing to step-away from his compulsive schedule, get off his success-driven treadmill so he could find and stay connected to his creator and Lord.

Jesus was not against hard work or wealth. What he was against was letting any all-consuming activity, no matter how good it was, separate people from their most important activity—being in an intimate relationship with their heavenly Father. He explained it this way, "First and most importantly seek (aim at, strive after) His kingdom . . . and all these things will be given to you also." Matthew 6:33 AMP.

Even with the multitudes of people daily pleading for his help and the constant pressures from his enemies, Jesus was able to stay connected to his heavenly Father. How did he do it? He practiced the discipline of pausing throughout each day. As I studied his activities and the ways he paused to stay connected, I saw five disciplines he used that will help you have a closer relationship with your heavenly Father.

SHORT MESSAGES. "He never tells me he loves me." Her husband's response was, "I told her I loved her when we got married. I haven't changed my mind. Why should I keep repeating myself?" Human-intimacy is not satisfied or developed by a few highly emotional moments, but by the consistent daily flow of meaningful moments. Intimacy demands some form of contact.

One way to stay intimately connected is to pause throughout the day and, from your mind and heart, send your Father a short, heartfelt message like, "I love you. Thank you Lord. Thank you, Jesus. Help me Lord." Like your loved-one, your Father will be more pleased when you send him several brief, sincere prayer-phrases each day, than one long note in a beautiful card a few times a year on national holidays.

HEART-ALERTS. When anything you see, hear, or read stirs your heart, pause and consider it a heart-alert. For example, if you're driving and notice an ambulance rushing to the ER and your heart feels for the one on the gurney, pause and share that heart-alert with your heavenly Father. It may be no more than, "Father, please take care of that person." Be on the lookout for any sight, sound or written message that stimulates your emotions. Turn that moment into a heart-alert opportunity. Remember, your heart-alerts may come from your own heart or from God's heart to yours. Be on alert.

PRIVACY. Another important way Jesus paused that helped him maintain his intimacy with his Father was privacy. Every morning, and sometimes in the evening, he slipped away from the crowd to a chosen, private place in a garden called Gethsemane. There he spent uninterrupted, just-the-two-of-us time with his Father talking and listening. If someone as close to the Father as Jesus was felt he needed a daily, alone-time with his Father to maintain their closeness, how much more do we need it?

Marriage research is clear—an important discipline every couple needs to maintain an intimately-close relationship is to practice privacy. It's that alone-time when two people are able to reconnect, refocus and get close again. It's their secret-time when they can count on no disturbances and feel comfortable sharing confidentially about anything they wish.

The same is true for spiritual-intimacy. For you to maintain an intimate relationship with your Lord, you need that same kind of private-time with him. But, where do you begin?

Because we have so much spinning around in our heads and hearts, often, when we begin to pray, we have no idea what to say or where to start. Once you establish your routine time and your personal Gethsemane, you might use the *acrostic* many veteran prayers have used. It helps keep us from wandering mentally in our prayers and guides us to include the same four major subjects Jesus used in his prayers. The acrostic is ACTS: ACKNOWLEDGE, CONFESS, THANK, and SUBMIT

A – ACKNOWLEDGE how humbled, amazed and grateful you are to be able to talk to him personally. Each day, let him know how much you appreciate Jesus coming to earth and dying an unspeakable death so that you can live forever. Speak to him about how much you love him, not just for what he has done for you personally, but for the kind of God his is--all-loving, all-powerful, all-knowing, and all-present.

C – CONFESS your sins to him. Don't hold back. He already knows all that you've done, thought and felt. Now is your time to be completely honest. To confess means to agree with. It's your chance to agree with him about what he has put on your conscience. Since he is completely merciful and forgiving, ask for his mercy and forgiveness. Ask him to give you the strength to not repeat those same sins.

T – THANK him for what he has done for your family, friends, church, work, country and anyone and anything else that's on your heart. Tell him how grateful you are for everything that happened yesterday and everything pleasurable and painful that is going on in your life.

S – SUBMIT your requests to him. First, make your requests for those you love. Briefly, tell him about every person and situation that is on your heart. You don't need to explain the problems to him as if he doesn't already know. But, he wants to hear your heart. Don't tell him what do to about the problems. He knows far better than you and I can imagine. Be humble and honest. Second, make your requests for your own personal needs. If you have so many that you can't remember them, make a list before you pray and go over them one at a time. Make your requests humble, responsible and honest. Seek his will in everything you pray.

MEDITATE ON HIS WORD. Another important way Jesus maintained his intimacy with his Father was to meditate on his Father's acts and words. In the Bible, God says we should read his word and, "Meditate on it day and night." Joshua 1:8 NIV. Jesus did just that.

David was called "a man after God's own heart." He said that he meditated on his Father's words, deeds, love, works and wonders. The Biblical call-to-meditation differs from all other forms of meditation, not so much in method as in purpose.

The main purpose of most ancient and many contemporary forms of meditation is to *free your inner-self* from outside influences. Non-biblical forms of meditation are supposed to put your mind in neutral so that your conscience can connect with the universal conscience or connect with nothing. Those kinds of meditation can be dangerous. Your mind and heart are never in neutral. When left without direction or purpose, they can come under the control of unhealthy thoughts, outside influences, and harmful desires. You should guard your heart and mind from such potentially hurtful forms of meditation.

Biblical medication assumes your inner self—mind, heart, and will—can only be free to work the way it was designed by coming under your heavenly Father's influence. When meditation assists you in getting your thoughts, desires, and behavior in rhythm with his, it is a powerful tool in helping you guard your heart.

How can you pause from your daily schedule and practice biblical meditation? One practical and simple way is to use part or all of your regular private time on some days to concentrate on a specific Bible story, sentence, phrases, or word from the scripture.

For example, after reading a Bible story, relax and close your eyes to avoid being distracted. Begin by mentally picturing yourself in the story. Ask the Lord to fill your mind and heart with his thoughts and desires as you think about each of the details of the story. Ask the Lord these four key meditation-questions:

- What does this story say about *you, Father*?
- What does the story say about *my past* and need for forgiveness or thanks?
- What does the story say about how *I should touch someone on my heart*?
- What does this story say about *your desire for my life*?

If you choose to meditate on one special sentence, phrase or word. To open your heart to hearing the Lord, ask him the same four questions.

5. SIMPLIFY
BE PASSIONATE ABOUT ONE. MAKE LITTLE THINGS MATTER. THE GREAT ONE.
Another way you can help deepen your intimacy with your heavenly Father and thus guard your heart is to simplify your inner and outer life. Biblical simplicity is the practice of reducing those things in your life that cause clutter, complexity, confusion, and complications while focusing on those matters that are most important. To live simply is to live with integrity. It's making your heart's desires easier to understand and satisfy. Brilliant Albert Einstein said it simply, "If you can't explain it to a six year old, you don't understand it yourself."

We crave simple plans. Trying to practice our faith in general and attempting to have a close relationship with God in particular are often discouraging. It can be so complicated and confusing that we just give up. What we all crave is a simple, easy-to-understand plan that will work. An early foundational teaching of Thomas Aquinas on knowing God was that God is infinitely simple. Jesus lived a simple life, taught a simple message and enjoyed a simple relationship with his heavenly Father. Members of the Christian group, the Religious Society of Friends (Quakers), practice their straightforward *Testimony of Simplicity* to help them stay close to the Father.

Outer-simplicity is not enough. Some people try to get closer to God by simplifying their physical surroundings. They move from the noisy city to the quiet countryside, give away most of their possessions, and shorten their to-do-list. For some, those kinds of external practices help make their outer-life less complicated and give them more time to work on their inner-life; but such efforts won't meet the basic needs and desires of their inner-life, their heart.

Jesus cut the long list to one. People have always sought to find God and get close to him. And, religious leaders have always put together long lists of laws, duties, desires, needs and things we should do and not do in order to please Him. And over the years, those lists have gotten longer and more difficult to remember, much less do. Jesus had the same long list of human desires and needs that we have, but he simplified his list and cut it down to one. Once he was asked what the single most important thing one could do to find God.

His answer was simple. "Love the Lord your God with all your heart and with all your soul and with all your mind." Matthew 22:36-39 NIV. So people could remember and could do what needed to be done, Jesus made it simple, clear and practical. You need to focus your entire self—your heart, mind and everything you do—on loving your Father. Simply put, if you want to satisfy every need and desire in your life and be close to God, give him your genuine love—love that is humble, responsible and honest.

No matter what, keep it simple. If you have any desire that is not satisfied, turn to him. If you feel insecure, lonely, brokenhearted, disappointed, confused or weak reach out to him. He alone knows what's best for you. He loves you as if you were his only child. He alone can satisfy any unfulfilled need you have or show you what to do to bring satisfaction. When you love him fully, he will give you an inner peace in the middle of any threat.

When you need direction, he will guide your mind to know what to think and do. He will bring people into your life to help you. He will never leave you, but will be with you through every problem. Together, you and your loving-powerful heavenly Father can handle any concern including death.

Don't make your relationship with your Father complicated. Just like a healthy, intimate human-relationship, your spiritual-relationship with your heavenly Father should not be complicated. If you simplify your desires, prioritize them, make your love for him your first and most important desire, he will see to it that all of the needs and desires of your heart will be met and exceeded. As long as you make your intimacy with him your most important desire, nothing can come between you, and nothing can harm your relationship. Unlike any human-relationship, your heavenly Father will always be there for you and will never let you down.

Exercises to Build and Maintain your Healthy Faith

Jesus was radical. When quizzed by the religious leaders about the greatest commandment in the law, he simplified all their rabbinical laws by saying, "Love the Lord your God with all your heart with all your soul and with all your mind. This is the first and greatest commandment. And the second is like it: Love your neighbor as yourself." Matthew 22:37-39. You want to build intimacy with God and guard your heart and relationships? Then let's get started with these exercises.

RECORD: From this chapter, record the Five Practices for Developing an Intimate Relationship with God. Write a one to two sentence summary of each practice. Keep this list accessible so that you can continue to review it.

REMEMBER: Talking with God in a personal way is essential for building intimacy with Him. Memorize the acrostic for the four elements of meaningful prayer, the kind Jesus prayed.

A – Acknowledge   C – Confess   T – Thank   S – Submit

Begin to practice using these elements in your daily conversations with your Father.

REFLECT: For your reflection, you will need your Bible and access to a dictionary. Read Proverbs 4: 23. These are words of wisdom from King Solomon, one of the wisest men who ever lived. He tells us what is the most important thing we can do and why we should do it. Now look up the words *heart, wellspring,* and *life* in the dictionary. Ponder their meaning as you re-read this scripture. If your heart is the wellspring of your life, what is flowing from you?

RE-EXAMINE: Look again at Jesus words in Matthew 22: 37- 39. Being intimate with God is the key to guarding your heart. In this chapter, you read that gratitude is a way to build intimacy. Spend some time making a list of things for which you are thankful, and tell God how grateful you are for each item on that list. Then think of someone special who makes a difference in your life. Write that special person a note of gratitude. Be specific about that for which you are grateful.

RELATE: Talk to your trusted friend and make a list of the ways that you are guarding your heart. Ask yourself the hard questions. Am I spending daily time with my Father? Am I reaching out and touching those who suffer, those who may seem to be untouchable? Do I ever just sit and quietly thank Him without asking for something? Are there ways I could simplify my life and uncomplicate my relationship to Him? Explore with your friend creative ways to guard your heart.

Moving on to the next Step

You are making good progress in your faith-development plan and have completed the first three steps, Now you are ready to go to work on learning how to Repurpose Your Behavior. For you to have a healthy faith you must have more than a healthy mind and heart, you will also have to develop and maintain healthy behavior and habits. That's what you will learn to do in Step 4. Let's get started.

Pray this prayer to your Heavenly Father.

Dear Father, The most important thing in my life is being close to you. I want you to be my first love so help me Lord Jesus. Thank you for your love and care for me. Fill my heart with your Spirit and give me the ability to make you proud of me. When you see anything that is about to harm our relationship, speak to my conscience and help me protect our relationship. Thank you, Lord, for all you do for me. Amen.

Repurpose Your Behavior

ℭℓ

Five Faith-Producing Acts

"Faith is taking the first step even when you don't see the whole staircase."

Martin Luther King, Jr., Civil Rights Leader, Preacher

"As the body without the spirit is dead, so faith without deeds is dead."

James 2:26 CEV

In the first three steps of your faith-development plan, you learned the meaning and characteristics of a healthy faith. So far you have seen how your *self*, the essence of who you are, is made of three parts—the head, the heart, and the hands. We have seen how what you think and what you feel determine the health of your faith. Since the effectiveness of your faith is dependent upon the health of all three parts of your personality, now it is time for you to put your hands to the task of practicing healthy behavior that will become healthy habits.

Genuine faith is more than what you think about life and its purpose. It's more than your feelings about God and others. Living the faith-life is more than talk, it's walking the walk. The clearest picture of your faith's health is painted by your habits.

If you want to evaluate your faith, think about your daily routines and habits. Look at your calendar. How are you really spending your time? Look at your checkbook. What you do with your time and resources will be real indicators of the health of your faith. Think about where your feet take you. Are your eyes seeing someone's need? Are your ears hearing someone's cry for help? Maybe you're in need of some new habits and routines that will produce a healthier faith.

Are you walking your talk? In 1926, Sinclair Lewis wrote <u>Elmer Gantry</u>, a satirical novel condemning the hypocritical practices of some of the clergy of his day. The story became a 1961 film classic, starring Burt Lancaster playing the role of the preacher-turned-con-man working with a female evangelist to sell religion to small town America. Gantry's golden, hypocritical speech was radically different than his dark behaviors. Even today, the name Elmer Gantry is a symbol of a sick, destructive, and unhealthy religion.

But hypocritical faith didn't start with Elmer Gantry. James, the brother of Jesus, observed sick, false faith and wrote, "Faith without works is dead." He also explained, "Someone might claim, 'You have faith and I have action.' But how can I see your faith apart from your actions? Instead, I'll show you my faith by putting it into practice in faithful action." James 2:19-29 CEB.

G. Ernest Wright, a world-renowned archeologist and theologian, wrote the classic, *The God Who Acts*, in which he emphasized how the God of the Bible is radically different from all other gods in all other religions. Other religions emphasize finding meaning in life and discovering the supernatural through the mind. The Bible emphasizes finding God through his acts, what he did in human history.

In the Bible, God did not reveal himself through contemplation or speculation, but through what he did. He appeared to Moses in a burning bush. He opened up the Red Sea, and his people walked on dry ground. He closed the mouths of lions to rescue Daniel.

Then, God stepped down out of heaven, took on flesh, and became a human. Jesus, the God-man, was fully human, and he was fully divine. And as he walked around sandal-footed and rough-bearded, he lived out his faith by doing. His habits and routines took him to quiet places to pray, to the synagogue, to the streets where the people lived, to the gates where beggars sat, to mountainsides where hungry hordes gathered to hear him teach, and to homes of sick ones needing healing. By faith, he walked on water, and he walked up to a hill where a cross awaited. Jesus had a healthy mind and a healthy heart, but it was his healthy habits that actualized, demonstrated, and authenticated his genuine faith.

Jesus didn't mind dirtying his hands doing. He worked, but he didn't do it all, and he didn't choose to do it alone. He invited and instructed others to participate. When it came time to feed the multitudes on the mountainside, he could have done it with the wave of his hand. Instead, he asked his disciples to help. When the stone needed to be rolled away from Lazarus' tomb, Jesus could have moved it with a word. But he didn't, he instructed someone else to do it. His last words to his friends before he ascended into heaven were instructions to go. Jesus knew that the doing of good work was necessary in being a healthy, whole person. His instructions to go and do are for us, too.

When I became a professor at a seminary, I was asked to teach a class instructing students how to lead people to a personal relationship with God through Jesus. I recalled having taken that same class as a young seminarian, and how I had studied the text book, had taken notes, memorized the lists, aced the tests, and made an "A" in the course. But then came the memory that became an indictment. I remembered that during the time I took the course, I never led a single person to Jesus.

That's when I changed the course. I required the ministerial students to spend one-third of their time in class learning the principles of leading someone to Christ, one-third of the time out in the neighborhood homes and on the streets practicing what they had learned in class, and one-third of their time back in class sharing what happened out in the field. By the end of the semester, most of the students reported helping someone find God as their personal Savior.

I especially remember one older student who told the class, "I've been a pastor for seventeen years and have never personally led anyone to God until Dr. Nichols required us to go out and practice what we learned in class. I am thrilled to report that I have lead four people to Christ this semester and helped them join a local church. Seeking to share my faith with others not only helped them, it helped my faith come more alive than it has ever been before."

Dr. Ruth Berggren, the daughter of medical missionaries and the Executive Director the Center for Medical Humanities and Ethics at the University of Texas Health Science Center in San Antonio, practices this same principle in teaching medical students. She knows the students must spend time in class and in intensive study, but she also knows the value of taking them to clinics serving the medical needs of refugees and to places of extreme poverty to take care of the hopeless and helpless. The "doing" brings about compassion and empathy and shapes the future medical practices of young doctors.

As a member of Dr. Berggren's Advisory Board, I have the opportunity and pleasure of interacting with her students. One of her students reported about his work in one of the student-run clinics, "Medicine is not about the lectures and the tests. It is about the people you meet and serve. I am surprised that one of the best ways to deal with the academic rigor of medical school is to volunteer at the clinics. It's like coming up for a breath of air after drowning in all the academia."

Like Dr. Berggren, I believe that healthy practices and habits are more caught than taught. A healthy belief-system and faith are more a result of hands-on practice than classroom study. Until your beliefs are practiced in the streets of heartache, pain, and suffering, they have no credibility or personal value.

Step Four is designed to help you actualize your healthy mind and healthy heart in healthy behavior. It will also help you transform your unhealthy habits into healthy habits. The Bible says, "*Offer your bodies as a living sacrifice, holy and pleasing to God—this is your true and proper worship. Do not conform to the pattern of this world, but be transformed.*" Romans 12: 1-2 (NIV).

Healthy faith requires more than an adjustment to your behavior. Your behavior and habits must be transformed—repurposed.

The term *repurpose* means to transform something so that it can be used for a different purpose. Buddy Clark, my father-in-law, enjoyed working in his woodshop. I was with him one summer when he took an old, discarded plank from a church pew and transformed it into a handsome mantel clock. He re-purposed that old pew, and now when I look at that handmade, functioning clock, I have sweet memories of the first church where I served as a pastor.

In the next five chapters, you will learn how to build healthy habits by repurposing your behaviors and by discovering answers to the following questions.

How do you DEFINE GOOD BEHAVIOR?
How do you VIEW YOUR BODY?
How do you TRANSFORM YOUR TROUBLES?
How do you OVERCOME YOUR BAD HABITS?
How do you GET IN ON WHAT GOD IS DOING?

As your behaviors and habits are repurposed, your faith will also become healthier.

CHAPTER 17

How do you DEFINE GOOD BEHAVIOR?

༯

"Doing good holds the power to transform us on the inside, and then ripple out in ever-expanding circles that positively impact the world at large."

SHARI ARISON, PHILANTHROPIST AND PUBLIC SPEAKER

"Let's not get tired of doing good, because in time we'll have a harvest if we don't give up."

GALATIANS 6:9 CEB

BEHAVIOR MATTERS. HABITS MATTER. ONE trip to the doctor's office for an annual physical and you're convinced. You cannot hide your behavioral patterns because they show up in lab results and health issues. Physicians know what to look for, and they give the dos and don'ts for modifying your behaviors to improve your health. Do exercise. Do eat a balanced diet. Do drink enough water. Don't neglect your blood pressure meds. Don't poison your body with harmful substances. Avoid stress.

There are lots of dos and don'ts in life because behavior matters. No doubt we perform dozens, maybe hundreds of seemingly insignificant and important acts in our walking-around-lives every day. In the so-doing, we are developing behavioral patterns and habits.

I recently attended the funeral of a dear friend and listened proudly to her successful young son speak about his mother. He began every sentence with the words, "Mama cared." His eulogy went something like this, "Mama cared when I was four and spat on someone. Mama cared when I misbehaved in church. Mama cared when I broke curfew as a teenager." If you've been a parent, then you have some idea of how this young man's mother might have expressed that she cared in these learning situations. He went on to say that his behavior mattered to his mother because she knew that it would shape his life and determine how he related to others. He described how his mother not only instructed him, but she demonstrated her care for him with selfless acts of love. What a tribute to his godly mother.

With all the instructions and suggestions we get from parents, teachers, preachers, spouses, friends, co-workers and the media, we find no shortage in messages about how we should behave. So many voices, so many instructions! They all perk our ears, but how do we know which ones will lead us to behaviors that will produce a wholesome life and a healthy faith?

Just as there are physical behaviors that produce optimal lab results, high energy, and good health, there are spiritual habits that will give your faith the vitality you want, will determine your inner peace, and will strengthen your relationship to God and others. Some behavior and habits are elective because they don't make much difference. However, there are critical habits essential to your faith-life that are not optional. It is in our best interest in our faith-building to know the difference between what's harmful, what's optional, and what's good for your spiritual health.

Like the young son delivering his mother's eulogy, we have a parent, a heavenly Father, who cares about our behavior. No doubt when he decided to give us our free wills, he knew that behavior would be the issue. So God provided all that we need to develop good behaviors that help us stay close to him, to overcome our challenges, and to live peacefully with those around us. He gives us principles, pictures, and his presence.

When God gave Moses the Ten Commandments, they weren't laws given just for the Israelites wandering around in the wilderness. They are timeless guidelines and principles for healthy behavior and relationships.

God knew that most of us would forget his laws or interpret them as we wish, so he went beyond words, laws, and rules and gave us a picture. Our God is active in human history and should be our model for healthy behavior. After centuries of studying the many ways God has acted on behalf of his children, Bible scholars chose five significant events they consider God's greatest acts in history: the Creation, the Exodus, the Incarnation, the Crucifixion, and the Resurrection. If we look at these historic spiritual acts more closely, they provide us with five magnificent models. We see how God desired and managed relationships, how he behaved when his creatures challenged him, and how love is at the core of his every act.

We were created by the God who acts, and we were created in his image. So if how we act is so important and crucial to living a wholesome life and developing a healthy faith, then we should define it according to the model the Life-giver offers.

Let's look at these actual God-acts as recorded in the Bible, and then let us look at the acts of some other real people as they fleshed out these principles in their own behaviors.

Five God-models that define GOOD BEHAVIOR

1. CREATION. God transformed NOTHING into SOMETHING.
God created all there is *ex nihilo*, out of nothing. God transformed nothing into something, darkness into light, chaos into beauty, and confusion into order. What was a lifeless void now teemed with living creation and creatures after God acted. We will never understand how God did all that, but we can understand it when he said that everything he did, all of his actions in creation, were good.

When God gets involved, good things happen. He does not leave things as they were or make them worse. He transforms what he touches into something better. That was his behavior in the Creation story, and that is what he has kept on doing throughout human history.

There was another scene of chaos and confusion on June 8, 1972 in the village of Trang Bang, South Vietnam, a village attacked and occupied by enemy North Vietnamese forces. Nine-year-old Kim Phúc joined a group of villagers and South Vietnamese soldiers as they fled from a temple to a safer place held by the South Vietnamese. As they ran, they were mistaken as enemy soldiers by a South Vietnamese pilot, and he dropped four napalm bombs which rained fire on the village and Kim. Several were killed, and Kim was severely burned as she ran, tearing off the chemical-soaked clothes that burned and melted her flesh.

Nick Ut was on assignment as a photographer with the Associated Press. He captured the unspeakable terror and pain when he photographed Kim as she ran screaming and naked through the village streets. His Pulitzer Prize-winning photograph became the symbol of the horrifying events of the Vietnamese war. But the story does not end there.

Ut had done his job in taking the photographs, but his transforming act took place when he put down his camera and carried Kim Phúc and other injured soldiers and villagers to a hospital in Saigon. He saw the chaos and the pain, and he acted. The fact that Kim Phúc survived was near miracle, and Ut visited her regularly until he was evacuated during the fall of Saigon.

Kim Phúc spent over a year in the hospital and underwent multiple surgeries and skin transplantations. Her experience as a patient made her dream of becoming a doctor, but the realities of her life made that impossible. Because of her physical pain and inner torment, Kim withdrew from normal activities and retreated to a library, where she spent her time reading, trying to find some purpose in her life. On Christmas in 1982, ten years after the bombing, Kim Phúc gave her life to Christ. She tells the beautiful story of learning to forgive, and how her body might have been scarred, but her heart was clean.

Fifteen years later, Kim Phúc established a foundation in the U.S. which provides medical help and counseling for children who are victims of war. Through the years, Kim Phúc has helped so many children and so many others as she speaks out publicly about her faith and the transformation in her life. And it's not surprising that even in 2015, Uncle Nick was at her side in a Florida dermatologist's office as she began treatment that will hopefully soften the scar tissue covering a third of her body and relieve some of her pain.

Nick Ut saw the chaos and acted. He could not have known when he took Kim Phúc's photograph and scooped her up to take her to the hospital where their journey would lead. But both their actions have brought goodness out of terror, light out of the hellish darkness of war and suffering, and hope for other victims.

Chances are you won't have an experience as dramatic as Nick Ut and Kim Phúc, but be reminded that you never know what God will do with that one simple action you take. This is a picture of good behavior, the kind of behavior like God's behavior in creating something good out of nothing. The Bible says Jesus went about doing good. Be like him, spreading light and encouragement and help. Look for people who live in darkness, confusion, meaninglessness, and depression and help them find light and goodness.

2. EXODUS. God transformed SLAVES into FREE PEOPLE.
Because God's children did not stay close to him and follow his leadership, they became slaves to their own bad choices and eventually to their Egyptian neighbors. After years of slavery and suffering, they cried out to God for mercy and for deliverance. God sympathetically heard their cries and acted. He called Moses as his representative, performed miracles in such a way that the Pharaoh freed his people, and God led them through the wilderness into the land he had promised them. God delivered them from their bondage and misery. You can read this dramatic story in the book of Exodus.

Alice met a young woman who lived in the bondage of her culture and in the prison of poverty. One Christmas, Alice's Sunday School class chose to provide Christmas for a poor family who lived in the inner city. A local help agency gave them Roxanna's name and described her situation.

Roxanna was one of five children, all who had different fathers who had never been a part of their lives. Following her mother's example, at sixteen

Roxanna was already a mother to two babies. She lived in a tiny apartment that she shared with her drug-addicted mother and her older siblings who dropped in when they needed a place to sleep. She had little to nothing and not much of a future to look forward to. That is until Alice showed up.

Alice wasn't satisfied to deliver a box of food and toys and sing Christmas carols. She assessed the situation and lead her Sunday School class to continue to help Roxanna. Over the next few months, Alice helped find better and safer housing for Roxanna and her two babies. It meant separation from some of the bad influences in Roxanna's life, but she loved her children and was willing to make the change and the commitment. That meant that Alice had to secure furnishings and utilities for the new apartment.

Roxanna returned to high school where she graduated with good grades and on time with her class. That meant that Alice had to find child care. Roxanna wanted to be a nurse. Alice went to work to help her fill out the necessary paperwork and get student aid to help her get into nursing school.

There were bumpy roads and a few difficult conversations along the way, but today, Roxanna is a nurse. She is married to a Christian man who adopted her two children, and now they have a son. She is showing her children a much different childhood than she had.

Alice followed God's way of behaving. She saw a young woman enslaved by her upbringing and the poverty, and she took her by the hand and the heart and helped her break those chains. She led her to a better place and a productive, satisfying life that will change the lives of future generations as well.

Perhaps you know a Roxanna. Maybe there is someone in your sphere of influence who is bound by bad habits, addictions, fear, anger or culture. When you relate to them, do what God did. Take them by the hand, and lead them to a new way of freedom in the Christ-life. Let that become your habit.

3. INCARNATION. God transformed LONELINESS into TOGETHERNESS.

After enjoying God's blessings, his children again forgot all he had done, and they stopped acknowledging God or showing their gratitude. Their behavior was habitually prideful, irresponsible, dishonest, and seemingly beyond hope. That is when God decided it was time for him to demonstrate to his children and to people of all times his greatest act of love. He, who was Spirit, came to earth to become one of us. He was God in flesh (in-carnate).

The Bible says God sent his son to be born of young virgin, Mary. With God as his father and Mary as his mother, Jesus became the God-Man, both fully divine and fully human. There is no suffering or temptation that we know that Jesus did not know, yet he lived without sin.

Through his teachings, and more importantly, through his behavior and habits, Jesus is the perfect model for healthy living. Jesus, though God, did not isolate himself in some comfortable tower to watch what was happening or continually sit in some synagogue among the learned. He walked the streets, no stranger to the poor, the disenfranchised, and the suffering. As he walked the streets, the seaside, and the mountainsides, Jesus transformed lonely, self-centered, sick, angry people by showing them a new way. That was his habit, giving them his Spirit so that he was always present with them. And Jesus transformed them so that these weak, isolated and hopeless humans were now united by his Spirit and became family.

I knew a man who followed Jesus' habit of bringing lonely people together. Sam was a man who had been a soldier in World War II. He came home, started a construction business, and married the love of his life. Sam was no stranger to seeing God at work in his life, so it was not surprising that in his early retirement, he studied at seminary and became a minister. Although, Sam found himself serving in churches that were in building programs and needed his construction expertise, his greatest joy was in leading someone to Christ and teaching God's Word.

Sam was a crusty old guy with a contagious laughter and a handshake that would rival a boxer's. He was ninety-eight, still teaching the Bible and serving his church, when his wife died. With his own health issues and no living children, Sam moved into a nursing home not long after his wife's death. One might think that Sam would just hang it up, but he didn't. He looked around him and saw some lonely people, some who had lost their life-mates, their homes, and their independence. So Sam started a Bible study in the dining hall, and it wasn't long before those same lonely people were not only show-ing up for Bible study, they were having conversations in the hallway and had caught Sam's infectious laugh.

Sam continued to teach the Bible study until he was nearly a hundred when an illness took him home. Whether in his life as a businessman or as a minister, Sam always said he was doing the Lord's business. He taught, he hugged, he built buildings for worship, and only the Lord knows how many folks are in heaven because Sam led them there. He followed Jesus' example and did his part to make people family, God's family.

Sam had a long life and a healthy faith, following God's behavioral habits. Maybe you weren't a soldier or a building contractor or a minister like Sam, but perhaps you know someone who is lonely or depressed or someone who has lost all hope. You could be the very person to be God's presence in that one's life.

4. CRUCIFIXION. God transformed DEFEAT into VICTORY.

The cross is the primary symbol of Christianity because it points to God's greatest act. God watched the waywardness and willfulness of his children over the centuries, and yet they continued to bring blood sacrifices to the temple. Perhaps God grew weary of all the blood sacrifices because in Isaiah, we read where God said he'd had enough of their sacrifices. So in time God, once and for all, became the sacrifice and paid for all their wrongdoing. What he desired was right living. God wanted the best for his children, so he gave himself. He still wants the best for us. He wants no one to live in hopelessness and defeat.

The Bible records Jesus' words in John 15 where he expresses his deep love for his disciples and explains that they were his friends, no longer servants. Then he tells them there is no greater love than when one gives his life for a friend. Jesus talked about it, and then he did it. He sacrificed his life for the lives of his friends. He died to give us a new beginning.

As a pastor I know that when the phone rings after midnight, it's never good. That particular night, it was Hank, a trusted friend and committed member of our church. I was accustomed to Hank's cheerful voice, but his voice quivered as he explained that he had a friend in deep trouble and needed help and wanted me to go with him. He picked me up a few minutes later, and on the way to a motel just on the outside of town, Hank told me Billy's story.

Billy had been a banker with all the trappings of success—a wife, two children, a large home, two cars, and a weekend boat. Alcohol had led him down a path to nothingness. His behavior drove his family away. He lost his house and his job, and with all gone, not even his drinking buddies were still around. Billy sat in a hotel room with a shotgun ready to end it all when he made a last desperate call to the one good man he knew, Hank.

I'd like to tell you that it was my wise pastoral counseling that saved Billy that night, but it wasn't. Yes, I talked to him and prayed with him, but it was Hank that embraced him, not just that night, but for the next several months. I listened as Hank tearfully apologized for letting Billy down and not reaching out to rescue him earlier. Billy went home with Hank that night and stayed there with Hank's family until he could get on his feet. Hank took him to church and to AA meetings. The men's Bible study group Hank taught became Billy's new family and his biggest cheerleaders.

Billy found a job, and after months of sober and clean living, he accepted an invitation to teach a youth Bible study at our church. He was honest with our youth about his own failures in hopes of keeping them from making the same bad choices. In time, Billy won back the hearts of his wife and his children. He never tired of telling how Jesus brought about victory out his self-made defeat. Billy changed his behavior.

This sounds like Billy's story, but it is Hank's story, too. Hank modeled Christ-like behavior. That's why Billy called him as a last resort before attempting to take his own life. Hank went, he talked, he prayed, and he sacrificed. He put Billy near the top of his priority list, gave him a clean, fresh start, and walked beside him until Billy was healthy again.

Do you know someone who needs a new beginning, a different path from the one their taking? Maybe you could be a Hank to that person and offer him a new path, God's path to wholeness and victory.

5. RESURRECTION. God transformed IMPOSSIBILITIES into
ETERNITIES.

The empty tomb is Christianity's symbol of God's character. It is a picture of
God's doing what only he can do, making the dead live again, overcoming seemingly impossible problems, and transforming lives and situations that no one else
could change. The Resurrection, God's greatest miracle of transformation, is his
habit and his continual way of helping people find the eternal in the temporal.

It was in 1999 when Lillian Klepp first heard the stories coming out of
war-torn Sudan—two million killed, six million homeless including widows
and orphans, disease and hunger. Lillian began to pray about what she could
do. She and her husband Dennis were very involved in their local church and
did short-term missions, but she felt there was more God wanted of her. It was
in 2001 when God answered her prayer with a clear call to sell all she had and
move to Sudan and give herself to work with the orphans.

Lillian had no idea when she began to pray that one day thousands of
Sudanese orphans would call her Mama Lilly and would speak with her
Wisconsin accent. In slightly less than fifteen years, what started with clearing of land is now a compound of housing for orphans, a school providing
a Christian education to more than five hundred students a year including
about one hundred school-age orphans who live on the compound, a medical
clinic serving a broad community, and land beyond the compound growing
vegetables to feed the children.

Mama Lilly nurses malnourished, abandoned children who would have
no hope. She makes certain that the children in school are instructed in Bible
study and discipleship and vocational skills so that they can carry Christ's
message to communities beyond. Mama Lilly's hope goes beyond their compound as they hope to duplicate their model throughout South Sudan and
other African nations.

Mama Lilly's work began as she prayed, but her prayers led to her God-
modeled behavior. Her faith-actions have brought hope to the hopeless, help
to the helpless, and vibrant life in an area of the world that smells of death.
And she is multiplying her efforts by teaching others to model God's behavior.

Chances are you will not be called to leave everything behind, sell out, and take off to Africa, but you don't have to go to Africa to find seemingly impossible situations. Maybe in your circle of friends and family there's a hopeless circumstance with a friend's health or a co-worker's home life. You could model God-behavior, giving them the assurance that God is present with them in their situation and showing them the eternal perspective of life beyond and after their present circumstance.

In this chapter, you've read about the five God-models for good behavior, his holy examples that picture healthy habits, and stories of modern-day people who have chosen to live their lives based on God's way. You won't get healthy behaviors and habits by comparing yourself to others. Just look to see how God behaves, and you'll find practical ways of dealing with your daily activities and responding to your challenges

Exercises to Build and Maintain your Healthy Faith

Now that you have these images in mind, you have a better understanding of how your Heavenly Father defines good behavior. It is time again to go to work and put these principles and pictures into practice.

RECORD: List the five great acts of God in history. Also write down five brief descriptions of how God wants you to define good behavior.

REMEMBER: Memorize this scripture which reminds you of the importance of doing good acts. "Little children, let's not love with words or speech but with action." 1 John 3:18 CEB.

REFLECT: You've already read the parable about a Good Samaritan and how the way he saw himself determined his actions. Re-read the story found in Luke 1: 25-37 and see how his actions compare to God's definition of good behavior. As you read, meditate on each phrase. At the close of the story Jesus said, "Go and do the same." Ask your Heavenly Father to put someone on your mind that you might go and "do the same."

RE-EXAMINE: In this chapter, you read about people who reached out to help others who experienced darkness, suffering, loneliness, failure, and other difficulties. Think back through what they did to help and what made their actions like the acts of God? Write down some ways their behaviors were similar to Jesus' responses to people in need? Perhaps you won't have to go through such traumatic problems, but how do you think you would respond if you did?

RELATE: Talk with your trusted friend about someone you know who is experiencing some difficulty and explore different ways you could do something to help that person. Make a decision to do one deed that will be good for that person and good for you.

Pray this prayer to your Heavenly Father.

Dear Father, as I look back over my life, you have been so gracious and caring in all that you have done for me, and I am deeply grateful. When I remember the many people in pain whom I have ignored or put down, I am humiliated and ashamed. Forgive me and help me change my behavior. I want to be more like Jesus. I want to change my way of responding to people in need. I give you myself and ask you to give me courage. Turn the love of my heart into the actions of my hands. Amen.

CHAPTER 18

How do you VIEW YOUR BODY?

❀

*"Your body is the home of the Holy Spirit God gave you . . . he
lives within you? Your own body does not belong to you."*

1 Corinthians 6:19 TLB

"A healthy body attends to the pain of the weakest part."

Paul Brand, MD, Author of *Fearfully and Wonderfully Made*

Your skin covers more than two-hundred bones, six-hundred muscles,
millions of receptors and fibers, billions of nerve cells, and sixty thousand
miles of tubing through which your heart, beating more than thirty-six million times a year, is pumping blood. As complex and marvelous as all that is,
simply put, your body is your way of existing in the world God created.

How you view your body greatly determines what you do with your body.
If you have an unhealthy way of looking at what God made your body to do
or how he made it to relate, then you will continually practice bad habits, and
your faith will be frail.

God put on flesh and walked around as a body to model for us what we
are to do and how we are to relate. But even with his example, first century
Christians in Rome were having a difficult time changing their old, deeply-
ingrained, pagan habits. The Apostle Paul explained what they needed to

do about their bodies to change their unhealthy habits. *"Present your bodies a living sacrifice . . . do not be conformed to this world, but be transformed . . ."* Romans 12:1-2 NIV.

Our heavenly Father wants the best for us, so he calls us to make a radical change from the way our culture views the human body. Body mania fills our media. Beauty fanaticism fuels a multi-billion-dollar cosmetic industry. Child beauty pageants, body-enhancement plastic surgery, primetime sensual promiscuity, airbrushed body advertising, and dangerous make-over procedures all reveal a cultural form of body worship. Social media is a continual ego-gallery of selfies. You want a miserable existence? Then accept what our culture has to say about your body. If you want a wholesome, fulfilling life, then live counter-culturally with God's instructions and live out his purpose for you.

Helen was a popular high school senior and an active member of the youth group in the church where I was her pastor. Helen dreamed and talked about becoming a nurse. So it surprised no one that she went to nursing school in a nearby university after graduation. After only three weeks of classes, Helen tripped on a street curb, fell, and shattered her knee.

Unfortunately, during the reconstructive knee surgery, Helen got an infection that resisted every prescribed antibiotic. Her aggressive infection led to other surgical procedures, excruciating pain, long days in bed, and hours of rehabilitation. Helen became angry at herself for falling, irritated at her family for pushing her to get out more, and mad at God for letting this happen to her. She dropped out of college and began taking high doses of prescription drugs to relieve the agony.

Helen's pain medications had side serious effects. She experienced panic attacks, insomnia, paranoia, and auditory delusions. Even with different medicines, she developed signs of depression. Slowly Helen lost control of her life. She was no longer the vivacious, ambitious, young nursing student with high aspirations of serving others. She became a young woman who was physically weak, emotionally-depressed, socially-isolated, void of hope, and under the control of her medications.

One day when Helen was especially low, her mother called and asked me to come by for a visit. She asked me to see if I could encourage Helen and help her get back to her old self. Helen's red, tired-looking eyes, her sallow skin, and her gaunt face made her a stranger to me. During our conversation, I asked Helen to describe, as best as she could, how she felt. With a weak voice and detached demeanor, she said, "Pastor, I don't just feel sad. I feel like I am living in some really dark, empty place. I'm tired all of the time and don't want to do anything. I'm just not me." She went on to tell me that she spent many days in bed crying because she felt so guilty about falling and causing her family so much trouble and expense. She believed they were all secretly angry at her.

Weeks later after a long, restless night, Helen, weary of her life and of being a burden, swallowed the entire bottle of her pain medication. Her mother found her and could not wake her. Helen, once a vibrant young woman, had lost all hope. Her pain, depression, and bad choices had robbed her of her sense of purpose. She had lost her ability to see herself, her total self, including her body the way God saw her and wanted her to see herself.

God invested his great, creative self in this world and in the design of our bodies. Since he is the master designer who also gives us purpose, then we should look at how he wants us to view and use our bodies.

THREE WAYS GOD WANTS YOU TO VIEW YOUR BODY

1. YOUR BODY AS A GIFT OF GOD

After God separated the light from the darkness, gave the earth shape, separated the waters, crafted the plants and animals, he fashioned us. God said his creation was good. Your body is not evil. It is not your enemy. It is a gift of God.

The psalmist says in Psalm 139 that you are awesomely and wonderfully made. Think of this. When you were conceived, and your cells started rapidly multiplying as God "knit you in your mother's womb," (Psalm 139:13 NIV) each cell carried your DNA. And yet as that multiplication continued, those cells differentiated and some became kidney cells and others became brain cells and so on, and they all carried their own instruction books inside them. But even with different purposes, every single cell still carried your DNA. Your DNA, like your fingerprint, is unlike any other human being's.

If God gave that much attention to detail in the design of your body, don't you think he has great purpose for the way you live your life and use your body? He invested himself in you, sacrificed himself for you because he desires a relationship with you. He were created you to be close to him, and to serve him as you serve others. Self-indulgence will lead to misery. Grateful service will lead to healthy faith.

What Jesus, the God-man, did for others was humanly limited by his times, resources, and abilities. Like everyone, you may have certain limitations, disabilities, and barriers, but do not compare yourself and what you do to others. Your Father only wants you to use your body, your gifts, and your abilities to fulfill your purpose. When you recognize that your body is a marvelous, creative gift of God and that you are born for relationship and service, then you will develop healthy behavior.

2. Your Body as a House of God

Historically, the world's major religions have led people to view their bodies in one of three ways. First, the body is viewed as a *house of pain*. Your body, as a place of evil and suffering, is viewed as your main problem. It is your soul's prison house and is evil and a hindrance to the spiritual. People with this view spend their lives disciplining their bodies in preparation for eternity.

The second way to view the body is as a *house of pleasure*. People with this view believe their bodies belong to them and come with the right to do with their bodies whatever pleases them. The body should be kept physically healthy and beautiful because it can get you all you want – personal pleasure, power, and financial success. The sole purpose of the body is for self-gratification.

The third and Biblical view of the body is as a *house of God*. Your body has a physical and spiritual dimension. Your physical body interacts with the rest of creation and performs physical activities. Your spiritual body is the collection of all that you do, think, and feel. When you die, your flesh-and-bones body deteriorates to nothing, but your soul, your spiritual body lives on for eternity.

Our heavenly Father wants to live in your house, laugh and cry with you, play and work with you, and at all times be with you in your walking-around home—your body. Does that sound strange or at least unclear? Let me explain a little bit. The Bible says,

> *"Haven't you yet learned that your body is the home of the Holy Spirit God gave you, and that he lives within you? Your own body does not belong to you. 20 For God has bought you with a great price. So use every part of your body to give glory back to God because he owns it."* 1 Corinthians 6:19-20 (TLB)

We cannot understand how God's invisible Spirit can live in us, but you can imagine God asking you to allow him to live with you so that the two of you can have an intimate relationship and work together to help others and help you reach your potential. As God's presence takes up residence in the house he gave you, he moves around in its various rooms—your mind, heart, hands, voice, eyes, ears, and all the rest, as he helps you repurpose how you use the body he gave you. This is a uniquely Hebrew-Christian way of viewing our bodies.

3. Your Body as an Instrument of God
Your body is a gift of God, and once his Spirit comes to live in you, you are his instrument. As a spiritual being, you live in and through your physical body. Your spiritual body is more than blood, bones, muscles and organs. It is the sum of all that you do. Your body is part of God's creation which he originally intended to be absolutely good.

However, when God made the choice to give us a will, we also received the capacity to choose to do good or to do evil. Take for instance your hand. Look at it. Its anatomy is quite complex, intricate and fascinating from its bony structure and musculature to the difference in the skin on the back of your hand and in your palm. That hand you're looking at is capable of chopping down a tree with an axe or playing a sonata on the eighty-eight keys of a piano. It can slap the cheek of a child, or it can caress the arm of a dying grandmother. It can bake a cake or construct a bomb. It can perform skillful, life-giving surgery, or it can hatefully pull a trigger. God's desire is that you make good choices about how you use your body.

When you invite God's Spirit to live in you, he will help you repurpose everything you do. When you partner with him, let him work through every part of you, you will be able to have healthy behavior and a healthy faith. Your body, the house of God, becomes an instrument of his Spirit.

> *"If the Spirit of him who raised Jesus from the dead is living in you, he who raised Christ from the dead will also give life to your mortal bodies because of his Spirit who lives in you."* Romans 8:11 NIV.

> *"I have been crucified with Christ and I no longer live, but Christ lives in me. The life I now live in the body, I live by faith in the Son of God, who loved me and gave himself for me."* Galatians 2:20 NIV.

> *"Do not offer any part of yourselves to sin as an instrument for wickedness. On the contrary, offer yourselves to God as people alive from the dead, and your various parts to God as instruments for righteousness."* Romans 6:13 CEV.

You may be asking yourselves, so how can I be God's instrument? How can make certain I am an instrument of right-living and right-doing? Here are seven ways that your physical body, God's gift and where he wants to live, can be God's instrument in his world.

1. *Do what honors him.* Be the brush not the artist. Use everything you do to bring your Father honor. Show your gratitude for his gift of your body and his presence in you. Get rid of the popular belief, "It's my body; I can do what I want with it."

2. *Take less so others get more.* In everything you do, take second place. Put others first. Get rid of the popular idea that you should be first and have the most. Use all you have to help others have more. Put others and God in the spotlight.

3. *Turn it around.* When you get rewarded for anything you do, be honest. Give your Father the credit he rightly deserves. Give praise you receive to the one who made it possible for you to accomplish what you did.

4. *Give every part away.* Give every part of your body to the Lord. Picture him working through your feet, hands, mouth, eyes, ears, and every other part of you. Think for a minute about your ears, those odd-shaped protrusions whose job is to make sense of what you hear. Imagine for a moment that you're sitting in a park. Simultaneously, you can hear the traffic speeding by, the park staff mowing grass, the music on your iPod, and that annoying mosquito buzzing around your head. Amazing sounds that you differentiate without conscious thought! But are you listening to a co-worker who's depressed? Do you really hear the cry in an aging parent's voice?

   And then there are your eyes, those small, one-inch orbs that are the most complex organ in your body. You can see a fly that lands on your nose and stars that are light years away, but when you focus on Jesus Christ, your peripheral vision will change. You'll begin to see people who are longing for someone to look at them, someone who'll see their loneliness or their fear or their needs. Is there any part of you that you have not given to your Father to use?

5. *Show gratitude for your weaknesses.* Stop complaining about your weaknesses and limitations. Instead, thank him for all you have and look for ways to turn your weakness into your advantage. Do acts of kindness to show your appreciation.

6. *Focus on function not appearances.* Your Father's purpose for your body is not to be impressive to others but to be useful to them and responsible to him. Instead of comparing the various parts of your body to someone else's, use every part to serve as gifts of God.

7. *Be love incarnate.* Use your body to demonstrate God's love to others through doing whatever you can, from hugging someone who hurts to giving food to someone who is hungry. God's love is delivered through the bodies of his children.

Before you move to the next chapter, I want you to know what happened to Helen. She survived her suicidal attempt, and her family met with a professional counselor, and they put together a recovery strategy. Even when Helen didn't want to, they got her out of the house and engaged with her friends. Her church friends took turns coming to visit her, always encouraging her back into her old healthy habits of listening to her favorite inspirational music, reading her Bible, and praying with them. When she was home alone, the church prayer coordinator gave her the names of people who needed prayer.

Before long, Helen was able to look at her continued time in physical therapy for her knee as an opportunity to get closer to God and to be more thankful for her family, friends and church. Her knee never fully recovered but when it got strong enough for her to stay up on it all day, she returned to college, got her degree, and became the nurse she always wanted to be. She also took on another job for free. She leads an ongoing recovery group for people who struggle with depression.

Helen decided to use her life to honor God. She quit complaining about her situation and allowed God to repurpose her body. She thanked God that he gave her friends and healthcare workers to help her understand her medical and emotional problems, but she also believed he gave her an opportunity to use her painful experience to help others. She began using her total self as God's instrument in the lives of other people.

EXERCISES TO BUILD AND MAINTAIN YOUR HEALTHY FAITH

Hopefully you have a better understanding of how you should view your body. When you begin thinking of your body the way God does, then your behavior will change. And with an improvement in behavior, there will come an improvement in attitudes and faith development.

RECORD: List the seven ways to use your body as an instrument of God. Beside each of the seven, write down at least one thought of something you are doing in your life to be God's instrument.

REMEMBER: Memorize this scripture which reminds you that Christ dwells in you and what that means. *"I have been crucified with Christ and I no longer live, but Christ lives in me. The life I now live in the body, I live by faith in the Son of God, who loved me and gave himself for me."* Galatians 2:20 NIV.

REFLECT: Your body is a marvelous creation and gift from God. Read Psalm 139: 1-14. Take time to read this passage in several translations. As you read, meditate on each phrase.

RE-EXAMINE: In this chapter, you read about Helen. God helped Helen transform her pain into purpose when she began to change the way she looked at herself. Think back through what she did in making positive changes and how her life demonstrated the seven ways we can be God's instruments.

RELATE: Take a good long look in the mirror. Now talk with your trusted friend about what you see. Talk about how viewing your body as God's gift, as a place he wants to live, and as his instrument can change how you really view your body. Talk about which parts of your body you will let God use tomorrow to make a difference in someone's life.

Pray this prayer to your Heavenly Father.

Dear Father, as I think about this marvelous creation of my body, I stand in awe of you and your attention to detail all the way down to the sub-cellular structure. You're the one who sprinkled the Milky Way and who thought of DNA. You made us all, everyone, and yet you made no one else like me. When I think of how I have mistreated my body and missed the opportunities to use it as your instrument, I hang my head in sorrow. Forgive me, Father, and help me see myself and others the way you see us, as creatures fearfully and wonderfully made and loved by you. Amen.

CHAPTER 19

How do you OVERCOME YOUR BAD HABITS?

"Our character is basically a composite of our habits.
Because they are consistent, often unconscious patterns,
they constantly, daily, express our character."

STEPHEN COVEY, AUTHOR, THE 7 HABITS
OF HIGHLY EFFECTIVE PEOPLE

"Don't let evil get the best of you; get the best of evil by doing good."

ROMANS 12:21

WHEN I WAS A BOY growing up in church, it was not unusual to hear the preacher deliver sermons about the bad habits of drinking, smoking, gambling, and being unfaithful to your spouse. Those were the four main ones, but I am certain if street drugs and prescription drugs and addiction to pornography had been prevalent, they would have been the next three. We didn't hear much about the bad habits of being critical, or ungrateful, or selfish, or greedy.

We all have habits that keep us from being spiritually and emotionally healthy. Sometimes they are called cravings, compulsions, or even worse, addictions. It is human nature to rate these habits according to their seriousness, but the truth is this—any bad habit we have stems from a root need that is not being met. Until we uncover that need, we will not be able to correct and replace those habits with good behaviors. Here are just a few of the most common bad habits that typically lead to more serious problems:

- Lying habitually
- Talking about yourself most of the time
- Cursing as a normal part of your conversation
- Complaining continually
- Being critical of most everyone and everything
- Procrastinating incessantly
- Being late frequently
- Striving for perfection
- Being lazy
- Working fanatically
- Spending compulsively
- Eating uncontrollably
- Compulsive sexual activities
- Drinking obsessively
- Gambling continually
- Taking drugs but cannot stop
- Secretly self-medicating

No doubt, we could come up with a longer list, but you get the picture. Whatever your negative habit might be, you will find it easier to overcome if you view it as a symptom of a bigger, underlying problem that must be solved before you can have a healthy faith. Obviously, some bad habits are more destructive than others, but they all have five things in common.

First, they all produce pleasure and pain. All bad habits are seductively pleasant at first, usually beginning as an insignificant, pleasurable act. Their potential of growing into an overpowering, painful problem is deceivingly unnoticeable. These habits provide temporary good feelings, satisfaction, and relief for one of our God-given desires or else we would not continue doing them, but eventually they become our normal, and they turn on us because they are not what they seem. They become controlling, sometimes perverted substitutes for what God intended to satisfy our basic desires. A bad habit is the cuddly baby bear that can grow into a man-eating grizzly.

Second, they all seem harmless. "What's the problem in being late? Who cares if I call in sick when I'd like a day off? So what if I have to yell at the kids to get their attention? What does it hurt to get another pair of shoes? They were on sale, and I had my credit card." We have no problem justifying our habits. We deceive ourselves into thinking that they do no harm. Little lies become the cracks in the foundation of trust. Bad habits become silent cancers eating away at your soul one little nibble at a time until you have become desensitized and sick. Don't forget. Bad habits are not harmless. They will distort how you see yourself. They will alienate you from God and others. They are silent killers of healthy faith and healthy relationships.

Third, they all overpower reason. How many people have come through the door of my office over the years to talk about their destructive habits or those of someone they love? Every one of those persons agreed with me that it makes absolutely no sense to continue a harmful habit. But rational thought is rarely the path to modifying behavior. If people could change their bad habits or overcome addictions by using common sense, counselors and drug dealers would be out of business.

Fourth, they all affect others. Since God created us as relational beings and unless you are the sole human on a deserted island, what you do affects someone besides yourself. Your actions are not insular. They have tentacles that reach sometimes into places and people you never dreamed. You may think your habits and your choices are private, personal, and no one else's business, but nothing could be further from the truth. Ask a mother whose child was killed by a drunk driver. Ask a husband who no longer can trust his wife. Ask a ten-year-old boy who cowers in the corner because his daddy is angry. All bad habits hurt others, and often their pain is the deepest. The great news is that good habits affect others, too.

Fifth, they all can be overcome. There is more good news. No matter what your bad habit or addiction, you can overcome it.

Now that we understand the common threads running through every bad habit, let's look at how to change them. Remember, every bad habit is fueled by some unmet desire. God created us with desires, but his plan is that we put those desires to use in healthy ways. His way of changing a bad habit is not just to stop the habit but to replace it. Replacing old habits with new ones requires more doing than thinking.

The Apostle Paul wrote about this approach to overcoming bad habits and difficult personal challenges. He emphasized the transforming power of being in a close relationship with the Spirit of God and following the example of Jesus. For example, he said,

> "¹⁻² *So here's what I want you to do, God helping you: Take your everyday, ordinary life—your sleeping, eating, going-to-work, and walking-around life—and place it before God as an offering. Embracing what God does for you is the best thing you can do for him. Don't become so well-adjusted to your culture that you fit into it without even thinking. Instead, fix your attention on God. You'll be changed from the inside out. Readily recognize what he wants from you, and quickly respond to it. Unlike the culture around you, always dragging you down to its level of immaturity, God brings the best out of you, develops well-formed maturity in you.*"
> Romans 12:1-2 MSG.

Do you have some bad habits that need to be replaced? Let's look at seven desire-transforming activities that will turn your bad habits into healthy habits.

1. Reposition your relationship with God as your greatest desire.

Begin every day admitting to yourself and to God that you cannot handle your bad habits alone. Offer your body and your desires to God as his instruments for good. Remind yourself that God created you with great detail, and he wants what is good for you. Ask yourself this question, "Is my (name your bad habit here) really what is best for me? Is it more important than my relationship with the one who made me and is preparing my eternity?"

2. Pinpoint your God-given desire that motivates your bad habit.

Usually, the source of your unhealthy behavior is not something external that abducts you. Remember, God made you with five basic human needs/desires: safety, love, respect, purpose, and God/eternity. You develop bad habits when one of those basic needs is not met in a healthy way, and you choose to fill it with unhealthy behavior. Observe what you are doing when you act out your bad habit. Of the five basic desires God has given you, which desire is not being met? Until you pinpoint that unmet need, you will not make better choices.

3. Look at your bad habits and behaviors as opportunities.

Your desires are like steam. They are looking for somewhere to go to find satisfaction. If you do not direct your desires, someone or something else will. Every problem or challenge you face is an opportunity for you to see God at work in you. Every bad habit is a chance for you to partner with God in doing something that is far more satisfying and lasting.

4. Make your problem a project, and work your desire-transforming plan.

The main reason we call ongoing behaviors *habits* is that they are so predictable. You do them more in certain situations and around certain people. Be attentive to the times, circumstances, and people you are around when you most often engage in your bad habit.

The Bible says, *"Keep a cool head. Stay alert. The Devil is poised to pounce, and would like nothing better than to catch you napping. Keep your guard up."* James 5:8-9 MSG.

Do not wait for your toxic behaviors to do their damage. Expect them. Keep an eye out for them. Be alert about their every move. Breaking bad habits requires more than just being aware of them and telling yourself to stop them. That's like telling a child to stop liking candy. You must make a plan to replace your patterns, and stick to your plan.

5. Now that you've named it and have a plan for overcoming it, don't try to hide it from God and others.

Just as living in denial about a disease keeps you from getting the healing help you need, hiding your bad habits makes them harder to overcome. If you want to transform your bad habits into healthy ones, you must do it God's way, the relational way. Pride says, "I don't need anyone. I can do this alone." God says, *"Two can accomplish more than twice as much as one, for the results can be much better. If one falls, the other pulls him up, but if a man falls when he is alone, he's in trouble."* Ecclesiastes 4:9-10 TLB.

We need a family of faith, a community of support, people we can lean on when we are weak and tempted. The most successful plans that help people break bad habits are those that involve building close, personal relationships with trusted friends who have already experienced the transforming power of Jesus and of living life God's way.

6. Give your new behaviors time to become life-building habits.

Deep, meaningful, and lasting transformations take time. Since habits are behaviors that have been repeated long enough that they have become normal, developing a new, healthy normal will also take time. You will need to set short and long-term goals and activities that will allow your new healthy habits time to become automatic ones. Share those plans and goals with a trusted friend.

7. TEACH YOUR TRANSFORMATION TO SOMEONE ELSE.

Nothing will solidify your new, healthy habits like teaching what you have learned and practiced to someone else. When you share your struggles, victories, and relationship with your Lord, every part of you will be strengthened, and you will be encouraging someone else to a life of freedom and wholeness.

There are several successful programs using similar principles for helping people overcome bad habits and addictions. Each one of those programs, just like these seven desire-transforming steps I've listed, require you to do something. Following these principles will put you well on your way to doing something about your behaviors and habits that are robbing you of a peaceful life and a healthy faith.

In the Old Testament, we see how Moses had to flee Egypt out of fear for his life. God had Moses spend the next forty years in Midian, part of Saudi Arabia's desert region. Moses had old pagan habits that needed transformation. God wanted him fully prepared for his return to Egypt and for all that would be required of him as God's chosen leader for his people. Moses developed some new healthy habits in his relationship with his Heavenly Father, habits that readied him to pick up his staff, to face evil adversaries, and lead to his wayward people through the Exodus, one of God's greatest acts in history.

In the New Testament, we see that Jesus recognized the importance of doing and becoming. We don't see Jesus confining himself to the synagogue, but we see him living out his good habits every day. He rose early and withdrew from the others to a quiet place to start his day with his Father. Then, he was out and about doing, and he taught his disciples to do the same. When he called them from their fishing nets to a new life, he didn't say to them, "Come sit at my feet and listen to what I say." Instead, he told them, "Come, follow me." He wanted them to do what he did, taking on his habits. Good faith-building behaviors and habits are critical to the kind of life you want and God wants you to have.

Exercises to Build and Maintain your Healthy Faith

Breaking old habits can be done but not without replacing them with new and better habits. Work through these exercises, trying as best you can to be honest with yourself about your behaviors.

RECORD: List the five things that all habits have in common. Which one of those characteristics do you have the most trouble believing?

REMEMBER: God wants you to live a fulfilling life, one of joy and peace no matter your circumstances. In John's Gospel, Jesus is speaking to the Pharisees and to the people and says of himself, *"I am the light of the world. Whoever follows me will never walk in darkness, but will have the light of life."*

John 8:12 NIV. Meditate on what it means in your life to follow Christ.

REFLECT: In looking at John 8:12, think about the difference between living in the light of God's presence and living in darkness. What real difference does God's light make in the world? What would the world be like if we took away God's presence? How would your life be different?

RE-EXAMINE: In this chapter, there are seven activities to do if you truly want to transform a habit or behavior. List those, and then think of one habit that you need to change. Based on these transforming activities, come up with a plan for changing that one behavior.

RELATE: Remember, we need community and relationship. That's why it is important for you to get involved in a Bible-centered church, a family of faith. Share your plan for changing one of your behaviors with your trusted friend. Talk to that person about your behavior, why it needs changing, and how you plan to make the change. Ask him or her to hold you accountable for sticking to your plan.

Pray this prayer to your Heavenly Father.

Dear Father, as I think about how I have squandered my time and what my habits are, I come asking for help to see myself honestly. Help me to put you and your ways above everything else in my life. Please let your Spirit prick my conscience when I fall into my old ways and habits. Father, I want to do better, but I need your help. Amen.

CHAPTER 20

How do you TRANSFORM YOUR TROUBLES?

"When it is dark enough, you can see the stars."

RALPH WALDO EMERSON, AMERICAN ESSAYIST

*"Watch what God does, and then you do it, like children who
learn proper behavior from their parents. Mostly what God does
is love you. Keep company with him and learn a life of love."*

EPHESIANS 5:1-2

HAVE YOU EVER MET JANICE? Sure you have. You may know her by a different name, but you will recognize her. When I met Janice, she was a receptionist with a big smiling façade, but underneath was an angry, critical heart. On a beautiful, sunny day, Janice complained that it was just too hot and too bright. On a rainy, cool day, she grumbled about the cold and dreary weather.

Every time I had a meeting where she worked, I engaged her in conversation and tried to spend a few minutes encouraging her. No matter how the conversation went, Janice was always able to find something she disliked and someone she detested. Talking negatively about family and company problems seemed to bring her pleasure, and she never figured out why people did

222

not enjoy being around her. Over the years, I noticed that her favorite phrase was, "I just hate that." Somewhere along the way, Janice had been wounded, her bitterness always oozing so that not even her big smile could hide it.

Then there's Stephen, my friend who gradually lost his eye sight as a child, becoming a legally-blind adult. Stephen could have decided to sit home, listen to radio or television, and complain, but he made a different choice. Like Janice, Stephen had a big smile, too, a real one and a laugh that would fill up a room. His laughter certainly filled many an elevator.

Stephen's favorite thing to do was to get on an elevator filled with people, tap his cane on the floor three times, and just start laughing. Although he couldn't see their startled faces, he knew they were staring; but after one of his wisecracks, his invitation to laugh had been accepted. An elevator full of people joined him for no reason other than it simply felt good. Stephen just had a way about him that drew people to him, especially his blind students. And with extremely limited vision, Stephen picked up a camera and took stunning black and white photographs of landscapes. He chose to let his telephoto lens become his eyes, and his hobby brought so many people pleasure.

We all have a *way* about us. Both Janice and Stephen had their share of troubles, but they responded differently, and their responses shaped their lives and their relationships. How you respond to your problems is not determined by your external circumstances. Your response is determined by your internal disposition or your way.

Are you like Janice? Perhaps you've been wounded, and your anger and bitterness just seep out all over those around you. Are you more like Stephen, accepting of your situation, living out your purpose in it, and wanting to spread a bit of joy? Or maybe you're somewhere in between and you're working on it.

Just remember, troubles do not make you happy or angry any more than they make your faith stronger or weaker, bitter or better, healthier or unhealthier. How you react from the inside out to those troubles is the determining factor and becomes the portrait of your faith's health. Since living a life of joy and peace, regardless of circumstances, is an "inside job," what you think and what you feel will need to be transformed. Keep these two things in mind:

1. *Stop being used by your troubles.* Just as allowing another person to dictate and control your behavior is unhealthy, so is allowing your problems to do the same. You may have no control over your circumstances, but you do have control over your responses. Your feelings will follow your focus. Good feelings follow good behavior. Regularly responding to troubles in positive, constructive, and gracious ways will always generate strong feelings of satisfaction that will motivate you to keep repeating those habits. Your faith will grow when you stop letting your troubles use you and start using them as opportunities to be the instrument of God.

2. *You will never make it alone.* In transforming your responses to your troubles, you need help because it's an inside-out transformation. Jesus' way must become your way. As you deepen your loving relationship with Jesus, whose Spirit wants to live in you and work through your body, you must let him live through you as you respond to your problems. He will help you replace pride with humility. You will experience your troubles through transformed eyes and ears. You can begin to see them, as real and painful as they are, as opportunities to see God at work in the situation and in you. What you say in response to your problems will be what you and Jesus choose to say together through your voice.

This is learned behavior, and with God's help, it will gradually become your new normal. You will no longer respond to troubles with anger, resentment, and confusion because your dominant desire will be to stay close to your loving God and to focus on his way.

Joyce was my friend. She was a committed Christian wife, mother, and educator who found herself in almost Job-like circumstances. Her daughter, a nurse, was infected with the HIV virus in a blood transfusion at the birth of her first child. Before the virus was identified, a second child was born. Over a period of a few years, Joyce dealt with the deaths of her daughter, two grandsons, and then the unexpected death of her husband, a fine Christian and denominational leader. Her grief was at times overwhelming. And as she aged with fragile health, I sat at her bedside multiple times, praying with her, listening to her heart.

There are so many Janices and Joyces who are looking for answers, trying to make sense of their suffering. As their problems became their focus, their behaviors followed. All through this book, I have held up Jesus as our model. Let's look at how Jesus, the God-man, responded to adversity. Let's examine how Jesus looked at problems and then some of his ways in dealing with problems.

First, and foremost, Jesus trusted his Father—his father's way. Jesus knew that his human feelings could and would change, but his Father's character, his unfailing love, and his purpose would never change.

The Apostle Paul found himself writing to the Roman Christians who were being persecuted in the first century. They were experiencing horrible harassment and devastating personal losses. Paul reminded them and us, *"We know that God is always at work for the good of everyone who loves him. They are the ones God has chosen for his purpose."* Romans 8:28 CEV.

When troubles come, and they will, focus on these facts—the facts of God's character.

1. Respond to the fact of *God's presence*, not just your feelings.

The Bible says, "We know that *God is* always at work." Usually we are not aware that we are breathing life-giving air, but it is real just the same. The Spirit of our life-giving God is always present even when we're not aware. Jesus knew that fact, so he focused on being one with his Father. Unless you stay close to him and partner with him in all you do, you will tend to follow your emotions rather than God's presence. Your troubles are real and painful, but his presence is also real and more powerful than your feelings. Your troubles are temporary and your emotions will change with the wind, but God's presence is eternal. You will not understand everything that happens in your life, but you can trust the fact that God is all-loving, all-powerful, all-knowing, and always present.

2. Respond to the fact of *God's plan*, not just your problems.

The Bible says, "God is always *at work.*" Jesus knew God was always actively working in his life and in all of his creation. So when he prayed in the Garden of Gethsemane before he was crucified, he trusted his father's will, God's purpose for his life. God is always working his plans for your life, too. He is never on vacation or unconcerned. Much of the time, you cannot see his invisible hand working behind the scenes. If you run into big bumps, shocking crashes, and even run off the road into the wilderness, remember, just because you cannot see the road or feel its peaceful way, you can know for a fact that God is at work. He may be clearing a new path, or creating a place for you to land, or holding your hand across the wilderness. It matters not, he is at work.

3. Respond to the fact of *God's blessings* not just to your circumstances.

The Bible says, "God is always at work *for the good.*" He sees the big picture and all of time is spread out before him. God sees more than the present moment. Jesus knew that his present suffering meant more than his personal pain. He was carrying out God's plan for his life and for the world. Your Father knows and shares your pain. There is nothing so horrible that God cannot bring some good out of it. There is no place so dark that he cannot bring light. Look at your pain as having meaning and purpose. You will find the good he is working through your troubles.

4. Respond to the fact of *God's love* not just to your loss.

God loves you even when he seems silent. Sometimes he speaks most clearly through silence and suffering to those he loves most. The scripture tells us that he works "for the good of *everyone who loves him.*" Never look at your pain or misfortune as God turning his back on you. Remember, he's the one who sacrificed himself for you so that you never have to know death. You can live eternally in his presence. Keep your mental eye on the cross, not just on your loss.

5. Respond to the fact of *God's call* and not just to your confusion.

God chose you to serve him and his children. As a child of God, you are on a holy mission to represent your Heavenly Father. When Jesus faced adversities, he stayed true to his mission, his primary purpose in life, the fact of God's call. The scripture tells us that God's children are "the ones *God has chosen for his purpose.*"

When faced with troubles, Jesus focused on the fact of God's love, power, knowledge, and presence. With that kind of focus, Jesus did not respond to adversity the way the world does. His response was counter-cultural. He didn't live by the "eye for an eye" philosophy; instead, he "turned the other cheek." What Jesus taught turned the world upside down, and his followers became known as people of the way, a new way of living. You want an inside-out transformation, then let's look at the Jesus-way, the extraordinary, above-the-normal way.

Mother Teresa summarized Jesus' revolutionary approaches to responding to life's difficulties and made them her ways of ministering in one of the world's most challenging places. Her memorable admonition, *Do it anyway,* was a synopsis of her nine classic, Jesus-like ways to respond to life's adversities. As a daily reminder, she wrote this list on the wall of her orphanage in Calcutta, India where she cared for some of the poorest people on earth.

1. People are often unreasonable, irrational, and self-centered. Forgive them anyway.
2. If you are kind, people may accuse you of selfish, ulterior motives. Be kind anyway.
3. If you are successful, you will win some unfaithful friends and some genuine enemies. Succeed anyway.
4. If you are honest and sincere people may deceive you. Be honest and sincere anyway.
5. What you spend years creating, others could destroy overnight. Create anyway.
6. If you find serenity and happiness, some may be jealous. Be happy anyway.

7. The good you do today, will often be forgotten. Do good anyway.
8. Give the best you have, and it will never be enough. Give your best anyway.
9. In the final analysis, it is between you and God. It was never between you and them anyway.

I know that when you read these things, you may be thinking this is too hard, I'm no Mother Teresa, and I'll never be able to get there. But this IS the Jesus-way, and with his help, you can do it. Let me tell you about someone who did.

Remember Joyce, the Christian woman who lost her daughter and grandsons to AIDS, her husband to an unexpected heart attack, and then had to deal with her own frail health? I marveled at her through the years as she was kicked down time after time. But each time, she got up, and in her quiet way, she responded like Jesus did. She and her daughter raised the funds to purchase a house where AIDS victims whose families had turned them away could come and receive care. Joyce started a ministry to seriously ill children who were hospitalized. She wrote children's books designed to help children deal with their grief. Joyce turned her problems into projects. She wanted her adversity to have purpose, and with God's help, Joyce, like Mother Teresa, did it anyway.

God never wants you to discard your pain or discount its purpose in your life. He wants you to deal with it in a healthy way, the Jesus-way. And the best news is that he is always present to work alongside and inside you.

EXERCISES TO BUILD AND MAINTAIN YOUR HEALTHY FAITH

The "inside job" of transforming how you deal with adversity is hard work that doesn't come naturally. Begin that work as you work through these exercises.

RECORD: Remember, it's always safer to trust God's character than it is to trust your own emotions. List the five God-facts you must keep in mind when you are experiencing troubling circumstances.

REMEMBER: Your pain does not mean that God has abandoned you. Memorize this scripture which will remind you that God is always present and he is always working things for good for his children. You might be surprised at how this scripture might be just what a hurting friend needs to hear. *"We know that God is always at work for the good of everyone who loves him. They are the ones God has chosen for his purpose."* Romans 8:28 CEV.

REFLECT: Truly reflect here over something that has happened in your life, something that brought you pain. Write it down. Now think about how God brought something good out of that situation. Write that down underneath it. Keep that in a safe place as a reminder to you that God is at work in your life.

RE-EXAMINE: Maybe you are experiencing some form of adversity right now. Perhaps it is a health issue, or a rebellious child, or a problem on the job, or some other significant loss. And if you're not, you're living in what I call the "in-between" times, and you can use your imagination. Look at the five God-fact characteristics, and evaluate how you are doing as you face this one adversity.

RELATE: Unless you live in a bubble, there is someone in your family or in your circle of friends who is hurting right now. Go to that person, and sit down, and talk with him or her. Share something you learned in this chapter that might help them deal better with their problems.

Pray this prayer to your Heavenly Father.

Dear Father, I know that you're no stranger to pain and problems. Help me to trust you and your ways when I cannot see my own way. Help me not to react with anger and bitterness, but to respond with humility and grace. Help me not to trust my feelings, but to do it anyway. Amen.

CHAPTER 21

How do you GET IN ON WHAT GOD IS DOING?

"We do not remember days, we remember moments."

CESARE PAVESE, ITALIAN POET, NOVELIST

"We throw open our doors to God and discover at the same moment that he has already thrown open his door to us".

EPHESIANS 5:1 ROMANS 5:1 MSG

ON A COLD FEBRUARY MORNING, Will had no idea when he picked up his fare at the Washington National Airport that he was in for a divine appointment. Neither did I, but I was Will's fare, and God showed up. As was my custom with all cab drivers, I learned his name and asked where he grew up and about his family. We had barely made it out of the airport when Will began his saga. I learned about his hardships, his finances, his three children, and about his wife who wanted a divorce. I had little opportunity to speak, but that wasn't my assignment. I was to listen.

Twenty minutes later, Will parked curbside at my destination. I paid him his fare and asked him if I could sit there for a moment and pray for him. I did my talking to God on Will's behalf. When I finished, Will turned to face me in the backseat. Tears ran down his cheeks, and he said. "No one has ever prayed for me in my whole life." I handed him my business card and asked him to give me a call or drop me a note sometime to let me know how he was doing.

Three months later, I got a letter from Will. He and his wife were back together, still struggling, but their whole family was attending church for the first time in years, and they were seeing a counselor at the church. Neither Will nor I knew that one simple act would become a life-defining moment for him. God had arranged a holy moment in time for one simple prayer.

God is always at work, and he wants you to join him. In Step Four of this book, I've talked about doing and developing healthy habits that will lead to a healthy faith. The last four chapters were more about defining, getting rid of unhealthy behaviors, and being on the defensive, but it's time now to go on the offensive. Let's get in on what God is doing. It's all about growing good habits.

Stop doing and start doing. People often stop bad habits but quickly fall back in to them because they choose the wrong new activities to replace the old ones. Hopefully, you have a better handle on what you should "stop doing," but you may not know what to "start doing." When there are so many choices, how can you know what you should do?

I killed too many roses until I learned the secret. For years I enjoyed planting and growing beautiful roses in my backyard. With great anticipation when I first got started, I carefully chose the plants according to color and enthusiastically, but unknowingly, planted those young, tender shoots in a way that practically assured their quick death. I just dug a hole in the existing, polluted soil and could not understand why my new roses kept getting sick and dying.

Later I learned that the best way to insure healthy growth was to amend the soil and create a healthy environment where roses could thrive. By planting them in the right soil, I had some of the healthiest and most beautiful roses you can imagine.

Do you want to get in on what God is doing and experience some life-defining moments with him? Then just like I had to make some choices and some changes in my rose garden to grow beautiful blossoms, you'll have to decide where to best plant your time, personality, and experiences to grow your new habits. Look for God's rich, fertile, healthy soil to get started. Be on the lookout for people already getting in on what God is doing. Watch for how God's spirit is already working, moving, and growing in them.

When you recognize something that his Spirit is doing or some door he is opening, stop right there and begin digging, planting, and thriving. As you see progress, your mind and heart will say to your hands and feet, "God is in this. Look what he is doing. I'll follow his lead." That is where you will have what I like to call your life-defining moments with God.

What are life-defining moments with God? Any time the Spirit of God opens a door of opportunity for you, and you step out on faith and get involved in what he is doing, that will become a life-defining moment for you. And because God is always at work, sometimes your simple acts of obedience might become someone else's life-defining moment.

So where are you most likely to see God opening doors for these moments that can re-shape your life? Over the years, I have studied what the people in the Bible and other spiritual leaders were doing when they had some life-defining moments. I concluded that there are at least three important elements—doing small acts of kindness, being obedient, and involving others.

1. Daily do Small Acts of Kindness in Jesus' Name.

Most big changes start small, and the same is true with your habits. You remember, Jesus is our model, and the Bible writers tell us that Jesus' daily routine was filled with small acts of kindness. In Acts 10:38, Paul reminds us that Jesus went around doing good. It is recorded how Jesus gave water to a thirsty woman, food to a hungry man, and encouragement to an outcast woman. These kinds of things were his habits.

Want to have healthy habits? Do what Jesus did. You were designed to do just that. *"He (God) creates each of us . . . to join him in the work he does, the good work he has gotten ready for us to do."* Ephesians 2:10 MSG.

With Jesus as our model, we know we are to join him in his work in the world. But why begin with small acts of kindness? There may be more, but here are eight reasons these acts are important.

Eight Reasons Why Small Spiritual Acts of Kindness are Important

1. They give God an opportunity to work through you.
2. They give you an opportunity to see God working.
3. They are easy for anyone to do.
4. They provide instant reward and motivation.
5. They can touch the heart of the most hardhearted.
6. They develop expectant eyes for seeing God at work.
7. They produce some unexpected defining moments.
8. They open some doors to additional opportunities.

So you may be asking yourself what you could do to get started. Below are some examples of small spiritual acts of kindness. Think about your interests, gifts and abilities and where you find yourself. These examples can and should be altered to fit your particular situation. Always remember, you are doing this in Jesus' name. Make certain you remind the one whose life you're touching with this act of kindness that God loves him, is with him, and that you are praying for him.

*   *Write a note.* Find a single mom who could use some encouragement. Write a note that says something like, "You are doing such a good job as a mother. I am so proud of your child, and I thank God for you."
*   *Use time that is otherwise wasted.* While you are waiting in line or in an elevator, say to the person next to you, "Have a good day, and God bless you in all you do today."
*   *Reach out to someone who doesn't expect it.* Find someone at work who might be going through a hard time, and give him or her a hug while saying, "Just wanted you to know that I am praying for you."

- *Give a small gift.* Look for someone who has failed at something and give him penny. Ask him to place it where he can see it throughout the day and say, "Every time you see that penny, let it remind you that I love you, God loves you, and I appreciate all you have meant to me over the years."
- *Take one flower.* Find someone who is lonely and take her one single rose or other flower. Ask her, "Every time you see this flower, will you remember that I love you, God loves you, and he is with you all the time?"
- *Deliver food to someone in need.*
- *Join a team that's repairing a poor family's house.*
- *Have a lonely soldier over for a meal.*
- *Call a lonely shut-in.*
- *Bring coffee to someone at the office that no one else likes.*
- *Call or write a teacher who made an impression your life.*
- *Give away some clothing or something else you have.*
- *Give a homeless person something to eat. Say a brief prayer.*
- *Mentor a child or teen and let them know God loves them.*
- *Offer to baby-sit for a single mom.*
- *Offer to pick up groceries for an elderly person.*
- *Out of the blue, send flowers to a friend.*
- *Pass along an encouraging spiritual book with a note.*
- *Read to someone who is lonely and needs to hear a human voice.*
- *Write a commendation letter to the boss of someone who went the extra-mile to serve or help you.*

Let me tell you how June Cheek got started. Now, June is my friend, and she may be short, but she's never short on energy and joy. Finding herself re-tired, she was looking and listening for something to do with her time when she learned about a ministry that her church supported. This ministry fed and mentored families living in poverty in a five-county area of the Texas Hill Country. It wasn't long before June was volunteering one day a week—long hours in a warehouse, packing up boxes of food and clothes to be delivered to these families in need. June sensed she was fulfilling her purpose in this ministry that started with packing one box of food.

Be like June, and get started doing something. Start out with at least one act of kindness each week, and you might even start with one a day. Just keep your eyes and ears alert to whom and what God places in your path. You never know which deed might turn into a long-term project that will shape your behavior and determine how you spend your time. God can turn some of your small spiritual acts of kindness into important good habits.

2. Go Through the Doors God Opens.

I grew up in a household with four kids—two girls and two boys. Both of my parents worked and believed in sharing the household chores. Although the family roles were a bit more defined during my growing up years, my parents gave each of us specific jobs that suited our abilities.

God is that way with his children. He has a specific assignment for each of his children at different times in their lives. He will never ask you to do something that he does not equip you to do.

Jesus saw his main purpose in life was to honor his Father by doing what God had assigned him to do. *"I glorified you on earth by completing down to the last detail what you assigned me to do."* John 17:4 MSG. No one else could do what Jesus did, and because you are a unique child of God, no one can do exactly what you can do.

Jesus talked to his Heavenly Father about his followers and how he was leaving them with a mission or ministry to do. *"They are no more defined by the world than I am defined by the world. . . . In the same way that you gave me a mission in the world, I give them a mission in the world."* John 17:18 MSG.

God has an assignment for you to do, and he gives you those opportunities to do them. When you go through a door he opens for you and begin serving his children, you have become a minister. The word minister comes from the Greek word that means, "one who serves others." When you let Jesus live through you, you are doing a ministry, a service for God, and you are a minister, a servant of God, carrying out your God-given mission.

Sometimes I think about the opportunities I have missed that God intended for me. I think about what would have happened to Will, the cab driver, if I hadn't stopped to pray for him. I'm not so naïve to think that God's work wouldn't get done if I don't do it. But when I don't step through the doors of opportunities to serve, then God has to tap someone else on the shoulder to do my part. I've disappointed him by not allowing him to use me, and I've missed the greatest blessing of having done one of the assignments God had for me.

Remember my friend June? Her one-day-a-week at the warehouse turned into three and sometimes four. This went on for quite a while until her knees just gave out, and she could no longer physically do the packing. What had started out as a simple act had grown into a significant part of her life and her habits over time, and now she could no longer physically continue her volunteering. But June began praying, and it wasn't long before one of the staff approached June about starting a new work. She asked June to think about how to acknowledge the birthdays of the children in these impoverished families.

June took that on, and it wasn't long before she had turned an area of her house into a mini-warehouse for birthday bags, curly ribbons, birthday cards, cake mixes, icing canisters, birthday candles, and small gift items. She was providing a birthday bag for over five hundred children a year. The making of those bags and stories that came back to her fueled her passion for her ministry—stories like the fifteen-year-old girl who received her birthday bag but had no working oven for her mother to bake her cake. She called her grandmother and asked if they could come to her home to use her oven. The young girl's mother and grandmother had not spoken for two years, but June's birthday bag brought them together and put them back on the road to forgiveness and relationship.

June started out packing boxes of food but had to quit, but when God opened another door, she walked through it and started a ministry that has touched the lives of hundreds of children. If you met June, you wouldn't be long into conversation with her before you'd hear her stories of these children and how God has blessed her through this ministry.

You may not be retired like June, but maybe you have just an hour or two a week for ministry. Look for God's open doors – they are always opportunities to serve others. Don't miss the assignments God has just for you, and don't miss the blessings that come with them either.

3. Multiply your Ministry by Involving others.

Look to Jesus once again. Jesus invested himself in his followers. He multiplied his life and ministry in the lives of others. He is still doing that, and he can use you to help.

As your ministry becomes your heart, your habit, and your lifestyle, engage others. Tell them about it. Share some of the special stories, those life-defining moments that came about as you ministered. If you need help, or if God shows you ways that your ministry could grow or expand, ask others to help you. As you engage others, you are inspiring them to start with small acts of kindness and find their own ways to serve and minister. You are becoming a multiplier, and you are increasing God's Kingdom on earth.

That's what June did. She went to local businesses and asked for help in providing cake mixes and icing. Other merchants helped by giving her a discount on items she purchased. She went to her church and asked for some assistance in being able to purchase items to go in the birthday bags. Her church started a special offering called the "Noisy" offering where church members were asked to bring their jars of change or empty the change in their pockets on the Sunday when this offering was collected. That change bought Bibles or wooden crosses on leather strings or some other gift to go in birthday bags.

Then God really surprised June with a whole new idea about the birthday cards. It came about when a Faith-in-Action Saturday, a church event, was suddenly rained out. But June had an idea. She quickly assembled some paper and craft supplies. The ladies who showed up thinking they would be doing some painting and yard work for the church's elderly neighbors found themselves sitting around tables making handmade birthday cards for children they would never meet. Out of that one Saturday rain-out, a group of retired teachers made a decision to meet monthly at June's house to make the birthday cards she needed for the month.

Do you see how all this works? Kids receiving birthday bags, merchants participating and feeling good about their involvement in the community, her church giving funds, and now a group of retirees who enjoy the fellowship gathering monthly to make cards. All of this because June engaged them. She gave them opportunities of service.

And June's face brightens as she talks about this ministry. She loves telling about filling her grocery cart with fifty boxes of cake mix and tubs of icing and heading toward the checkout lane. She says it never fails that someone makes a wisecrack, and she gets to tell them about the birthday bags and the larger ministry this organization does to meet the needs of impoverished families in her community.

The birthday bags don't go with just birthday wishes. June finds creative ways to let these children know they are special to God and that Jesus loves them. June is a multiplier and an investor, and only God can calculate the exponential returns of what she is doing.

Start with simple acts of kindness in Jesus' name. Then watch to see how God opens other doors for you to serve and engage others. Over time, not only are you experiencing life-defining moments and building good habits for developing your own healthy faith, but you are fulfilling your God-given purpose and serving his children.

EXERCISES TO BUILD AND MAINTAIN YOUR HEALTHY FAITH

It's time to get started and time to get busy. God has expectations of you, a job designed just for you and the ways he has equipped you.

RECORD: Look back at the list of examples of small spiritual acts of kindness that you can do in Jesus' name. Write a few of them down that interest you, or perhaps you've come up with some others that suit you and your personality better. Put that list in your Bible where you can see it every morning in your quiet time.

REMEMBER: Memorize Ephesians 2:10 from The Message. *"God creates each of us … to join him in the work he does, the good work he has gotten ready for us to do."* You might substitute the word "me" for "us" in this passage.

REFLECT: Ephesians 2:10 reminds you that God has a purpose for you, a job for you to do. Meditate on that phrase *"to join him in the work he does."* What does that mean to you? What work do you see God doing? What door is he opening for you and inviting you to come through where you can join him?

RE-EXAMINE: Think back over the last seven days. Can you think of an opportunity to do a small act of kindness in Jesus' name that you just missed? Maybe you were too busy, or maybe you were uncertain as to how to handle it. How do you think that missed opportunity might have affected someone else? How might that missed opportunity have affected you?

RELATE: Make a commitment to do at least three small acts of kindness in Jesus' name in the next week. You might look back over the list you made, but God might surprise you with opportunities that you have never considered. Share your commitment with a trusted friend, and ask that friend to hold you accountable for doing those deeds. Then share with your friend what happened when you did them and how God surprised you.

Pray this prayer to your Heavenly Father.

Dear Father, I know that you're at work in the world. I understand that you made me with a purpose and you invite me to join you in your work. Help me daily to see what that work is. Help me to be sensitive in looking around for opportunities. And then, Lord, when I see them, help me to be bold enough to walk through the doors you open for me. Amen.

Revitalize Your Lifestyle

Two Musts to Maintain Your New Way

"You can revitalize your wilted faith."

BILLY GRAHAM, INTERNATIONAL EVANGELIST

"Jesus said to him, "I am the way, the truth, and the life."

JOHN 14:6 NIV

*"Take on an entirely new way of life—a God-fashioned life,
a life renewed from the inside and working itself into your
conduct as God accurately reproduces his character in you."*

EPHESIANS 4:24 MSG

CARL WAS VERY SICK, AND he knew it. For a few months he had been experiencing gastro-intestinal problems. Even with an increase in his appetite, he was losing weight. Then he lost his appetite, and the weakness, sickness, and the pain in his abdomen set in. Soon after came the flu-like symptoms that rendered him unable to get out of bed. Carl's doctor admitted him into the hospital, and I was in Carl's room when his doctor came in with the test results.

Carl was expecting the worst, and he wanted straight answers. "Doctor, I want the truth, no soft-soaping and coddling me. I want the straight-up truth."

The doctor responded, "The straight-up truth is that you have an intestinal parasite that has caused all this trouble. We'll be giving you an anti-parasitic drug to kill the parasites, then we'll put you on a nutrient program to rebuild your strength. You'll be as good as new in a few weeks."

With the fear of life-robbing cancer gone, Carl took the medicine, his intra-venous nutrients, and was out of the hospital continuing his regimen at home in just a couple of days. In a few weeks, Carl looked like the healthy Carl I had known before, with his weight back and some color in his ruddy cheeks. He was working and returned to the church basketball league. His health was restored, and he was revitalized.

Doctor, I want the truth. Over the years, I have found that people faced with health or relationship problems, no matter how serious, want to be told the truth. They don't want the news sugar coated or minimized. They want to know two things, what their problems are and how they can be fixed.

From the beginning of this book, I told you that I would be honest with you about faith issues, and that is what I must do now. Carl was sick, he was diagnosed, he took his medicine, and he was fixed. It's not quite that simple and straightforward with your faith. Your deep-seated old lifestyle got you where you are today, and just reading this book and doing a few exercises over a short time will not change all that history, or keep your faith effective and healthy.

Faith is a relationship, an ever evolving relationship. Faith is not just something you have, it is something you do. You now have some good, foundational information upon which you can build a life-long healthy faith, but you know that there is a big divide between knowing and continually doing what you know.

I heard a different tone in Dr. Hamilton's usually-composed, just-the-facts voice that night she called me at home well past bedtime. Although I had performed Marion and Jordan's wedding eight years before and had numerous conversations since then, that night I didn't recognize the voice from her heavy sobs.

Their wedding was the social event of the year in our city. Marion was a respected cardiologist, and Jordan an environmental engineer with a PhD in geology. They were the complete package—highly educated, financially successful, magazine-page attractive, active church members, physically fit, owned a large home near the country club, and had twin girls as beautiful and bright as their mother. By our culture's standards, this couple could have been the poster-couple for the model marriage. That picture faded when I got that late night call.

Jordan wanted a divorce. When Marion came for help, she said they had started out so intimate, open, caring, and close. They made time for each other, but over time with changes that come in everyday living, their relationship changed and their closeness, openness, and caring had evolved into distance, discontent, and coldness. When they were together, it seemed like all they did was argue. Their once happy and healthy marriage was in serious trouble. Their problems didn't stem from lack of knowing, they stemmed from lack of doing. Their relationship had deteriorated and needed revitalizing if they were going to make it.

Did you know that science tells us that it is normal for a healthy body to constantly rebuild, regenerate, restore, or revitalize old cells in response to injury or natural deterioration? God made us so that even the cells in our bodies naturally deteriorate and must be revitalized. To *revitalize* means to bring back life (vital) to something that is dying or failing.

Like our bodies' cells, our relationships and faith must continually be revitalized to stay alive. It is a never ending process. With all you have done so far in reading this book and doing the exercises, you are probably feeling pretty proud of your progress, and you should. I am also proud of you because few people are willing to do the work you have already done, but be careful because you have only just begun.

Building and maintaining a healthy body requires living a healthy lifestyle, and building and maintaining a healthy faith requires a healthy faithstyle. Don't do like those who read books on dieting and work hard to lose weight but gain it all back because they never change their lifestyle. They have new knowledge, new exercises, and new good feelings about their weight loss, but their old lifestyles do not support their new desire for a healthy body, so they slowly get pulled back into their old habits.

You can make this new way a lifestyle instead of a brief course. With so many challenging conditions and the negative parts of your past working against you, you could have quit long before now. So, I commend you for faithfully continuing to peddle up the hill of faith. You are about to begin a dangerous turn in your faith-journey where many drop out. Don't think of this faith development plan as a course you are taking, or a retreat you went on. Think of it as a new way or lifestyle you are constructing that will continually support and revitalize your healthy faith for the long haul.

Two essential priorities. Because of your new approach to this lifestyle of faith, you will now face many new challenges and alternatives that will force you to decide on your priorities. If you choose the wrong priorities, your faith with fail. That's why this last step focuses on helping you choose healthy priorities.

In the next three chapters you will learn the elements of a strategic lifestyle plan and how to develop you personal plan that will keep your faith and relationships effective and healthy the rest of your life. How do you establish those critical priorities and follow them? Let's go to work.

CHAPTER 22

How do you CREATE a Strategic Lifestyle Plan?

☙

"Your mission statement becomes your constitution, the solid expression of your vision and values. It becomes the criterion by which you measure everything else in your life."

STEPHEN COVEY, AUTHOR

"In the same way that you gave me (Jesus) a mission in the world, I give them a mission in the world. I'm consecrating myself for their sakes so they'll be truth-consecrated in their mission."

JOHN 17:18 MSG

THERE'S AN OLD SAYING THAT if you fail to plan you plan to fail. What kind of person would attempt to accomplish an important task without first putting together a well thought out plan?

I had a good friend who built a company that tested new aircraft. Chet, himself, crawled into the cockpit of seventeen different planes and flew them for the very first time. Think about what courage that took. One day in conversation, I asked him how he prepared for such an assignment. I assumed he would want to meet with the engineers who built the plane to make certain that it was well-constructed. His answer surprised me, "No, I don't talk with the engineers, I want to talk to the designer. I want to know what was in his mind when he designed the plane and what makes him think it will fly."

There is no trial run for life. There is no test pilot who's willing to try out your life for you, but the good news is that you have a Master Designer who made you and who has a plan for your life. It is your job to discover that plan or way, learn it, and follow it.

In the Psalms, King David told how he learned that truth the hard way. He said the people end up in slavery to their own bad plans "because they rebelled against God's commands and despised the plans of the Most High." Psalm 107:11. So, it behooves us to seek our Master Designer because the best strategic plan is one that is consistent with His plans for us.

Let's look to the Bible for a story about planning. King David desired to build a temple for God. For centuries his people, the Israelites, had wandered in the wilderness, had lived through war-torn years, and had to worship in the Tabernacle, a tent-like structure that moved with them when they moved. After this turbulent history, Israel finally settled into the period of rest God had promised, and it was time to build the Temple. But building was not in God's plan for David, the warrior king. Instead, God gave the job to Solomon, David's son.

Wise Solomon knew how critical proper preparation is. "Plan carefully and you will have plenty; if you act too quickly, you will never have enough." Proverbs 21:5 GNT.

The Scripture tells us about the meticulous plans Solomon made and how he carried them out. He called out thirty-thousand men to help harvest the cedars from Lebanon. He assigned more than one-hundred-fifty thousand workers to quarry and transport the stone needed to build the Temple. It took twenty years of hard work to complete the magnificent structure with its cedar walls, solid gold floors, and olive-wood carvings of angels and flowers. Solomon oversaw all of this with careful planning and without telephones and email.

Solomon wanted to build a dwelling place worthy of their God, a place where people would think of God when they came there. And when it was finished, God made it known that his presence was there, but his presence was conditional. God told Solomon that the people must obey him and follow his teachings or else the Temple was worthless.

God wasn't then nor is he now limited to a building. The Bible says that we are his temple. His plans for you may not be as elaborate as the plans for the Temple, but building a life where you know that God is present takes planning and work. There are those who would say that you don't need a plan, you just need to follow the Spirit. There are others whose lives are so structured and rigid that they don't recognize the leading of God's spirit. God is spirit, yet he is the author of order and detail. It is your job to focus and balance a lifestyle plan that is structured, orderly, and yet open to the leading of God's spirit.

Since life is so complex and there are so many negative influences trying to pull you away from your relationship with your Heavenly Father, there is little chance that you will succeed in maintaining a healthy faith unless you have good strategic plan that is in line with God's plan for your life.

Most strategic plans fail. Will yours? When I checked this morning, there were 74,613 books listed on Amazon.com on how to build a strategic plan. Greg Bustin, contributor to the Forbes Leadership Forum, reminds us that most strategic plans fail. Studies indicate that less than five percent of those who create strategic plans actually follow their plans.

With so many plans out there, so many that don't work, and so many people who do not follow the plans they make, how can you be sure you have a quality plan that *will* work and *will* help you continually revitalize your lifestyle? What you need is not some impersonal, mechanical business plan. You are a spiritual, relational creature, so an effective lifestyle plan must go beyond rules, laws, and activities. It must have spirit and structure, passion and order. It must be a partnership between you and God, who lives in you.

Jesus' Father had a plan for his life. Jesus followed that plan. The Bible writers call his plan, the Way. Over the years I have studied the Jesus' lifestyle and his unique way of living. From that study, I developed a strategic plan for my life. You can easily customize it to fit your personality and needs. I admit this plan has not made my lifestyle or relationship with God perfect. I fail many times and have a long way to go in reaching the goals I believe God has for me, but I don't know of another strategic lifestyle plan that is as effective and comprehensive.

Remember, it took Solomon twenty years to build the Temple. It will take you a life time and a lifestyle change to become God's temple. This is a healthy, uncomplicated, practical, strategic lifestyle plan that will work for you if you will make three essential commitments:

1. ADMIT YOUR ABSOLUTE NEED FOR A STRATEGIC LIFESTYLE PLAN.

Countless people suffer daily with disease and addiction because they will not admit they need help. Too often, people think they can make it on their own so they wait until it's too late.

That's exactly what happened with Sheila. By the time I reached her, she grasping for life. The undercurrent had swept her out into the deep before she realized how far she was from the shore. As a part-time lifeguard that summer of my last year in high school, I saw her thrashing at the water in desperation. I knew she was in trouble and was able to reach her before she went down for the third time. When I got her to the shore and pumped the water from her lungs, I asked, "Why didn't you call for help when you knew you were in trouble?" She simply said, "I didn't want anyone to know that I couldn't swim, and I thought I could do it on my own."

Anosognosia is an obscure word that means "denial of illness." We all know someone who is a heavy drinker, eater, smoker, gambler or drug user who says, "I can quit any time I want. I don't need help." They live in denial. They cannot stop. They need help, but they can't or won't admit it.

Remember Solomon. God gave him a job to do, but Solomon could not build a magnificent temple all by himself. He needed help. Remember, you're building your faith and constructing a temple where God resides. None of us can handle all the challenges of life and enemies of faith without God's help. If we try, we are in denial, and we will fail. We need God's help. He offers us help through his indwelling Spirit and through his *way*, his plan for our lives as best demonstrated in the life of his son, Jesus. Are you ready to admit that you need a plan to help you? See if you feel like these who found the value of having a strategic lifestyle plan.

* Nicole – Protects Priorities

   "I hate to admit it, but I'm the kind of person that is easily distracted. My plan has helped me become more self-disciplined and really helps me stay close to the Lord. I feel better about myself now and know I am growing in my faith."

* Jerome – Clarifies Values

   "It seems I'm so busy that I get off on too many things that don't really matter that much. Since I started using my plan to keep me focused, I find it easier to major on my highest values."

* Cecelia – Simplifies Choices

   "Making decisions is hard for me. There are just too many options and opinions for me to try to figure out without a guide. Having my own spiritual plan makes me more prepared to make good choices. I'd never go back to my old way."

* Sophie – Resists Temptations

   "I would never again try to live without a written strategy that guides my life because there are so many ungodly temptations around me. My strategic plan is like a shield that keeps me from falling back into my old ways. I don't know what I would do without it."

* Amanda – Channels Emotions

   "My friends say that I am easily excited and discouraged. Having a solid plan for my life helps me respond to emotional situations in a Christ-like way. It helps me channel my emotions to support things that mean the most to me."

● Lawrence – Maximizes Resource

"Before I had a specific map to follow, I had a vague sense of direction in my everyday activities. I wasted a lot of my time and resources on things that were not important. As I look back, I was a poor steward of all the Lord gave me until I started following the way he helped me put together."

● Zoe – Organizes Activities

"I never liked rules, laws, or people telling me what I should do. Then God showed me that I had a problem with pride. I needed to be a servant surrendering all my activities to him. My strategic plan helps me organize my schedule around his will not mine."

These people had all experienced life trying to do it by themselves, and only when they admitted their weaknesses and their need for help did they find the peace and satisfaction they so desired. It came in a strategic lifestyle plan.

Confess your need for a strategic plan. Admit your complete inability to have and maintain your faith by yourself. Remember, you're constructing a life, a valuable life. Once you have admitted your inabilities and your need for help, you are ready for the next important commitment.

2. ASPIRE TO GOD'S WAY AND ABANDON YOUR WAY.

I remember one summer when my cousin David visited us in South Florida. He was from the north and had never seen the Atlantic Ocean or the Intracoastal Waterway. We hopped on bicycles and rode over so that he could see the water and take a swim. In his eagerness as we approached the canal, he stopped his bike and decided to take a swim before we reached the ocean. I told him to wait and that he couldn't jump in there because of the barnacles underneath the water. He argued that he didn't see any barnacles and jumped in while I yelled from the sea wall. David thought he knew best and needed no instruction. He did it his way in spite of my warning, and he spent his vacation time in the Broward County hospital with shredded feet.

I did it my way is not the best way. When we were kids, many of us handled life like my cousin David. We made decisions with a glance and a chance, and we gave little thought to planning. Children are born self-centered, crying when they're hungry, kicking and screaming when they're uncomfortable, without a thought for their futures or anyone else's feelings. But we don't stay children, and trying to live adult lives with childish ways leaves a string of messes and broken relationships. Somewhere along the way, we begin to see that jump-then-look, carefree, careless lifestyle is dangerous and painful.

When the time comes that you admit your way is not best and that you need help, you are almost ready to make a big change. Notice, I said, "almost ready." You must desire God's way more than you do your old way.

Jesus says of himself, "I am the WAY." John 14:6 NIV. Those who followed him, those early Christians, were called "people of the way."

The Bible says to be totally committed to God's way, God's plan for your life, you must abandon your old ways and to die to them. When the Apostle Paul became a follower of Jesus, he stood before the governor of his region and said, "I am a follower of the Way." Acts 24:14 CEB. He later explained this idea of abandoning or dying to his old way by saying, "For me to live is Christ, to die is gain." Philippians 1:21 NIV. And again, "I have been crucified with Christ and I no longer live, but Christ lives in me." Galatians 2:20 NIV.

Remember, dying to *self* does not mean that your *self* disappears. It simply means that God is in charge now, and you're allowing him to use your *self* in ways that will bring peace and contentment in your life.

Abandonment of your old ways is not easy, but it is a necessary part of true change and genuine commitment. Think of Solomon again. God gave him the task of building that first Temple in Jerusalem. That meant change. That meant abandoning the old idea of a tent-like tabernacle, leaving their old ways behind. The Bible shows us that Solomon's greatest aspiration was to follow God's plan down to the minutest detail. Solomon allowed God to use his *self*, his wisdom, and his abilities to create something magnificent, so magnificent that we're still reading about it thousands of years later. Somehow, I think Solomon preferred the new Temple and the new palace over his old tents and wandering ways.

Don't be like my cousin David who missed his opportunity for a rewarding experience and instead spent his time caring for his wounds because he had to do things his way and ignored sound instruction and counsel.

You will keep on doing what you desire the most. You will work the hardest for what you want the most. When you aspire with all your mind, heart, and body to follow God's way, you will abandon your old way. It is then that God will begin to lead you into a new lifestyle that will bring you the joy, peace, and contentment that you desire.

3. ADHERE TO EVERY ELEMENT OF YOUR NEW STRATEGIC LIFESTYLE PLAN.

The elements for a successful strategic plan are not optional. It is not a pick and choose proposition if you really want your plan to work.

Research has shown that for patients undergoing heart bypass surgery, their greatest fear is stopping the heart and going on by-pass. So for years, doctors worked developing a type of heart surgery where the heart would not have to be stopped. On February 23, 1999, Dr. Lawrence Hamner made medical history when he performed the first beating-heart bypass surgery while it was being broadcast live over television and the internet. At that time, I was the CEO of the television network that produced the historic program from the Methodist Hospital in San Antonio, TX.

What impressed me most was not the actual surgery, but the decades of detailed research on heart surgery and then months of meticulous planning that preceded this procedure. I'm certain Dr. Hamner performed that surgery in his mind many times before this successful application. These surgeries are practically routine now but still follow the detailed, tested, and perfected plans. Built into those protocols are even protocols for unexpected events during surgery. The surgeons know that people's lives depend upon this kind of adherence to proven protocol.

Your faith-life depends upon your complete and whole-hearted commitment to the non-negotiable, must-do elements of your new lifestyle strategy. Just as Dr. Hamner performed a successful surgery because he followed every step in the protocol, you must follow each step in the plan you'll be developing.

Neglecting or leaving out a part would be like trying to develop a loving relationship with your spouse while doing it with a tentative or selective commitment. You remember that a loving relationship is built on three essential, non-negotiable ingredients: humility, responsibility, and honesty. Without all three, you don't have a genuine, satisfying love. Let's say you choose to be unselfish and responsible, but you are not honest, your loving relationship will eventually crumble. So make a commitment now to adhere to every part of your plan.

Life is all about choices. You can choose to live your life as if you were a corked bottle afloat on the ocean, being tossed by the waves, crashed onto the rocks, and winding up wherever the winds and currents take you. Or you can choose to build yourself a boat that has a much greater chance of getting you to your choicest destination.

I hope you're at the point where you can admit that you need help, and that you have the highest aspiration for a meaningful life, and that you are committed to adhering to every step of building a lifestyle strategy that will work for you. You will see there are no exercises for you to complete in this chapter because it is in this step that you will be building your own lifestyle plan. If you're still with me, then in the next chapter, it's come down to developing your personal strategic plan.

CHAPTER 23

How do you DEVELOP a Strategic Lifestyle Plan?

༄

*"I believe each of us has a mission in life and that one cannot
truly be living their most fulfilled life until they recognize
this mission and dedicate their life to pursuing it."*

BLAKE MYCOSKIE, AUTHOR AND PHILANTHROPIST

*"Nothing, not even my life is more important than completing my mission.
This is nothing other than the ministry I received from the Lord Jesus."*

ACTS 20:24 CEV

WHEN DR. BENJAMIN SOLOMON "BEN" Carson, Sr., the internationally-
famous neurosurgeon, gives motivational addresses to young people, he challenges them to use their God-given, uniquely-human abilities to prepare them
for their futures. As an expert on the brain, Dr. Carson reminds his youthful
listeners that we are the only creatures on earth that God gave large frontal
lobes, the part of the brain that enables humans to make rational decisions.
He explains that our frontal lobes give us the ability to make plans and greatly
determine our lives rather than becoming victims of our past, present or future circumstances.

Since your frontal lobe gives you the capacity to analyze, strategize and prioritize information from your past and present, you have the ability, with God's help, to design a new lifestyle that will support your new healthy faith rather than allow your old lifestyle to pull you back into your old ways of thinking, feeling, and behaving.

It is interesting that the word *strategy* comes from the Greek word *strategos*, meaning "the art of the general." It is a military term and came out of the need for people to overcome their enemies. The first recorded strategies were in the Chinese manuscripts of Sun Tzu's The Art of War, written in 400 B.C. and still admired by military experts. The principles of any good strategic plan are timeless.

I want to make a distinction between a *plan* and a *strategy*. For purposes here, a *plan* is a detailed proposal to achieve a short-term, specific goal. A *strategy* is a master plan designed to achieve a long-term goal. So the term *strategic plan* is a detailed proposal with long-term goals. A general may have a battle plan for protecting the city, but his strategic plan would be to defeat the enemy through a series of battles, thus protecting the city and the country and securing their future.

You face enemies every day—enemies that would rob you of peace and joy and healthy relationships and a faith that will see you through, all those good things that God desires for you. So in this chapter, you will learn the elements to build your strategic plan to keep you safe from these enemies.

While you have been reading this book and doing the exercises at the ends of the chapters, you have actually learned the meaning and importance of some of these principles. You have already begun to develop some habits that will become a part of your plan.

You are about to make some changes in your life and your daily routine. Perhaps the best way to get started is to take a close look at each of the elements of a strategic plan. As you read through these elements, be thinking of how they relate to your life and what you have already learned about yourself—about your mind, your heart, and your behavior. Begin to imagine how you will personalize each of these elements so that you can transform this generic plan into a unique, customized strategic lifestyle plan that is yours.

As an educator and a businessman, I am well aware of the terminology and jargon associated with plans. I have deliberately tried to make this streamlined and simple for you.

THE SIX ESSENTIAL PARTS OF AN EFFECTIVE LIFESTYLE PLAN

Your plan will become a highly personal, dynamic document with six essential parts that are designed to affect every fiber of your daily life and routine.

1. VISION STATEMENT: *Your most important, non-measurable aspiration.*
Every plan begins with a vision. It is that single, most important target that you keep your mind's eye on at all times. It is by far the greatest desire of your mind and heart. If you had to give up everything and everyone in your life except this one thing, what would it be?

To have and work your strategic lifestyle plan, you must be able to put into a one sentence your vision-statement which reflects the primary guarding principle in your life and eternity. In the next chapter, you will be asked to write your vision-statement. It might begin with these words, "More than anything else, I want . . . ."

2. CORE VALUES: *Your beliefs that dictate how you live your life.*
Your core values are those few beliefs, morals, and principles that you use to live by. They help you evaluate the worth of everything. They determine how you make the decision as to whether a thing or idea is good or bad, important or not, and how you should respond. These core beliefs also determine how you value and relate to others.

In the next chapter, you will be asked to make a list of your core values. You might want to review Chapter Nine which addresses the three basic morals and Chapter Thirteen which helps you understand your heart – your passions and emotions.

3. MISSION STATEMENT: *Your most important, non-measurable life-purposes or goals that will enable you to accomplish your vision and maintain your values.*

Every effective plan must have a simple, clear, concise mission-statement. Because of its practical importance, I will spend a bit of extra time describing the value and content of a mission statement.

Major corporations and organizations of all kinds pay experts millions of dollars to help them condense the essence of who they are and what they do into a concise mission statement. They do this because it is a proven fact that just the right, memorable, and succinct statement brings great returns on the money they spent.

I have sat on the board of a major non-profit organization that went through such an exercise. The consultants made recommendations on everything from logo to letterhead, from colors to consistency in communications, and from methods to mission statement. When management accepted this concept, they quickly became focused on who they were and what their priorities were. It helped them with every corporate decision made as it became their single target, their primary goal, their ultimate desire, their gold standard, and their priority.

If a mission statement is that crucial in helping an organization succeed and in keeping it focused and from getting off track, isn't a mission statement as important for you in developing your strategic lifestyle plan? After all, you are in the business of building and maintaining something far more valuable to you—a healthy faith and healthy relationships with God and those you love.

Your mission statement becomes your standard, your hitching post, that purpose against which you evaluate your thoughts, feelings, and behaviors. Before you make major decisions, you will ask yourself, "Will what I am thinking of doing keep me from carrying out any part of my mission statement?" It will help you in advance for whatever comes as it will keep you from second guessing or reacting emotionally to what you should or should not do in every situation.

As I have often in this book, I point you to Jesus. He is the best model to follow in writing your personal mission statement. Before he began his mission on earth, he made this very clear and concise announcement. This comes after Jesus had spent forty days and nights in the wilderness to commune with his father and clarify his mission.

While in the wilderness, Jesus was tested and tempted by Satan. After this experience, Jesus returned to his hometown of Nazareth and went to the meeting place on the Sabbath. As was his custom, he read from Isaiah, *"God's Spirit is on me; he's chosen me to preach the Message of good news to the poor, sent me to announce pardon to prisoners and recovery of sight to the blind, to set the burdened and battered free, to announce, this is God's year to act!"* Luke 4:18 MSG. And thus began Jesus' ministry on earth. Everything he did from that moment on was in sync with his purpose in life proclaimed in his mission statement.

No one else can write your mission statement, for it is yours and yours alone. It is personal. It should show responsibility, stewardship of who you are and what God has given you, and commitment. As an example, here is my personal mission-statement:

> *To have an intimate, healthy relationship with Jesus, who now lives in me, and to gratefully let him use everything he has given me, to serve him responsibly and to help others in all circumstances so that they may also know, serve and have a personal relationship with Jesus.*

4. YOUR PERSONAL RESOURCES: *Your unique gifts, skills, and experiences for accomplishing your mission statement.*

Often times, a SWOT, which is an industry-term for a tool or analysis used to determine your strengths, weaknesses, opportunities, and threats, can be helpful. If you do not have access to that, have a conversation with a friend or family member who knows you well and can help you come up with that list.

Remember God uses the talents he gave you. He uses your personality and your life circumstances. Look at where you are; look at the relationships you have; look at the access you have. Identifying those resources making you uniquely you are critical in designing your lifestyle plan.

5. ACTION STEPS: *What you do to live out your mission statement.*
Your vision, values, and mission statement are your non-measurable desires, but your action steps are calculated and measurable. It is the list of your activities that can be checked by you and your trusted friend to hold you accountable to your lifestyle plan.

Obviously, these activities require time, and they will need to be scheduled. Some of these activities need to be on your daily schedule, and others, although routine, will not likely find a designated time on your calendar. Some of these activities require time alone for Bible study, prayer, and meditation. Others require a commitment to an organization or involve relating to others. Think of your gifts, abilities, interests, contacts, your life experiences and time as you begin to make your list.

In completing the exercises in this book, you already have a list of action steps, and you've already begun to develop some practices in carrying them out. You will find a detailed list and examples in the next chapter.

6. ACCOUNTABILITY: *Your trusted friend/s who hold you accountable and help you be responsible in living your new strategic lifestyle plan.*
If you have been doing the exercises in this book, you are already accustomed to communicating with a trusted friend or family member—one who is interested in helping you build and maintain your healthy faith. You can continue that relationship and maybe develop others as you engage in your Action Steps. Just remember, you don't have to nor should you do this alone.

These are the elements of a strategic lifestyle plan. As you learned in the previous chapter, you must be committed to each and every element. If you develop and work your plan, not overnight, but over time, you will develop a lifestyle with a faith that works. It takes a real commitment to learn a new way of living.

For over thirty years, New Yorker, Sheryl Imperati, was a yo-yo dieter. Oscillating between one-hundred-forty and two-hundred pounds, she started and stopped numerous diet plans. When Sheryl turned thirty-nine, she stopped trying to lose weight and started trying to get healthy. She found just the right strategic plan, made a commitment, and unreservedly adhered to every element of the plan. Over time, she stopped yo-yo dieting, became physically fit, lost weight, and became an energetic, happy and most importantly, a healthy woman. Sheryl became successful when she stopped the yo-yo way of trying and developed nd worked a strategic plan.

Frank Newport, Editor-in-Chief of the Gallup Poll, reported that research from Gallop's Annual Consumption Habits Poll indicated that although people try multiple times and different plans to change their bad habits, most do not stick to their plans. They become yo-yo dieters, yo-yo smokers, yo-yo drinkers, or maybe they even become yo-yo faith builders. Don't let this discourage you about starting your strategic lifestyle plan. Let those facts be honest warnings and powerful motivations.

There are three common reasons why people give up on their plans. The first reason many people quickly lose heart and give up is because their plans are too complicated, too confusing, or too idealistic. The second reason is they attempt to do it alone, and the third is they work their plan in a tentative or halfhearted way.

You're aware now of these stumbling blocks, so avoid them. As you construct your personalized, strategic lifestyle plan, keep it simple, easy to understand, and street-practical. That's the kind of plan I use, and it works.

Don't go it alone and deliberately keep your plan a secret. That could be an indicator in itself that you plan to fail, and you don't want others to know. Or it could be a sign that you still have a problem with pride and believe you can do it your way. Don't be so independent. Depend upon God and others whom you trust. And don't go into this with a selective commitment, choosing the easy parts or the ones that are more convenient. Do it all with your whole heart.

Again, no exercises here because in the next chapter, you will be writing out your lifestyle plan. I will help you. Do this for yourself, for your life now and for your eternity. Could anything you do be more important than that?

CHAPTER 24

How do you CONSTRUCT your Strategic Lifestyle Plan?

❧

"When you discover your mission, you will feel its demand. It will fill you with enthusiasm and a burning desire to get to work on it."

W. CLEMENT STONE, AUTHOR

"Planning is bringing the future into the present so that you can do something about it now."

ALAN LAKEIN, AUTHOR

"The plans of the Lord stand firm forever, the purposes of his heart through all generations."

PSALM 33:11 NIV

EVERYTHING I HAVE WRITTEN THUS far in this book is to get you to this chapter. I don't know if you're a teacher, a student, a business executive, a stay-at-home mom, a mechanic, a medical professional, young or old, just starting out in your faith walk, or in the middle years of your life as a person of faith, but I have written the truth; and Truth fits everyone no matter your station in life.

If you have been serious and accepted my call to action as you began this study, you have been reading, writing, memorizing, meditating, and conversing about your faith-building activities. You have learned about your core values and your passions and the parts of your *self*. You have learned about God-alerts and prayer-alerts. You have written notes to others. You have sought out ways to practice your faith. You are much farther along the way in developing your strategic lifestyle plan than you realize.

I am aware that different people have different learning styles, and I know that you're not going to remember the numerous lists in this book even though you've read them, and written them down, and you might even be carrying around a few of those lists in your wallet. I hope you will continue to use this book as a resource and that you will use the Resources I have included to help you design your plan and most importantly to create your action steps.

It is critical that you write your plan. Writing helps you to sift through and record what is most important. The physical act of writing will help you remember. And when finished, you will have a document that you can refer to for years to come. It will become your reminder and your checklist to see how you are doing.

The material in this book comes from decades of study, of counseling, and of practicing what I teach. As an example to help you construct your plan, I have included my own strategic lifestyle plan that has served me well in the development of my faith and my relationship to God and others.

My Strategic Lifestyle Plan: A Practical Outline
Written by: Bill Nichols

1. MY VISION STATEMENT:

The single greatest desire of my life is . . .

To please my Lord and Savior Jesus.

2. MY CORE VALUES:

The most important values that guide everything I think, desire, and do.

- The Bible is my source for truth for my life and eternity.
- God's character is my guide for truth.
- God created everything good and pride caused evil.
- We are created in God's image and can relate to him.
- God wants to have an intimate relationship with us.
- Jesus died for my sins and rose to live in and through me.
- Jesus' life and words are my best examples for living.
- Eternity with God and loved ones impacts all my choices.
- Being humble, responsible, and honest are my primary values to determine how I relate to God, my wife, family, and others.

3. MY MISSION STATEMENT:

My most important goals (what I want most) . . .

- To have an intimate relationship with my Heavenly Father.
- To love my wife like Christ loved me and gave himself for me.

- <u>To love my family and family of faith like Christ loved me.</u>
- <u>To serve God with all my resources no matter the circumstances.</u>

4. MY PERSONAL RESOURCES:

My gifts/abilities and experiences I will use to accomplish each goal in my mission statement.

My Gifts/Abilities:

- <u>Comfortable talking with people</u>
- <u>Trained counselor</u>
- <u>Gifted and trained in art</u>
- <u>Trained in public speaking, preaching</u>
- <u>Bible teacher</u>
- <u>Strategic planner, administrator</u>

My Experiences

- Relationship Experiences

<u>Grew up with loving mother, Dad, brother and sisters</u>
<u>Loving, supportive church family</u>
<u>Several spiritual friends who encouraged me</u>
<u>Loving Christian wife and family members</u>

- Educational Experiences

- <u>Grew up in church with good Bible education</u>
- <u>BA degree in sociology and psychology</u>
- <u>Seminary studied theology, counseling, planning,</u>
  <u>Bible study</u>

- Vocational Experiences

- <u>Several labor jobs as a teenager</u>
- <u>Pastor of rural and city churches</u>
- <u>Counselor</u>
- <u>Seminary teacher</u>
- <u>Television executive, administrator</u>

- <u>Significant God-Moments</u>

- <u>My conversion experience. God spoke to my heart.</u>
- <u>God called me to be a minister.</u>
- <u>My ordination experience</u>
- <u>My near-death experience</u>
- <u>Witnessing a woman seeing angels as she was dying</u>
- <u>Witnessing my best friend seeing Jesus as he was dying</u>
- <u>Witnessing miracles of healing and character</u>
  <u>changing conversions</u>

- <u>Failures and Painful Experiences</u>

- <u>Life-altering auto accident when I was a young minister</u>
- <u>Battle with cancer and cure</u>
- <u>Death of mother, dad, and best friend</u>
- <u>Suffering with friends with addictions</u>
- <u>Suffering with friends, in death of loved ones</u>

My SWOT: Strengths, Weaknesses, Opportunities, Threats

- Strengths: My three main resources of all my gifts, abilities, and experiences

<u>My intimate relationship with the Lord</u>
<u>My Bible knowledge and experiences using his Word in life</u>
<u>My loving, devoted Christian wife and her constant</u>
<u>friendship</u>

- Weaknesses: My main character problems that harm my faith

<u>Not enough awareness of God's Spirit moving in and</u>
<u>around me</u>
<u>Procrastination. Do not follow through with all plans</u>
<u>Overextending myself. Trying to do too much</u>
<u>Hard to stay focused. Easily to get distracted</u>
<u>Worry too much about unimportant things</u>
<u>Time management of my personal schedule</u>
<u>Too quick to express frustration</u>

- Opportunities: Areas where I can now begin to improve my faith

I can practice more ways of staying in touch with God.
I can improve looking for God's Spirit moving in and
around me.
I can spend more time serving God's hurting children.
I can focus more on overcoming my weaknesses.

- Threats: Potential greatest problems that may weaken my faith

My lack of being close to God and being under his influence
My lack of involvement in the lives of those who suffer
My lack of recognizing God's presence and following him
My tendency to accept my old habits and not desire change

5. **My ACTION STEPS:**
Detailed action-steps I will do to accomplish each goal in my mission statement.

Goal 1: To have an intimate relationship with my Heavenly
Father

- Daily Quiet Time

  Schedule a set time and place each morning
  Read some Bible story or a parable of Jesus
  Follow a plan for reading and meditating on
  some scripture

Read from a daily devotional book
Plan to apply something from my quiet time
to my dail activities
Pray using the acrostic ACTS (page 230)

- Daily practices for staying in touch with God

I will . .

Listen to hear the voice of God through others.
Thank God periodically throughout the day for
experiences.
Let God's Spirit use me to touch someone in need.
Watch for God-alerts and stop to thank God or
ask for help.
Pause and step aside throughout the day to
talk to God
Read a scripture or repeat a memorize scripture
during the day
Ask God for forgiveness at the moment I sin and
ask for his help.

- Daily do some small act of kindness (Review Chapters 16 and 21)

I will . . .

Touch those who are hurting in the ways Jesus
touched them.

Say a silent prayer for anyone who is hurting
Speak a word of encouragement to anyone who
is hurting

- Periodically go on a planned spiritual retreat
  Go alone or with a small group to focus on reviewing your Strategic
  Lifestyle Plan and revitalizing your spiritual life.

I will . . .

Explore with other Christians possible
spiritual retreats.
Schedule some time on my calendar to take a
spiritual retreat
Schedule a brief time with my trusted friend for
a brief retreat

Goal 2: To love my wife, or closest friend, like Christ
loved me.

- Daily Quiet time

  I will . . .
  Schedule a set time and place to pray with
  my wife
  Pray using the acrostic ACTS (page 230)
  Discuss our daily schedule and how we can serve
  the lord

- Daily practices for staying in touch with my wife, or closest friend.

I will . .

Thank her every time I have opportunity
Pause and step aside throughout the day to
contact her.
Ask her for forgiveness at the moment I
disappoint her
Ask for her suggestions and listen attentively
Inform her of what I am thinking, feeling, and doing
Pray for her throughout the day and ask for
her prayers

- Daily spend private time.

I will . . .

Schedule private time each evening to do what
she wants
Take a long walk with her and enjoy God's
creation together
Ask her about her day and listen attentively
Let her know that I care about how she feels and thinks
Let her know how I feel and think about my day
and hers
Share my experiences with God from the day

Help her feel safe, cherished, important to me
Show affection by hugs, squeezes, pats, and
kisses she likes

- Periodically serve others with her

I will . . .

Go with her to help someone who is in need
Schedule serving others in one of our church ministries
Schedule an annual trip to minister to others

- Periodically surprise her

I will . . .

Schedule times to surprise her with small gifts
or notes
Cook her a meal or take her out
Plan a short trip or do an activity she enjoys
Leave a written prayer for her or send a prayer-
message

Goal 3: To love my family and family of faith like Christ loved me

I will . . .

- Pray for each of them every morning
- Stay in touch with them through various media means
- Share in their struggles, sorrows, and joys
- Send them notes with a scripture and prayer
- Periodically ask them to pray for me
- Keep them informed of my prayers for them
- Be by their side when they need me.
- Express my gratitude and love for them regularly
- Surprise them with small acts of kindness to encourage them

Goal 4: To serve God and others with all my resources

Daily or weekly I will . . .

- Visit people in the hospital and nursing homes
- Counsel people the Lord brings into my life
- Paint pictures to inspire and encourage
- Paint note cards to send messages of faith

- <u>Preach in churches and other venues</u>
- <u>Teach the Bible each week in a class in our church</u>
- <u>Write a Bible centered blog weekly and write articles and books</u>
- <u>Help faith-based ministries with their strategic plans</u>

<u>Periodically I will...</u>

- <u>Work on a church local ministry project helping the poor</u>
- <u>Serve on a committee or ministry in the church</u>
- <u>Travel on a short term mission trips out of the country</u>
- <u>Travel to preach or teach a series of messages</u>

My Strategic Lifestyle Plan: A Practical Outline

Written by: _____

1. MY VISION STATEMENT:

_____

_____

2. MY CORE VALUES:

The most important values that guide everything I think, desire, and do.

_____

_____

_____

_____

_____

3. MY MISSION STATEMENT:

My most important goals (what I want most) . . .

_____

_____

_____

_____

_____

4. MY PERSONAL RESOURCES:

My gifts/abilities and experiences I will use to accomplish each goal in my mission statement.

My Gifts/Abilities:

_____
_____
_____
_____
_____
_____

My Experiences

- Relationship Experiences

_____
_____
_____
_____
_____
_____

- Educational Experiences

_____
_____
_____
_____
_____
_____

- Vocational Experiences

_____
_____
_____
_____
_____
_____

- Significant God-Moments

  _____
  _____
  _____
  _____
  _____
  _____

- Failures and Painful Experiences

  _____
  _____
  _____
  _____
  _____

My SWOT: Strengths, Weaknesses, Opportunities, Threats

- Strengths: My three main resources of all my gifts, abilities, and experiences

  _____
  _____
  _____
  _____
  _____

- Weaknesses: My main character problems that harm my faith

  _____
  _____
  _____
  _____
  _____

- Opportunities: Areas where I can now begin to improve my faith

  _____

  _____

  _____

  _____

  _____

  _____

- Threats: Potential greatest problems that may weaken my faith

  _____

  _____

  _____

  _____

  _____

5. My ACTION STEPS:

Detailed action-steps I will do to accomplish each goal in my mission statement.

Goal 1: To

- Daily

  _____

  _____

  _____

  _____

  _____

- Daily

  I will . .

  _____

  _____

  _____

  _____

  _____

  _____

- Daily

  <u>I will . . .</u>

  _____

  _____

  _____

  _____

  _____

- Periodically

  I will . . .

  _____

  _____

  _____

  _____

  _____

  _____

<u>Goal 2: To</u>

- Daily

  I will . . .

  _____

  _____

  _____

  _____

  _____

- Daily

  I will . . .

  _____

  _____

  _____

  _____

  _____

- Daily

  I will . . .

  _____

  _____

  _____

  _____

  _____

- Periodically

    I will . . .

    _____

    _____

    _____

    _____

    _____

    _____

- Periodically

    I will . . .

    _____

    _____

    _____

    _____

    _____

    _____

Goal 3: To

    I will . . .

    _____

    _____

    _____

    _____

    _____

    _____

Goal 4: To

Daily or weekly I will . . .

_____

_____

_____

_____

_____

Periodically I will . . .

_____

_____

_____

_____

Goal 5: To

Daily or weekly I will . . .

_____

_____

_____

_____

_____

Periodically I will . . .

_____

_____

On This Journey Together

WHEN I WALK THROUGH HEAVEN'S door, I would love to hear our Father say to me what he said to Jesus, "You are My beloved Son; in You I am well pleased." Luke 3:22 NKJV.

The scriptures remind us that "Without faith it is impossible to please him." Hebrews 11:6 KJV. But, we both know that not just any kind of faith pleases him or produces the life we so greatly desire. That is why we are willing to do the demanding work of developing a Healthy Faith that does please our Father.

Since you are reading this final note, I imagine you have joined me on the most important journey in your life, and I am proud of you for doing the work you have done thus far. But you have only just begun. As I said from the start, building a healthy faith is not a sprint, it is a marathon.

When you read the Strategic Lifestyle Plan form I filled out, maybe you thought it was merely a made-up example. But it's not, and I do hope it offers you a few ideas when you filled out your form. For years I have updated my Strategic Lifestyle Plan to help me grow in my faith and be able to handle anything life throws at me.

The auto accident I mentioned at the beginning of the book was not my last crash. Like most people, I continue to experience bumps along the journey, health struggles, disappointing turns in the road, and a variety of challenges to my faith. But as it was with our Lord, I have not been surprised by such experiences and am grateful for God's unfailing and all-sufficient presence in every situation. That is why our Strategic Lifestyle Plan must be a dynamic document that we revise from time to time to conform to changes in our lives.

At the end of each chapter you have prayed for our Father's support. And now that you have come to the end of the book, I offer this prayer for you and ask you to pray for me as I join you in continuing to develop a healthy faith.

Dear Father, Thank you for leading me throughout the writing of this book and for leading this reader to join me in taking this important journey of faith. I am grateful for your love and presence our lives. At this important juncture, kindly provide wisdom, insight, and encouragement every step along the way. As we seek to follow you, we confess that we depend on you to guide our minds, hearts, and bodies as instruments of your indwelling Spirit. Thank you, in the name of our Lord Jesus, your Son and our Savior, Amen.

Forty Great Faith-Building Bible Stories

༭

Old Testament Stories – From Creation to Jesus

1.	The Story of Creation	Genesis 1-2
2.	The Story of Noah and the Ark	Genesis 6-9
3.	The Story of Abraham, Isaac and Jacob:	Genesis 12-30
4.	The Story of Joseph	Genesis 37-46
5.	The Story of Moses	Exodus 3-13
6.	The Story of Joshua and the Battle	Joshua 3, 6
7.	The Story of Samson and Delilah	Judges 13-16
8.	The Story of Ruth	Ruth 1-4
9.	The Story of Hannah and Samuel	1 Samuel 1-3
10.	The Story of David's Call	1 Samuel 16
11.	The Story of David and Goliath	1 Samuel 17
12.	The Story of Solomon and His Temple	1 Kings 3-5
13.	The Story of Elijah and Three Miracles	1 Kings 17-18:39
14.	The Story of Elisha and Three More Miracles	1 Kings 4-5
15.	The Story of Esther	Esther 1-10
16.	The Story of Daniel, Shadrach, Meshach and Abednego	Daniel 1-3
17.	The Story of Daniel and the Lions' Den	Daniel 6
18.	The Story of Jonah and the Whale	Jonah 1-4

19. The Story of Job   Job 1-2, 42
20. The Story of Isaiah's Prophecy of Jesus   Isaiah 53

New Testament Stories – From Jesus' Birth to His Return

1. The Story of Jesus' Birth   Luke 1-2
2. The Story of the Boy Jesus at the Temple   Luke 2:41-52
3. The Story of Jesus' Temptations in the Wilderness   Luke 4-6
4. The Story of Jesus Feeding the 5000   Matthew 14
5. The Story of Jesus Walking on the Water   Matthew 14:22-33
6. The Story of Jesus and the Little Children   Mark 10
7. The Story of Jesus Calming the Storm   Mark 4
8. The Story of the Rich Young Ruler   Luke 18
9. The Story of the Farmer who Scattered the Seeds   Luke 8
10. The Story of the Bridesmaids and Lamps   Matthew 25
11. The Story of the Prodigal Son   Luke 5
12. The Story of the Good Samaritan   Luke 10
13. The Story of Mary, Martha and Lazarus   John 11
14. The Story of the Little Man, Zacchaeus   Luke 19
15. The Story of Peter Walking on Water   Matthew 14:22-33
16. The Story of Jesus' Death   John 19
17. The Story of Jesus Coming Alive After Death   John 20
18. The Story of Paul's Conversion   Acts 9:1-31
19. The Story of Paul's Release from Prison   Acts 16:16-34
20. The Story of Jesus' Return   Acts 1:1-11

Principles for a Healthy
Bible Study

ℛ

A HELPFUL WAY TO STAY close to your Father is to listen to his Spirit speak to you through your daily Bible study. However, not just any kind of Bible study is healthy intellectually, emotionally, and practically. For you to have a *healthy Bible study* you will need to follow some basic principles that produce the results God wants for you.

1. *The Principle of Personal Responsibility.* Like love, truth cannot be handed down. It must be personal. For you to realize truth and hear God speak to you through the Bible, you must accept your personal responsibility to read, interpret, discover, apply, and share God's truth.

2. *The Principle of Authority.* As you read, study, and memorize verses in the Bible, approach scripture with a desire to find truth and a closer relationship with God that will help you have a healthy faith. Your ultimate authority for truth is the living God, and your written authority is the Bible. Truth is what you can count on, rely on, or depend on for every situation in your life and death. As you engage in your Bible study, anticipate that God will speak to you and let his word be your authority for what you think, desire, and do.

3. *The Principles of Literary Interpretation.*
    You want your Bible study to be accurate, as dependable as possible, and as helpful as conceivable. But we know that Bible study can

be shallow, confusing, and even harmful unless basic literary principles of interpretation are followed. These are principles you would use to properly understand any piece of literature including the Bible. Before you study any piece of Scripture ask yourself these kinds of questions

- ♦ WHO was the author? (Background and personality)
- ♦ WHO received the material? (Area, persons, or groups)
- ♦ WHAT is the context? (The verse's relation to overall book and section)
- ♦ WHEN was the literature written? (Historical setting)
- ♦ WHERE was it written? (Cultural setting)
- ♦ WHY was it written? (Purpose of writer, problems faced)
- ♦ HOW was it written? (Type of literature: poetry, letter, history and others)

4. *The Principles of Biblical Interpretation*

Although the Bible is literature, it is a special kind of literature. God is its ultimate author. He used real people in real history to write the Bible through the each of the author's own personality; but he guided them to write the truth for his children of all times. So, as you study and memorize the scriptures, keep these unique principles of biblical interpretation in mind.

- ♦ *Accommodation.* Your Heavenly Father chose to limit Himself (accommodate himself) by using the language and symbols of us humans to write the Bible. As you read the Holy Scriptures, be careful to not think of God as just a "Big Man in the sky." He is our creator and is Spirit. His Bible only gives us a glimpse of God and his truth. His clearest representation is found in the life and words of Jesus as revealed through his Spirit.

- ♦ *Limitation.* Since we are God's created and loved children, not little gods, we are limited in time, space, and attitude and can never completely understand the Bible. We are all sinners and have a tendency to interpret his word to our advantage. That's why it is important for you to approach his word with humility and dependence on his Spirit and those who have for years faithfully studied Scriptures and lived a godly, Christ-like life.

* *Progression.* The more we study and live out God's Word, the more we hear God speaking to us through it and experience God guiding our daily lives. The Bible provides God's acts in history over centuries and his truth becomes the clearest to his children through the life and words of Jesus and the coming of His Holy Spirit.

* *Consistency.* When you read the Bible or what someone says about the meaning of scriptures, always ask these questions before you accept any interpretation or conclusion: "Is this teaching consistent with the .

  Overall MESSAGE of God's Word?
  Overall CHARACTER of God as seen in Jesus?
  Overall TEACHINGS of the early churches and apostles?
  Overall PURPOSE of God?

5. *The Principles of Practical Discipline.*
   * TRUST AND OBEY. The authors of the Scriptures take for granted that you are a follower of the Lord and trust what the scriptures say. As you study your Bible, always expect God to speak to you personally, trust His word as absolute truth, and do your best to follow what you learn.
   * SET A TIME. Your personal discipline in Bible study is as important as your need for food. Set a specific time, choose a place, and schedule all of your other activities around your quiet time.
   * HAVE GOOD TOOLS. The use of proper tools for any job usually makes the task more enjoyable and the results better. Some of the most important tools you need for your Bible study include:
     (1) A good standard translation of the Bible like the New International Version (NIV) and at least one or two other translations for comparison.
     (2) You may choose to use an online Bible website that provides multiple translations of each scripture.
     (3) Since we are so far removed from the events reported in the Bible and from the time the scriptures were written,

you should have a good compact Bible dictionary that will provide you helpful historical background information and the meaning of some of the key words in the passage you are studying. Zondervan's Compact Bible Dictionary and Nelson's Compact Bible Dictionary are favorites, but there are several other good ones available.

(4) Keep a pen handy to make notes in the margins of one of your Bible or in a separate notebook.

(5) Have a color highlighter ready to mark words and phrases which are especially meaningful to you at the time or your reading.

* HAVE A PLAN. Find a good study guide or workbook on themes, subjects, or books of the Bible. Many good guides are available in Bible bookstores and online. You may choose to focus on one book in the Bible and go through it systematically; or you may decide to select a topic, such as love, truth, or graced and study it throughout the Bible. The key point is to have some systematic plan of study.

* RECALL THE PRINCIPLES. After a brief period of Bible study, we are all tempted to ignore the important principles mentioned earlier. A good discipline for you to adopt early on is to periodically examine your Bible study habits and the conclusions you are making in light of the great principles of interpretation.

* QUESTIONS ARE GOOD. When you experience some questions concerning the Bible or a particular passage, be glad. That means you are taking your Bible study seriously. At the same time, remember you begin your Bible study with the conviction that God's Word is your authority and not the other way around. Therefore, look at your questions and concerns as opportunities for more study. God's Word does not need to be improved; we need improvement. In some cases, you will want to discuss your questions and concerns with others whom your respect in spiritual matters.

- SAY IT SIMPLY. When you decide on what a passage means to you, write the essence of the passage in your own words.
- APPLY IT THOROUGHLY.

Ask these questions of every passage to help you apply His truth to you.

KEY OCCASION: What was the situation that brought about this text? How does my situation compare?

KEY PURPOSE: What was the author's central idea?

KEY WORD: What is/are the key word/words in this text?

KEY MESSAGE ABOUT GOD: What does this passage say about how God feels about me?

KEY MESSAGE ABOUT YOU: What does this passage say about how I should act towards God?

KEY MESSAGE ABOUT OTHERS: What does this passage say about the way I should relate to others?

KEY INSIGHT: What new insight do I now have I can use today?

Scriptures When Your Faith Needs Encouragement

✾

We all need encouragement at times; and, for centuries, people around the world and in every imaginable situation have found hope, inspiration, and support from some of these sample Bible verses.

I have chosen fifty of my favorite short scriptures that you may find strengthening when your faith needs encouragement or when you want to support a friend with a word from God.

The list is presented alphabetically representing common themes.

When you or someone feels . . .

1. Abandoned. *God has said, never will I leave you; never will I forsake you.* Hebrews 13:5

2. Afraid. *Even though I walk through the valley of the shadow of death, I will fear no evil, for you are with me; your rod and your staff, they comfort me.* Psalms 23:4

3. Afraid. *God has not given us the spirit of fear; but of power, and of love, and of a sound mind.* 2 Timothy 1:7

4. Afraid. *Thus says the LORD. Fear not, for I have redeemed you; I have called you by name, you are mine.* Isaiah 43:1

5. Alone. *I have been crucified with Christ and I no longer live, but Christ lives in me. The life I live in the body, I live by faith in the Son of God, who loved me and gave himself for me.* Galatians 2:20

6. Angry. *Walk in the way of love, just as Christ loved us and gave himself up for us.* Ephesians 5:1-3

7. Angry. *Love your neighbor as yourself.* Matthew 22:39

8. Anxious. *Do not be anxious about anything, but in every situation, by prayer and petition, with thanksgiving, present your requests to God.* Philippians 4:6

9. Anxious. *Be strong and courageous. Do not fear or be in dread of them, for it is the LORD your God who goes with you. He will not leave you or forsake you.* Deuteronomy 31:6

10. Brokenhearted. *Peace I leave with you; my peace I give you. I do not give to you as the world gives. Do not let your hearts be troubled and do not be afraid.* John 14:27

11. Brokenhearted. *The Lord is close to the brokenhearted and saves those who are crushed in spirit.* Psalm 34:18

12. Confused. *For we live by faith, not by sight.* 2 Corinthians 5:6-8

13. Confused. *We know that all things work together for good to them that love God, to them who are the called according to his purpose.* Romans 8:28

14. Confused. *In everything give thanks: for this is the will of God in Christ Jesus concerning you.* 1 Thessalonians 5:18

15. Discouraged. *I praise you because I am fearfully and wonderfully made; your works are wonderful, I know that full well.* Psalm 139:14

16. Discouraged. *Love the LORD your God with all your heart and with all your soul and with all your strength.* Deuteronomy 6:5

17. Guilty. *If we confess our sins, he is faithful and just and will forgive us our sins and purify us from all unrighteousness.* 1 John 1:9

18. Hopeless. *It is by grace you have been saved, through faith — and this not from yourselves, it is the gift of God.* Ephesians 2:8

19. Impatient. *They that wait upon the LORD shall renew their strength; they shall mount up with wings as eagles; they shall run, and not be weary; and they shall walk, and not faint.* Isaiah 40:31

20. Indecisive. *For where your treasure is, there will your heart be also.* Luke 12:34

21. Insecure. *Trust in the LORD with all your heart and lean not on your own understanding.* Proverbs 3:5

22. Insecure. *Be on your guard; stand firm in the faith; be courageous; be strong.* 1 Corinthians 16:13

23. Insecure. *By faith in Christ you are in direct relationship with God.* Galatians 3:24-26

24. Lonely. *In him you too are being built together to become a dwelling in which God lives by his Spirit.* Ephesians 2:21-22

25. Lonely. *In him and through faith in him we may approach God with freedom and confidence.* Ephesians 3:11-13

26. Lonely. *The LORD is my shepherd; I shall not be in want.* Psalms 23:1

27. Needy. *My God shall supply all your needs according to his riches in glory by Christ Jesus.* Philippians 4:19

28. Pressured. *Consider it pure joy, my brothers, whenever you face trials of many kinds.* James 1:2

29. Sad. *Ask, and you will receive, that your joy may be full.* John 16:24

30. Sad. *Cast your burden on the LORD, and he will sustain you.* Psalms 55:22

31. Stressed. *Humble yourselves therefore under the mighty hand of God, that he may exalt you in due time: Casting all your cares upon him; for he cares for you.* 1 Peter 5:6-7

32. Stressed. *The peace of God, which transcends all understanding, will guard your hearts and your minds in Christ Jesus.* Philippians 4:7

33. Stressed. *We know that in all things God works for the good of those who love him, who have been called according to his purpose.* Romans 8:28

34. Tempted. *I have hidden your word in my heart that I might not sin against you.* Psalms 119:11

35. Troubled. *God is our refuge and strength, a very present help in trouble.* Psalms 46:1

36. Troubled. *The LORD is a stronghold for the oppressed, a stronghold in times of trouble.* Psalms 9:9

37. Undecided. *So whether you eat or drink or whatever you do, do it all for the glory of God.* 1 Corinthians 10:31

38. Unloved. *For God so loved the world that he gave his one and only Son, that whoever believes in him shall not perish but have eternal life.* John 3:16

39. Unloved. *The Father himself loves you because you have loved me and have believed that I came from God.* John 16:27

40. Unloved. *God demonstrates his own love for us in this; while we were still sinners, Christ died for us.* Romans 5:8

41. Upset. *Jesus Christ is the same yesterday and today and forever.* Hebrews 13:8

42. Upset. *You keep him in perfect peace whose mind is stayed on you, because he trusts in you.* Isaiah 26:3

43. Useless. *Let your light shine before men, that they may see your good deeds and praise your Father in heaven.* Matthew 5:16

44. Weak. *What shall we then say to these things? If God be for us, who can be against us?* Romans 8:31

45. Weak. *I can do everything through him who gives me strength.* Philippians 4:13

46. Weak. *The Lord is a refuge for the oppressed, a stronghold in times of trouble.* Psalm 9:9

47. Weary. *Come to me, all who labor and are heavy laden, and I will give you rest. Take my yoke upon you, and learn from me, for I am gentle and lowly in heart, and you will find rest for your souls.* Matthew 11:28-29

48. Worried. *Trust in the LORD with all your heart and lean not on your own understanding.* Proverbs 3:5

49. Worried. *For I know the plans I have for you, plans to prosper you and not to harm you, plans to give you hope and a future.* Jeremiah 29:11

50. Wounded. *Weeping may tarry for the night, but joy comes in the morning.* 1 Peter 5:6-7

Fifty-two-week Faith-building Scripture Memory Plan

༒

WE ARE LIVING IN A post-memorization age, but in earlier days, it was not unusual for devout believers to memorize great quantities of Scripture. Is Scripture memory worth your time? It has been for me and many others. What are some of the values of memorizing key Bible passages and some simple instructions that will make memorizing easier and more effective?

1. VALUES OF MEMORIZING SCRIPTURE

* A RESPECT FOR GOD'S WORD: Memorizing Bible scripture shows our respect and obedience to God. In reference to His Word, God said, "*These words which I command you this day shall be upon your heart.*" Deuteronomy 6:6 RSV.

* A WAY TO TRUE WISDOM: God's Word encourages us to memorize key scriptures so we have wisdom available for any situation, "*Do not forget my teaching, but keep my commands in your heart, for they will prolong your life many years and bring you peace and prosperity.*" Proverbs 3:1-4 NIV.

* A KEY TO GENUINE SUCCESS: Material success is possible without God's word. But spiritual success is measured by deeper qualities of life such as peace, love, joy, assurance, and purpose. Referring to God's Word, our Lord, said, "*You shall meditate on it day and night,*

so that you may be careful to do according to all that is written in it; for then you will make your way prosperous, and then you will have good success." (Joshua 1: 8) NIV Our Lord Jesus often used the key Bible verses he had learned.

- A GUIDE TO GOD-PLEASING PRAYER: One of the reasons some people never feel comfortable about what to pray is they do not have God's words in their minds and hearts to guide them. Jesus said, *"If you abide in me, and my words abide in you, ask whatever you wish and it shall be done for you."* John 15:7 NIV. Jesus told us to have His words in us before we ask, lest we ask wrongly.

- A CHANNEL TO CONFIDENT SHARING: Sometimes our lack of confidence in communicating our beliefs and ideas with others is due to our lack of memorized Scripture. We wonder what to say when simple problems and questions arise. James, the brother of Jesus, urged followers of Jesus to *"Receive with meekness the engrafted word which is able to save your soul."* James 1:21 KJV. When lawyers, religious leaders, powerful people, even Pilate, who had Jesus Crucified, interrogated Jesus, our Lord simply quoted Scripture. Can we do any less?

2. Instructions For Following The Plan

This scripture-memory plan is divided into four 12-week sections with one review-week in between each section (totaling 52 weeks). Find a friend to whom you can repeat your assigned memorized scriptures at the end of each week. This may be done in a meeting or on the phone. This will aid in your motivation, accuracy, and accountability. Follow these helpful hints and your memory work will be easier and more effective.

- DON'T HURRY. You'll be tempted to close your eyes and see if you can memorize the passage in one day. Don't do it. Just read aloud the scripture slowly and clearly seven times in the morning, seven during the day, and seven in the evening (preferably just before bedtime).

- KEY THOUGHT: Each time you say the scripture, include the *key thought* appearing just before the scripture.
- TEXT LOCATION: Each time you say the scriptures, include the name of the book, chapter, and verse at the close of your memory. By memorizing the scripture locations, you will be able to find the context of the scripture or share it with anyone.
- AFTER MEMORY: By repeating this procedure for 14 days, you will have the scriptures memorized without putting pressure on yourself. By taking time and repeating them often, they will become a part of your permanent mental records. When you finish the first scripture, read the new verses aloud like before. When you no longer need to read the scripture, just recite it at the same time each day for the 12 week period. This practice will help you retain them for quick use for the rest of your life.
- REVIEW WEEK: After completing one 12 week section, a full week (seven days) should be given to reviewing that section of twelve promises.
- SHARE PROMISES: Share what you have experienced in your memory work by getting someone else involved in this process. A friend can help you be accountable; and, he or she may take decide to memorize the scriptures.

Week 1: "Your word is a lamp to my feet and a light for my path." Psalm 119:105

Week 2: "Trust in the LORD with all your heart and lean not on your own understanding." Proverbs 3:5

Week 3: "Pray without ceasing." 1 Thessalonians 5:17

Week 4: "Therefore, if anyone is in Christ, he is a new creation; the old has gone, the new has come!" 2 Corinthians 5:17

Week 5: "Be on your guard; stand firm in the faith; be courageous; be strong." 1 Corinthians 16:13

Week 6: "And whatever you do, do it heartily, as to the Lord and not to men." Colossians 3:23

Week 7: "For where your treasure is, there will your heart be also." Luke 12:34

Week 8: "I can do all things through Christ who strengthens me." Philippians 4:13

Week 9: "My God shall supply all your need according to his riches in glory by Christ Jesus." Philippians 4:19

Week 10: "For I know the plans I have for you," declares the LORD, "plans to prosper you and not to harm you, plans to give you hope and a future." Jeremiah 29:11

Week 11: "You keep him in perfect peace whose mind is stayed on you, because he trusts in you." Isaiah 26:3

Week 12: "In him you too are being built together to become a dwelling in which God lives by his Spirit." Ephesians 2:21-22

Week 13: "In him and through faith in him we may approach God with freedom and confidence." Ephesians 3:11-13

Week 14: "Walk in the way of love, just as Christ loved us and gave himself up for us." Ephesians 5:1-3

Week 15: "By faith in Christ you are in direct relationship with God." Galatians 3:24-26

Week 16: "The LORD is my shepherd; I shall not want." Psalm 23:1

Week 17: "For we live by faith, not by sight." 2 Corinthians 5:6-8

Week 18: "And we know that all things work together for good to them that love God, to them who are the called according to his purpose." Romans 8:28

Week 19: "What shall we then say to these things? If God be for us, who can be against us?" Romans 8:31

Week 20: "In everything give thanks: for this is the will of God in Christ Jesus concerning you." 1 Thessalonians 5:18

Week 21: "For God hath not given us the spirit of fear; but of power, and of love, and of a sound mind." 2 Timothy 1:7

Week 22: "Jesus answered, "I am the way and the truth and the life. No one comes to the Father except through me." John 14:6

Week 23: "For all have sinned and fall short of the glory of God." Romans 3:23

Week 24: "For by grace you have been saved through faith. And this is not your own doing; it is the gift of God." Ephesians 2:8

Week 25: "I praise you because I am fearfully and wonderfully made; your works are wonderful, I know that full well." Psalm 139:14

Week 26: "Love the LORD your God with all your heart and with all your soul and with all your strength." Deuteronomy 6:5

Week 27: "Love your neighbor as yourself." Matthew 22:39

Week 28: "Do not be anxious about anything, but in every situation, by prayer and petition, with thanksgiving, present your requests to God." Philippians 4:6

Week 29: "And the peace of God, which transcends all understanding, will guard your hearts and your minds in Christ Jesus." Philippians 4:7

Week 30: "Every word of God proves true; he is a shield to those who take refuge in him." Proverbs 30:5

Week 31: "So whether you eat or drink or whatever you do, do it all for the glory of God." 1 Corinthians 10:31

Week 32: "In the beginning, God created the heavens and the earth." Genesis 1:1

Week 33: "The heavens declare the glory of God; the skies proclaim the work of his hands." Psalm 19:1

Week 34: "The LORD knows the way of the righteous, but the way of the wicked will perish." Psalm 1:6

Week 35: "Thus says the LORD... Fear not, for I have redeemed you; I have called you by name, you are mine." Isaiah 43:1

Week 36: "I, even I, am the LORD, and besides me there is no savior." Isaiah 43:11

Week 37: "You are the light of the world. A city set on a hill cannot be hidden." Matthew 5:14

Week 38: "Let your light shine before men, that they may see your good deeds and praise your Father in heaven." Matthew 5:16

Week 39: "Seek ye first the kingdom of God, and his righteousness; and all these things shall be added unto you." Matthew 6:33

Week 40: "Let the word of Christ dwell in you richly in all wisdom…" Colossians 3:16

Week 41: "Jesus Christ is the same yesterday and today and forever." Hebrews 13:8

Week 42: "They that wait upon the LORD shall renew their strength; they shall mount up with wings as eagles; they shall run, and not be weary; and they shall walk, and not faint." Isaiah 40:31

Week 43: "Peace I leave with you; my peace I give you. I do not give to you as the world gives. Do not let your hearts be troubled and do not be afraid." John 14:27

Week 44: "Commit your way to the LORD; trust in him and he will do this: He will make your righteous reward shine like the dawn." Psalm 37:4

Week 45: "Ask, and you will receive, that your joy may be full." John 16:24b

Week 46: "For God so loved the world that he gave his one and only Son, that whoever believes in him shall not perish but have eternal life." John 3:16

Week 47: "Beloved, let us love one another, for love is of God; and everyone who loves is born of God and knows God." 1 John 4:7

Week 48: "Let us think of ways to motivate one another to acts of love and good works." Hebrews 10:24

Week 49: "Whatever is noble, whatever is right, whatever is pure, whatever is lovely, whatever is admirable – if anything is excellent or praiseworthy – think about such things." Philippians 4:8

Week 50: "If they obey and serve him, they will spend the rest of their days in prosperity, and their years in contentment." Job 36:11

Week 51: "Forget the former things; do not dwell on the past. See, I am doing a new thing!" Isaiah 43:18-19

Week 52: "Let everything that has breath praise the LORD. Praise the LORD." Psalm 150:6

Recommended Reading

ॐ

1. Faith and the Uniqueness of the Christian Worldview

Collins, Francis S. *The Language of God*. New York: Simon & Schuster, 2006.

Colson, Charles. *Burden of Truth: Defending Truth in an Age of Unbelief*. Wheaton, IL: Tyndale House, 1997.

Colson, Charles, with Nancy Pearcey. *A Dance with Deception: Revealing the Truth Behind the Headlines*. Dallas: Word, 1993.

Craig, William Lane. *Reasonable Faith: Christian Truth and Apologetics*. Wheaton, IL: Crossway, 1994.

Evans, C. Stephen. *Philosophy of Religion: Thinking About Faith*. Downers Grove, IL: Inter-Varsity, 1985.

Heschel, Abraham J. *God In Search of Man*. New York: Meridian, 1959.

Holmes, Arthur F. *All Truth Is God's Truth*. Grand Rapids, MI: Eerdmans, 1977.

Hutchison, John A. *Faith, Reason, and Existence*. New York: Oxford University Press, 1956.

Kaufman, Gordon. *Relativism, Knowledge and Faith.* Chicago: Univ. of Chicago Press, 1960.

Keller, Timothy. *The Reason for God: Belief in and Age of Skepticism.* New York: Penguin Group, 2008.

Lewis, C. S. *Mere Christianity.* New York: Macmillan, 1953.

Macquarrie, John. *In Search of Humanity: A Theological and Philosophical Approach.* New York: Crossroad, 1985.

Newport, John Paul. *Life's Ultimate Questions: A Contemporary Philosophy of Religion.* Dallas, TX: Word Publishing, 1986.

Stott, John R. W.. *Basic Christianity.* Downers Grove, IL: InterVarsity, 2012.

Tillich, Paul. *Dynamics of Faith.* New York: Harper & Row, 1957.

2. Faith and the Evidences for the Supernatural

Bendall, Kent, and Frederick Ferre. *Exploring the Logic of Faith.* New York: Association, 1962.

Brown, Colin. *Philosophy and the Christian Faith.* London: Tyndale Press, 1969.

Carnell, Edward John. *Christian Commitment: An Apologetic.* New York: Macmillan, 1957.

Craig, William Lane. *Apologetics: An Introduction.* Chicago: Moody, 1984.

Dymess, William. *Christian Apologetics in a World Community.* Downers Grove, IL: Inter-Varsity, 1983.

Geisler, Norman. *Christian Apologetics*. Grand Rapids, MI: Baker, 1976.

Geisler, Norman, and Ronald M. Brooks. *When Skeptics Ask: A Handbook of Christian Evidence*. Wheaton, IL: Victor, 1998.

Glynn, Patrick. *God the Evidence: The Reconciliation of Faith and Reason in a Postsecular World*. Rocklin, CA: Prima Publishing, 1997.

Howe, Frederic R. Challenge and Response: *A Handbook of Christian Apologetics*. Grand Rapids, MI: Zondervan, 1982.

Lewis, Gordon R. *Testing Christianity's Truth Claims*. Chicago: Moody, 1976.

McDowell, Josh. *Evidence That Demands a Verdict: Historical Evidences for the Christian Faith*. Vols. 1 and 2. San Bernardino, CA: Here's Life Publishers, 1990.

Yancey. Philip. *Reaching for the Invisible God*. Grand Rapids, MI: Zondervan, 2000.

3. Faith and the Modern Mind

Arterburn, Stephen. *Faith That Hurts, Faith That Heals: Understanding the Fine Line Between Healthy Faith and Spiritual Abuse*. Nashville, TN: Thomas Nelson, 2015.

Baillie, John. *The Belief in Progress*. London: Oxford Univ. Press, 1950.

Ferre, Frederick. *Language, Logic and God*. New York: Harper, 1961.

Frankl, Viktor. *Man's Search for Meaning*. Boston: Beacon Press, 2014.

Gill, Jerry H. *Faith in Dialogue: A Christian Apologetic.* Waco, TX: Word, 1985.

Henry, Carl F. H. *God, Revelation and Authority. Vol. 3, God Who Speaks and Shows: Fifteen Theses, Part Two.* Waco, TX: Word, 1979.

Hordern, William. *Speaking of God: The Nature and Purpose of Theological Language.* New York: Macmillan, 1964.

Kania, Walter. *Healthy Religion: A Psychological Guide to a Mature Faith.* Bloomington, IN: AuthorHouse, 2009.

Newport, John P. *What Is Christian Doctrine?* Nashville: Broadman, 1984.

Niebuhr, Reinhold. *Faith and History.* New York: Scribner's, 1949.

Ramsey, Ian T. *Religious Language.* London: SCM, 1957.

Scazzero, Peter. *Emotionally Healthy Spirituality.* Grand Rapids, IL: Zondervan, 2006.

Schaeffer, Francis. *How Should We Then Live?* Westchester, IL: Crossway, 1983.

Schaeffer, Francis A., and C. Everett Koop. *Whatever Happened to the Human Race:* Westchester, IL: Crossway, 1983

Tilley, Terrence W. *Talking of God.* New York: Paulist, 1978.

Walsh, Brian J., and J. Richard Middleton. *The Transforming Vision: Shaping a Christian World View.* Downers Grove, IL: InterVarsity Press, 1984.

Williamson, Wm. B. Ian Ramsey. *Makers of the Modem Theological Mind.* Waco, TX: Word, 1982.

4. Faith and Science

Bube, Richard H. *The Human Quest: A New Look at Science and Christian Faith.* Waco, TX: Word, 1971.

Henry, Carl F. H. *God, Revelation and Authority, Vol. 6, God Who Stands and Stays, Part Two.* Waco, TX: Word, 1983.

Hummel, Charles E. *The Galileo Connection: Resolving Conflicts Between Science and the Bible.* Downers Grove, IL: InterVarsity, 1986.

Hyers, Conrad. *The Meaning of Creation: Genesis and Modern Science.* Atlanta: John Knox, 1984.

Noll, Mark A., and David F. Wells, eds. *Christian Faith and Practice in the Modern World: Theology from an Evangelical Point of View.* Grand Rapids, MI: Eerdmans, 1988.

Ramm, Bernard L. *The Christian View of Science and Scripture.* Grand Rapids, MI: Eerdmans, 1954.

Richardson, Alan. *The Bible in the Age of Science.* Philadelphia: Westminster, 1961.

Rust, Eric C. *Science and Faith.* New York: Oxford Univ. Press, 1967.

Torrance, Thomas F. *The Christian Frame of Mind.* Colorado Springs, CO: Helmers & Howard, 1988.

5. Faith and Miracles, Prayer, and Providence

Brown, Colin. *Miracles and the Critical Mind.* Grand Rapids, MI: Eerdmans, 1984.

Brown, Colin. *That You May Believe: Miracles and Faith, Then and Now.* Grand Rapids, MI: Eerdmans, 1985.

Lewis, C. S. *Miracles: A Preliminary Study.* Hammersmith, London: Fount, 1974.

Moody, Dale. *The Word of Truth: A Summary of Christian Doctrine Based on Biblical Revelation.* Grand Rapids, MI: Eerdmans, 1981.

Phipps, William E. *Death: Confronting the Reality.* Atlanta: John Knox, 1987.

Thielicke, Helmut. *Living with Death.* Grand Rapids, MI: Eerdmans, 1983.

6. Faith and the World Religions

Anderson, J. N. D. *Christianity and Comparative Religion.* Downers Grove, IL: Inter-Varsity, 1970.

Copeland, E. Luther. *Christianity and World Religions.* Nashville: Convention Press, 1963.

Cragg, Kenneth. *The Christ and the Faiths: Theology in Cross-Reference.* London: SPCK, 1986.

Farmer, Herbert Henry. *Revelation and Religion: Studies in the Theological Interpretation of Religious Types.* London: Nisbet and Co., 1954.

Hick, John. *God and the Universe of Faiths.* New York: St. Martin's Press, 1973.

Kraemer, Hendrik. *Religion and the Christian Faith.* Philadelphia: Westminster, 1956.

Neill, Stephen. *Christian Faith and Other Faiths: The Christian Dialogue with Other Religions.* London: Oxford Univ. Press, 1961.

Newport, John P. *Christ and the New Consciousness.* Nashville: Broadman, 1978.

Smart, Ninian. *The Phenomenon of Religion.* New York: Macmillan, 1973.

Vos, Johannes G. *A Christian Introduction to Religions of the World.* Grand Rapids, MI: Baker, 1965.

Wright, G. Ernest. *The Challenge of Israel's Faith.* Chicago: Univ. of Chicago Press, 1944.

Zaehner, R. C. *Mysticism, Sacred and Profane.* New York: Oxford Univ. Press, 1971.

7. Faith and Reason

Carnell, Edward John. An *Introduction to Christian Apologetics: A Philosophic Defense of the Trinitarian-Theistic Faith.* Grand Rapids, MI: Eerdmans, 1948.

Casserley, J. v. Langmead. Graceful *Reason: The Contribution of Reason to Theology.* Greenwich, CT: Seabury, 1954.

Hazelton, Roger. *On Proving God.* New York: Harper, 1952.

Holmes, Arthur F. *Faith Seeks Understanding.* Grand Rapids, MI: Eerdmans, 1971.

Hutchison, John. *A Faith, Reason, and Existence.* New York: Oxford Univ. Press, 1956.

Jenkins, Daniel. *Believing in God*. Philadelphia: Westminster, 1952.

Kroner, Richard. *Speculation and Revelation in Modern Philosophy*. Philadelphia: Westminster, 1961.

Moreland, J. P. Love *Your God with All Your Mind: The Role of Reason in the Life of the Soul*. Colorado Springs: NavPress, 1997.

Nash, Ronald H. *Faith and Reason: Searching for a Rational Faith*. Grand Rapids, MI: Zondervan, 1988.

Plantinga, Alvin, and Nicholas Wolterstorff, eds. *Faith and Rationality: Reason and Belief in God*. Notre Dame: Univ. of Notre Dame Press, 1983.

Ramm, Bernard. *After Fundamentalism: The Future of Evangelical Theology*. San Francisco: Harper, 1983.

Wolfe, David L. *Epistemology: The Justification of Belief*. Downers Grove: InterVarsity, 1982.

Wright, G. Ernest. *The Rule of God: Essays in Biblical Theology*. Garden City, NY: Doubleday, 1960.

8. Faith and the Moral Laws

Baillie, John. *Our Knowledge of God*. London: Oxford Univ. Press, 1939.

Bloesch, Donald G. Freedom for Obedience. *Evangelical Ethics in Contemporary Times*. San Francisco: Harper, 1987.

Fletcher, Joseph. *Situation Ethics: The New Morality*. Philadelphia: Westminster, 1966.

Grisez, Germain G. *The Way of the Lord Jesus. Vol. 1, Christian Moral Principles.* Chicago: Franciscan Herald Press. 1983.

Grisez, Germain G. *The Way of the Lord Jesus. Vol. 3, Different Moral Questions.* Quincy, IL: Franciscan Press, 1997.

Grisez, Germain G. *Beyond the New Morality: The Responsibilities of Freedom.* Notre Dame, IN: University of Norte Dame Press, 1988.

Henry, Carl F. H. *Aspects of Christian Social Ethics.* Grand Rapids, MI: Eerdmans, 1957.

Henry, Carl F. H. *Christian Personal Ethics.* Grand Rapids, MI: Eerdmans, 1957.

Holmes, Arthur, ed. *The Making of a Christian Mind: A Christian World View & the Academic Enterprise.* Downers Grove, IL: Inter-Varsity Press, 1985.

Kaye, Bruce and Gordon Wenham, eds. *Law, Morality and the Bible.* Downers Grove, IL: InterVarsity, 1978.

Lewis, C. S. *God in the Dock: Essays on Theology and Ethics.* Grand Rapids: Eerdmans, 1970.

Lillie, William. *Studies in New Testament Ethics.* Philadelphia: Westminster, 1961.

O'Donovan, Oliver. *Resurrection and Moral Order: An Outline for Evangelical Ethics.* Grand Rapids, MI: Eerdmans, 1986.

Plantiga, Cornelius, Jr. *Not the Way It's Supposed to Be: A Breviary of Sin.* Grand Rapids, MI: Eerdmans, 1995.

Ramm, Bernard. *The Right, the Good and the Happy.* Waco: Word, 1971.

Harper & Row, 1981.

Wright, G. Ernest, and Fuller, Reginald H. *The Book of the Acts of God: Christian Scholarship Interprets the Bible.* Garden City, NY: Doubleday, 1957.

Made in the USA
San Bernardino, CA
08 June 2016